W9-CQS-619

PRAISE FOR *SCHOOLS THAT DELIVER*

"I'm pleased to recommend *Schools That Deliver* as an exceptional work to inspire, rejuvenate, and engage your school staff along a powerfully aligned trajectory toward success. Reimagine your school through the lens of these transformative authors."

—Jill Gildea, Superintendent
Fremont School District 79
Mundelein, IL

"*Schools That Deliver* is long overdue in the midst of too much focus on testing and accountability. It has the potential to provide a practical guide coupled with the underlying philosophy to assist school leaders in making their schools engaging environments for all students and staff."

—Richard A. Simon, Retired Superintendent
of Schools, Adjunct Professor
Stony Brook University and Long Island University Post
Stony Brook, NY

"A common thread that separates *Schools That Deliver* from others is the focus on remaining loyal to the unique personality of each individual school while providing specific tools and procedures to focus on."

—Delia McCraley, Principal
Southgate Academy
Tucson, AZ

"John Edwards and Bill Martin write about the reality of authentic school issues using proven research and from their own experiences."

—Bonnie Tryon, Mentor/Coach
SAANYS Representative to NYS Education
Department's NCLB Committee of Practitioners
SAANYS Representative to the NYS Teacher of the Year Council
Past President, School Administrators
Association of New York (SAANYS)
Latham, NY

To Sandra and Vicki

SCHOOLS THAT
DELIVER

JOHN EDWARDS | BILL MARTIN

Foreword by Arthur L. Costa

CORWIN
A SAGE Publishing Company

FOR INFORMATION:

Corwin

A SAGE Company

2455 Teller Road

Thousand Oaks, California 91320

(800) 233-9936

www.corwin.com

SAGE Publications Ltd.

1 Oliver's Yard

55 City Road

London EC1Y 1SP

United Kingdom

SAGE Publications India Pvt. Ltd.

B 1/I 1 Mohan Cooperative Industrial Area

Mathura Road, New Delhi 110 044

India

SAGE Publications Asia-Pacific Pte. Ltd.

3 Church Street

#10-04 Samsung Hub

Singapore 049483

Program Director: Dan Alpert

Senior Associate Editor: Kimberly Greenberg

Editorial Assistant: Katie Crilley

Production Editor: Melanie Birdsall

Copy Editor: Diane DiMura

Typesetter: C&M Digitals (P) Ltd.

Proofreader: Christine Dahlin

Cover Designer: Rose Storey

Marketing Manager: Charline Maher

Printed in the United States of America

ISBN 978-1-5063-3347-2

This book is printed on acid-free paper.

SUSTAINABLE FORESTRY INITIATIVE

Certified Chain of Custody
Promoting Sustainable Forestry
www.sfiprogram.org
SFI-01268

SFI label applies to text stock

16 17 18 19 20 10 9 8 7 6 5 4 3 2 1

Contents

Foreword

This book was written by two good friends of mine. They write about the joys and frustrations, the successes and disappointments, the realities and dreams of working in learning organizations. In some ways, this book is a documentary about their sometimes brutal, often humorous and consistently touching realities as front-line school administrators. And in other ways, this book is about their mission as educational provocateurs to draw upon their Personal Practical Knowledge to liberate teachers, administrators, and students' capacities for autonomous growth, learning, and adaptability: a noble cause.

I remember meeting John Edwards in 1982 at the first International Conference on Thinking in Fiji. What struck me about this young Australian researcher were his insights about education and his daring to question and seek to transform many of the sacred practices currently in vogue (such as homework, compartmentalization of subject matter, and theories of learning). During his sabbatical, I invited him to spend half a year with me at Sacramento State University. As a single parent, he came with his four children. The impact on my graduate students was profound. Like the irritating grain of sand that creates a pearl, he modeled risk taking, thinking critically about the educational status quo and questioning practices that were "politically correct" but educationally faulty. As a result, my students gained confidence as agile leaders. I introduced John to consulting work and the response from schools was that John was "refreshingly sound." Since that time, John has matured from a brave, delightfully "brash" young man into a powerful, internationally respected, thinking changemaker.

In 1990, as principal of Bleyl Junior High School near Houston, Texas, Bill Martin, complete with cowboy boots, invited me to spend time with his staff to explore the teaching of Habits of Mind. I came prepared to introduce the staff to the need for teaching students to think more skillfully and how the Habits of Mind were dispositions of successful, efficacious thinkers that could be taught and learned by students. Habits of Mind flourish in schools where there is trust, where staffs share a common vision, and where the Habits are not only taught but also modeled by all the staff—where they are the norms of the school culture. Much to my amazement, I was greeted by the professional development lead teacher who introduced me to the staff's motto: "The United Mind Workers." Amazed, I put my planned presentation notes away, packed up my PowerPoints, and spent the next three days observing and learning from them. They were indeed united as they shared a common vision, were committed to teaching thinking, and supported each other in the process. They went far beyond my expectations due to Bill's "down-home," unassuming but powerful, leadership style. I learned how, working in conditions of trust, being focused on students' needs, having access to resources and given freedom, teachers will liberate their ingenuity and creativity to network, collaborate, and develop a vision that results in programs to which the entire staff and community become committed. As a result, students' dispositions of persisting, problem solving, collaborating, empathizing, questioning, and continual learning were enhanced.

Over the years, these two friends found each other, formed an alliance, and have influenced school staffs and business leaders around the world. Based on their leadership experiences, they are dedicated to a few simple but profound concepts which they articulate well for those who read, apply, and live by this book.

"THE KNOWLEDGE IS IN THE ROOM"

Considering the job's long hours, generally low pay, mandated curriculum, unpopular testing requirements, and unruly students, I wonder why, despite all the reasons to quit, so many teachers keep at it. Reported by Liz Riggs (2013) from the research by Richard Ingersoll, professor of education at the University of Pennsylvania, 68 percent said that supportive leadership was "absolutely essential." Only 34 percent said the same about higher salaries. I have observed that the main reason why teachers quit is they feel they have no say in decisions that will ultimately affect their teaching. Ingersoll concludes that this lack of classroom autonomy is the biggest source of frustration for teachers nationally.

Autonomy makes such a difference because micromanagement, the opposite of autonomy, puts people in a threatened state. They become primed to respond quickly and emotionally. Productivity falls and the quality of decisions is diminished. Over time, sustained lack of autonomy is an ongoing source of stress, which causes more reactivity than reflectivity, more "conformativity" rather than creativity. When teachers feel they are being micromanaged their executive thinking (e.g., self-control, paying attention, innovating, planning, and problem solving) become less active (Newton & Davis, 2014).

In *Schools That Deliver*, a major driving concept is that "the knowledge is in the room." Teachers who achieve genuine respect for their skillfulness, stamina and efficacy, and school staffs that achieve collective autonomy, reduce the frequency, duration, and intensity of this threat state. The perception of increased choice makes people feel liberated, committed, and collaborative.

CREATING A CULTURE OF TRUST AND THOUGHT-FULL COLLABORATION

Working internationally with numerous schools over the years, I have found that the "glue" that holds the staff and the community together is relational trust. Research by Anthony Bryk and Barbara Schneider (2002), not surprisingly, confirmed that trust was a necessary for improved student learning. Chicago schools whose test scores were increasing over the period of this seven-year study had high levels of relational trust. In contrast, low-performing schools had low levels of trust. Relational trust is the trust that is developed through the interpersonal social exchanges that take place in a school community: principal to teacher, principal to parent, teacher to teacher, teacher to student, and teacher to parent. In *Schools That Deliver*, the leader, or principal, is instrumental in fostering a climate in which relational trust can flourish. Relational trust means respect, competence, personal regard for others, and integrity. It is built by being visible and accessible, behaving consistently, keeping commitments, sharing personal information, keeping confidences, revealing feelings, expressing personal interest in other people, acting non-judgmentally, listening empathically, admitting mistakes, and demonstrating professional knowledge and skills.

In *Schools That Deliver*, skillful thinking is prized and practiced. Staffs in which sharing a common language, dialogue, planning, reflecting, and problem resolving are routinely done are those that experience success in adapting to continuing environmental changes while maintaining a sense of personal and collective efficacy (Ritchhart, 2015).

Thinking interdependently is a leading resource for their responsiveness to change. Collaboration is strengthened by finding, recognizing, and cherishing the interconnections among individuals, schools, communities, and cultures. Interdependence includes a sense of kinship that comes from a unity of being, a sense of sharing a common habitat, and a mutual bonding for common goals and shared values.

LIBERATING LEADERSHIP IN OTHERS

Schools That Deliver emphasizes that the best part of leading is developing and bringing out the leadership capacities in others. The source of a facilitator's satisfaction shifts from being the problem solver to developing others' capacity to solve their own problems and helping others learn from situations, from giving unsolicited expert advice to helping others self-prescribe, from evaluating others to developing others' disposition for self-evaluation, from holding power to empowering others, from telling to inquiring, and from finding strength in holding on to finding strength in letting go.

Schools That Deliver is not only sprinkled with numerous testimonies of administrators in schools around the world who have experienced the shift to a new paradigm of leadership, but also laced with powerful, thought-provoking questions that school leaders must ask themselves about their roles as well as deciding on what is the real work of their school.

The contemporary leader possesses a belief in his or her capacity to serve as an empowering catalyst for building trust in the school culture, for fostering a shared vision among all members of the school community, and for developing the intellectual growth of others. A facilitative leader refrains from giving advice unless asked for, believing in what Cicero stated: "Nobody can give you wiser advice than yourself."

WHAT DO "SCHOOLS THAT DELIVER" DELIVER?

The answer to this question is fairly simple and direct: They enhance student learning! Enhanced student learning, however, depends on the expertise of the teacher (Hattie, 2003). The expertise of the teacher, however, depends largely on the school community in which that teacher operates (Hargreaves & Fullan, 2012). And the power and effectiveness of the school community depend largely on the skills and dispositions of its educational leaders (Leithwood & Seashore Louis, 2011). Schools that deliver, therefore, are dedicated to this consistency of enhancing others, who, in turn, ultimately produce maximum growth in students' acquisition of desired outcomes.

Russian psychologist Lev Vygotsky observed that children grow into the intellectual life of the community in which they live. A school that delivers is one in which learning, fulfillment, and becoming more humane are the primary goals for all students, faculty, and support staff. It is the concept of a learning organization in which self-development, intellectual empowerment, collaboration, and lifelong learning are esteemed core values and all institutions within the culture are constructed to contribute to those goals. What is required for schools that deliver is the emergence of a new kind of leadership—leaders who passionately communicate and reinforce high aspirations for students, who ignite and focus teacher energy, who develop the leadership capacities of teachers, who distribute informed decision making within their schools, and who foster the development of work cultures whose dominant features are self-directedness, collaboration, and inquiry. In a "school that delivers," the principal carries the vision, sensitivities, and skill sets of cultural change and creates the conditions in which teachers become the leaders of instruction and students become the leaders of the future.

WE ARE NOT IN THIS ALONE

Having worked across many countries in my career, I share with John and Bill strong insights into the power of shared international experience. Readers of this book should be strengthened by the knowledge that our frustrations are not isolated. We are not in this alone and can learn deeply from each other across national boundaries. This book, with its rich international examples, is a powerful start on this journey.

—Arthur L. Costa
Emeritus Professor of Education
California State University, Sacramento

REFERENCES

Bryk, A., & Schneider, B. (2002). *Trust in schools: A core resource for improvement.* New York, NY: The Russell Sage Foundation.

Hargreaves, A., & Fullan, M. (2012). *Professional capital: Transforming teaching in every school.* New York, NY: Teachers College Press.

Hattie, J. (2003, October). *Teachers make a difference: What is the research evidence?* Auckland, New Zealand: Australian Council for Educational Research. Retrieved from https://cdn.auckland.ac.nz/assets/education/hattie/docs/teachers-make-a-difference-ACER-(2003).pdf

Leithwood, K., & Seashore Louis, K. (2011). *Linking leadership to student learning.* San Francisco, CA: Jossey-Bass.

Newton, J., & Davis, J. (2014, July 14). Three secrets of organizational effectiveness: How the practices of "pride builders" can help you build a high-performance culture. *Strategy + Business, 76.* Retrieved from http://www.strategy-business.com/article/00271?gko=d819d

Riggs, L. (2013, October 18). Why do teachers quit? And why do they stay? *The Atlantic Monthly.* Retrieved from http://www.theatlantic.com/education/archive/2013/10/why-do-teachers-quit/280699/

Ritchhart, R. (2015). *Creating cultures of thinking: The eight forces we must master to truly transform our schools.* San Francisco, CA: Jossey-Bass.

Acknowledgments

This book has grown out of the rich lives of productive people inside school communities that deliver. The narrative of the text is carried by these collective voices, and we acknowledge this shared ownership.

Inside our tight writing team, Sandra Russell has been our constant ally, helping us keep ourselves true to what we believe. Her contribution to the manuscript has been deep and inspiring. Dr. Jim Butler, an absolute master of creating powerful models, has his influence spread throughout this book. Lisa Wolford has been our internal editor, solid as a rock, clear and fearless in her collegiality and leadership. Vicki Martin's gentle presence has kept us together as a team throughout the writing journey we have shared.

Art Costa has been our mentor for over twenty years. He has always shown us great generosity of spirit both professionally and personally. His foreword is highly valued by us both.

When we started on our writing, we invited ten respected colleagues to be "friends of the book." We asked them to bring their experience into the book and to challenge us to be our best. As we finalized the manuscript, their eyes and intellects have been our final checkpoint. Together with Sandy and Lisa, Jon Saphier, Brendan Spillane, Mary Wilson, Greg Morgan, Fredrik Höper, Bitte Sundin, Bengt Lennartsson, and Ragnhild Isachsen have been our friends of the book. Once we formed our partnership with Corwin, Dan Alpert, Kim Greenberg, Melanie Birdsall, and their team have provided insight, challenge, and support. Their professionalism is reflected in this book.

PUBLISHER'S ACKNOWLEDGMENTS

Corwin gratefully acknowledges the contributions of the following reviewers:

Sean Beggin
Associate Principal
Anoka-Hennepin Secondary
    Technical Education Program/
    Anoka Technical College
Anoka, MN

Ruthanne Bolling
Elementary School
    Instructional Coach
Fairview Elementary School
Richmond, IN

Jill Gildea
Superintendent
Fremont School District 79
Mundelein, IL

Jeff Ronneberg
Superintendent
Spring Lake Park Schools
Minneapolis, MN

Richard A. Simon
Retired Superintendent of
    Schools, Adjunct Professor,
    Stony Brook University and
    Long Island University Post
Stony Brook, NY

Bonnie Tryon, Mentor/Coach
SAANYS Representative to NYS
    Education Department's NCLB
    Committee of Practitioners
SAANYS Representative
    to the NYS Teacher of
    the Year Council
Past President, School
    Administrators Association
    of New York (SAANYS)
Latham, NY

About the Authors

John Edwards has always been fascinated with the beauty of the human mind. He began his working life as a research metallurgist. He has worked as a teacher and department head in schools and in state, national, and international curriculum development roles; and he has written textbooks for schools. Through his extensive university career, he has been one of the leading research grant recipients in cognitive science in Australia.

John's research began in his own classrooms, which led to publications in the areas of the direct teaching of thinking and what children are thinking while teachers are teaching. He has explored areas including how people think, what tests really test, ways to measure the intellectual demand of learning, how to generate successful change in organizations, innovation and creativity, leadership, internally driven transformation of schools, and creating productive feedback environments. He worked on a major project using Piaget's clinical method to reveal how Southeast Asian children develop science and mathematics concepts.

John is Managing Director of Edwards Explorations, an Australia-based company concerned with exploring and developing human potential. He has worked inside many leading Australian and international companies and sporting organizations, to research and deliver powerful cultures of learning. He has dedicated a large part of his life to the work that forms the basis of this book: helping school communities create the schools they know are right for their children.

Dr. Edwards is one of the few international researchers to turn his research into award-winning practice in education, in business and industry, and in high-performance sport.

Bill Martin loves working inside schools to build positive learning environments for children. He has done this for forty-nine years. He taught in primary and middle schools for seventeen years and was a secondary assistant and high school principal for sixteen years. On two occasions, he led large schools to win State and National Blue Ribbon awards for excellence. Since 2003, he has worked with over 180 schools across six countries to support efforts to create powerful learning cultures.

He has earned personal awards for educational leadership. In 1991, he was one of five finalists in the first National Secondary Principal of the Year competition sponsored by the NASSP and Metropolitan Life. In 1993, he was named one of ten Principals of Leadership by the National School Safety Center. In 2000, the Michigan State Legislature proclaimed a Special Tribute to Bill's leadership as principal of Monroe High School.

He has presented invited addresses at International Conferences on Thinking in New Zealand, the United Kingdom, the United States, Australia, Sweden, Spain, and Malaysia. He has been a keynote presenter at the International Conference on Ignorance. Bill has served on a United Nations team to make recommendations for the reform of secondary education in Kuwait. He has designed and facilitated long-term professional development programs to grow leadership capacity for the Tønsberg Kommune in Norway and the Varberg and Kungsbacka Kommunes in Sweden. In Lexington (Kentucky) Public Schools, Bill served as the Smaller Learning Community Technical Advisor for the district's five high schools.

Introduction

For us: why write this book?

For you: why read this book?

This book is based on the confidence we share that teachers and their communities know how to create the schools needed for their children.

Both of us have worked in schools most of our lives. This has brought us face-to-face with the current challenging culture within which schools must deliver. This is work demanding courage, authenticity, and character. Most importantly, it demands of us all to be different tomorrow than we are today.

At the core of our profession is a hunger to be part of learning environments that deliver brilliantly for all involved. We have seen such schools and worked in them and with them. They are a joy. As well, we have listened to many stories of frustration within schools. Teachers share that their school starts on new initiatives, with passion and energy, only to have this fade away with no delivery. The school then starts on another initiative with the same result: nothing absolutely mastered, nothing deeply embedded. Teachers need a sense of completion and achievement as much as their students.

"Posttraumatic initiative fatigue" (PTIF) would be a great descriptor for what is being experienced in many schools across the world. People with high ideals, desperate to do the job they have trained for, are grieving to see their vision lost. This book is about honoring those visions and bringing sanity to the here and now.

Within an evolving culture of disrespect for the people who dedicate their lives to the education of our children, few are questioning systems that no longer serve the interests of our children and society at large. This has resulted in a culture of blame, which creates paralysis. To fill this vacuum, there is a growing body of international literature supplying external processes. Everyone has an answer. This book does not bring definitive answers. Let's be honest: No one size fits all schools. We share skills, models, processes, and insights that enable schools to deliver. These come from real school experiences of successful delivery across six countries and in single schools containing many cultures. They define an approach that works in our times, facing our constraints and our complexity.

We stand with schools to acknowledge their challenges and face them with courage. This book is based on processes that break negativity and tap the potential currently buried under the weight of external myopia. In the end, only you can discern what is needed in your context. Different contexts demand different approaches. Knowing your own context provides a thread of authenticity. This lights pathways of growth and softens the pressure of external voices. Schools that deliver weave a powerful path between the competing voices and demands from outside. They draw on their inner resources to satisfy both learners and teachers.

Processes clarifying what is in the hearts and souls of your community for your school are at the core of our work. Having the understandings and processes to then make this a reality on your school site is what we mean by delivery.

We work with school leaders, staff, parents/caregivers, and their communities to create the schools they have long wanted. They describe what they have developed, in rich interaction with us, as being a fresh and liberating approach. This book reveals how people are working productively together within schools to deliver what really matters for their children. This collective voice provides one valuable benchmark.

Seeing beyond our own context is difficult for all of us. Our ongoing action research inside schools keeps us in touch with contemporary schooling and the issues faced internationally. Our aim here is to share a rich range of alternative approaches you can use to reflect on your experiences of your own unique school culture.

Everything in this book has passed the litmus test of working across diverse cultures and situations. We provide quotes and examples throughout the book from colleagues we are learning from and working with. These are schools that deliver.

We focus on the six central areas for delivery:

1. Alignment, which enables our school to better tap the potential of our people

2. The Real Work, which puts energy into what really matters for delivery

3. Leadership, a disposition that helps us all hold our true course

4. Authentic Action, through which we deliver on our promises

5. Core Values and Culture, which are at the root of our actions, both effective and ineffective

6. Community, the rich human web in which schools are wrapped

Voices

Friday, September 20, 1985, 12:05 p.m.

My buddy Marvin and I are deputies on lunch duty in the cavernous eating commons of Langham Creek High School in Houston, Texas. The student population mirrors the toughness and diversity of this oil-driven city. The school has tough kids during this booming time. There are 650 teenagers finishing the last lunch session of the day. Marvin and I have been chatting on our walkie-talkies about two things: what bar we are going to after work, and about the rising tension in our boys as we have been pushing them really hard to enforce the new hair length rule that our district has introduced.

"Crack!" a noise I have never heard before rings out and the kids, as they are wont to do when they think something is brewing, stand up on the stools of the cafeteria tables, blocking the view. I begin to slowly walk along the wall next to where I am on duty toward the sound.

A boy races around the corner of the cafeteria tables toward me, dressed completely in black, with a 357 Magnum in his hand. He draws down on me in a police stance. My racing thoughts tell me I am about to die. I take a step toward him. The gunman fires, "Craaaack!!!" The shot flies past my head and ricochets off the cement wall next to me, slamming into a student standing behind me, shattering his leg.

Pandemonium—all the students standing atop stools dive under the tables for protection. The gunman turns and runs back toward where he has come from. I slowly follow his path, eyes fixed on him as he races up to the mezzanine floor. I think: He is going to shoot down at us. I shout at the students nearest me to "Get out!" As these kids race toward the two exit doors opposite the shooter's location, everyone else does the same in utter panic. In a nanosecond, the cafeteria empties as students flee into the cornfields behind the school.

I continue to walk slowly around the end of the cafeteria tables, watching the shooter. As I turn the corner, I see the product of the first "Crack." Marvin lies on the floor in a small pool of blood. As I bend down to cradle his

(Continued)

(Continued)

hand in mine, a useless question ventures from my mouth, "Marvin, what happened?" Marvin says, "I've been shot and it's serious. I want to be life-flighted to Hermann Hospital." Marvin's fingers are swelling and his wedding ring has started to tighten on his finger . . .

What seemed like "hell on earth" started for all of us at that moment. You see, the first bullet had been shot into Marvin's back, smashing his tailbone and paralyzing him instantly.

When our school district introduced the hair length rule, I had enforced it strongly, as was expected. I felt the growing anger in our boys, I knew the rule was stupid, but I enforced it anyway. The tension in the school was palpable. I did not speak out against this stupidity; I just did my job. This shooting was one young man's unskilled and brutal response. I had colluded.

Never again would I avoid telling the truth.

This incident is about much more than a hair code. When I talk about telling the truth, about integrity and speaking up, I am not talking about mundane rules. I am talking about school culture. Why did the boy bring a gun to school? It was not simply because of the hair code, I can guarantee you that. Was it because he had been marginalized in such a large school? Was it because he had a mental illness that went unrecognized or unreported? Was it because "Keep one another safe" was not a value of the school, and his buddies who had an inkling of what he was up to did not let anyone know? Was it because he or his family were not connected to the school as a part of a community and had no one to turn to?

We are still unsure what caused him to act as he did, but our collusion connects to the principles in this book. Culture, connectedness, and community deliver schools that are safe. These are what really mattered back in 1985, as they do now.

This book for me is about culture, courage, and voice.

It is December 1959. I am fifteen. It is the summer holidays before I am to start my university studies in metallurgy. Towering above me is a long row of huge, fire-breathing, open-hearth furnaces in the steelworks of one of Australia's largest mining companies. They have given me a scholarship.

It is searingly hot and heavy steel dust is in the shafts of light that cross the room as we enter the beaten-up, galvanized iron hut. Peering into the shadowed corner, I see the outline of a wrinkled, weather-beaten old man.

I hear the depth of his sigh as he looks at this young boy with long red 1960s hair flowing over his shoulders.

The besuited, well-ironed executive officer begins: "This is young John, one of our scholarship holders; he will be working with you for the next three months, OK?" The old eyes roll.

"Just don't get under my feet!" he barks at me.

"Kit him out" is the next missive; no pleasantries here.

Within minutes, I have a shiny new grey outfit with black buttons down the front, large safety boots, safety glasses, and gloves that have to be tucked up inside my sleeves, so that if molten metal hits me, it will run outside my gloves, not inside.

As I stand, trying to force a large quantity of red hair inside a safety helmet, he slowly rises. Out from the gloom, I feel a massive presence emerge. I will never forget the sight—baggy dark blue dungarees and a blue and black striped woolly shirt with holes in it. Each hole fringed with a brown burn mark where the molten metal has blown through. The scars beneath match the holes. No hard hat here, no safety clothing.

He pushes past me gruffly and with a "Follow me" we are up on the furnace floor. He is barking orders in every direction as we go. The full force of the man is now on display. He strides to the front of one of the furnaces. The heat is excruciating. After a quick look, he bellows, "Throw in fifteen bags of ferromanganese and ten bags of coke."

With notebook in hand, I timidly ask, "Why did you say that?"

"Looks like it needs it" and he strides on. "Have a look for yourself!"

I can smell my eyebrows singeing as I peer into the furnace.

It is molten orange.

But you see, for me, it is always molten orange.

My task was to follow this man, their top steelmaker, for three months and make detailed notes on how he made steel. He was about to retire and he could cook a batch of steel like no one else in the plant. They need to know his secrets; they are worth millions. I still have those detailed notebooks and I still have no idea how he made steel.

I learned from this old steelmaker about the importance of delivery. This man had exquisite Personal Practical Knowledge, and he delivered magnificently. He could not articulate what he knew and we could not capture it. He retired and pure gold went with him. This experience helped form my lifelong quest to understand how people think and how to value the power and depth of what people know.

This book for me is about delivering and about deep respect for the knowledge that people carry with them. For us, these blend seamlessly with the culture, courage, and voice mentioned above. Over our years working together the alignment in our thinking is palpable. We have come to our beliefs through very different trajectories: one research based and the other practice based, and we have learned to keep each other honest.

OUR LEARNING JOURNEY

Between us, we have almost one hundred years of research and practical experience inside schools. Between us, we have worked in over twenty countries. We are currently working in schools across six countries. As we work, we are constantly responding to challenges alongside our colleagues in schools. Together with them, we observe what works in their context. Over time, we look for what works across different contexts. We tentatively generalize, then continually observe, share, and test more broadly. Ours is a shared never-ending, collaborative learning journey, with each other and with respected teachers and school leaders. We invite you on board.

For us, theory emerges from practice, not the other way around. We are constantly exploring what works with real teachers and school leaders in real classrooms and real schools. We extend and strengthen our work with every new school experience. We are clear that we do not have "the answers." We have powerful insights and many questions. This book is made up of elements of practice, each one of which we have observed in lived successful school practice. Many of them our colleagues have reported as transforming their schools and their classrooms. For us, many promising approaches do not stand the heat of practice. This was the screening test for this book.

Nothing gets into our shared practice until we have used it successfully in our own lives for at least three years. If you cannot make it work yourself, why share it with others? The schools that deliver, around which this book is based, operate in similar ways. Their practice is robust and continuously road tested.

We are both action learners, so our practice is constantly evolving. Both of us regard feedback as a gift and we are totally open to fresh insights. We have each created strong feedback environments for our own growth and learning. This is central to our professional lives. Respected colleagues have critiqued and recritiqued the many drafts of this book and enriched our writing.

This book is woven around the voices and experiences of hundreds of teachers, school leaders, and community members. Our action research with them forms the ongoing reality of our work. As you encounter their examples, quotes, and voices, you are accessing the up-to-date manifestations of what we live every day. They keep our work fresh and relevant, in the here and now.

We robustly challenge each other and invite our colleagues to do the same. We are not "shrinking violets." Both of us work hard to expose flawed assumptions behind our work and we are constantly on the lookout for unhelpful inferences. Our shared history is littered with these. Thankfully, our history is also filled with delightful moments. We share the joy of what works to create the learning and growth that each child and each teacher deserve.

This book is our most up-to-date iteration, the 2016 version—what we use today in our daily practice with schools. The book has been written for anyone interested in how schools can better deliver:

for children,

for families,

for teachers,

for school leaders, and

for the community.

OUR WORDING

We have written this book together, using *I*, using *we*, and using *you*.

We do not want to confuse you as our reader, so let us explain.

When we say *I*—this could be John or Bill writing from his heart. It does not really matter to us which of us is the *I* in any of what we write and we hope it will not matter to you, as our reader.

This is a genuinely coauthored book, with two strong core voices. We have also included the voices of many of the people we have learned from and with. To respect these voices, we have used their language and spelling in our quotes.

When we say *we*, it could be both of us saying something that we have talked about in our twenty years together or in the many joyful months writing together. We have loved this process. We have deep respect for each other and writing this book has been an absolute professional and personal joy. We are only stopping so that we can write the next one.

We also write *we* when we are talking about the education community. We have been part of that community for most of our lives: as school children, teachers-in-training, teachers, leaders in schools, principal, educational researcher, university professor in education, teachers of adults, parents of many children and grandchildren. So we are often using that collegial *we*—we are in this together, you and us—people who care deeply about education and learning.

When we say *you*, we are talking to you, our reader. Reading a book is a deeply personal experience and we want to make it as valuable for you as we can. Part of that for us is establishing a rich interaction between you as our reader and us as writers.

This is our current best practice.

—John and Bill

1

The Hidden Power of Alignment

As a school principal, continuously working with change, Bill knows that any time a group forms to do work together, they create a unique organism. Each person has travelled their own signature path to get to this school. How do you tap this unique collective resource to grow a school?

As a cognitive science researcher, John works to understand how people think and how to tap human potential. This brings him up against context. People do not live and learn in a vacuum. He is continuously exploring and testing learning processes internationally across organizations of all types.

How does the clinical clarity of well-tested research match with the complex messy reality of life in schools? Each of you will have faced this.

The researcher and the practitioner came together to work inside Bill's schools. We needed a process that was robust enough to provide a rock solid base for effective school change. To be of real value, any such process must be flexible enough to work across many school contexts and cultures. We have learned that the change process must encompass the beliefs and experience of all of the school community if it is to have any chance of lasting the distance.

Sometimes change works beautifully; sometimes it enthuses us all at the start and fades to leave us bereft; and sometimes it is slow to begin and develops real bite over time. Change in schools is always working inside a fluid medium. Principals come and go, staffs change, mandates come and go, as do theories and funding.

Despite all of our practical experience, reading, and research, and that of our many colleagues, we all continue to struggle with the complexities and frustrations of school growth. There is no one formula. Each particular school context demands unique insights. As one observes any school, characteristics jump out. We may see strong teamwork, weak literacy skills, a strong multicultural community, tired staff development activities. Most staff will openly share these and they can form a strong basis for analysis. The challenge is to match this sharp analytical focus with the equally important big picture synthetic view of why this school exists. It is a delicious productive tension that tests and enriches us all. This balance of analysis and synthesis you will find throughout this book.

The best change processes are simple, powerful, and elegant. This requires stripping away artifice, the distractions that can derail thinking.

- We are only interested in this book in processes that drive action.
- We are only interested in models that give people explanatory power to understand what is happening to them.

Jerome Bruner (1986, p. 132) put it beautifully:

If one fails to develop any sense of reflective intervention in the information one encounters, one operates continually from the outside in—information controls you.

If you develop a sense of self, premised on your ability to penetrate information for your own uses, and you share and negotiate the results, then you become a member of the culture-creating community.

From the base of our rich experience and that of the thousands of people we have worked with, what is the distilled essence? What are the lessons and the pathways that lead to the creation of a culture of delivery? This first chapter takes you on a change journey.

ALL OF US HAVE A STAKE IN THIS

A new teacher enters her classroom. She holds a dream for the way she wants her class to soar; she holds a dream for the teaching life that lies ahead for her. Over time, this evolves; reality reshapes all of our dreams. We see teachers living the joy of a teaching career, being filled daily by the nobility of the life teaching can provide. We also meet teachers grieving for the loss of their dreams, the loss of the career they envisioned.

The new principal enters the school, filled with dreams for the school. We know principals flourishing in their leadership career and we know principals grieving for their loss.

Parents have dreams for that child they held in their arms. They want the best for their child and will do almost anything to help achieve that. We know parents filled with the joy of family and the richness this brings to their lives. We also know parents grieving for the child they feel has somehow missed out.

This bridge between dreaming and grieving is crossed regularly throughout life. What stance we take on this bridge impacts our life and our career.

Every child has their own unique personality. Our children have precious lives ahead of them. They hold dreams for their own lives. Richard Ryan and Jennifer La Guardia (cited in Ryan & Deci, 2000, p. 71) report,

> Much of what people do is not, strictly speaking, intrinsically motivated, especially after early childhood when the freedom to be intrinsically motivated is increasingly curtailed by social pressures to do activities that are not interesting and to assume a variety of new responsibilities.

What message does this hold for us in education? Take some time to reflect on this.

What have you dreamed?

What have you lost?

What do you hold dear and will never let go?

Ryan and Deci (2000) reviewed the research on self-determination and what facilitates intrinsic motivation, social development, and well-being. Personal responsibility and self-determination are at the core of who we are. If we are to have the courage to address what best promotes organizational and individual richness of life and learning, here is a space to invest energy.

How can we address this deeply felt need for self-determination, the basis for any effective change process in our lives? And how do we balance this with the needs of the group?

THE CORE OF CHANGE

At the core of any effective change is what people's lives have already taught them. All of us act out of what we know, what our life has taught us. My experiences with change have been positive, so I look forward to it and embrace it. That is all very well for me, but if your life has taught you that change is unpleasant and hurts you, then that is the reality you work from.

We all have "school of hard knocks" knowledge etched into us. Jim Butler (1994) calls this **Personal Practical Knowledge (PPK). This is my knowledge from living my life**, practicing my craft. It is personal because it comes from my unique life; it is practical because I can drive my performance from it; and it is true actionable knowledge. We explore PPK in more detail in Chapter 4.

My PPK comes from my experiences and my reflections on those experiences. And that should not be easily disregarded.

Because my parents moved home many times during my school years I developed PPK about how to deal with bullies in schools. That PPK is still with me. We each have our own unique PPK. My wife, Sandra, has loads of PPK about art, movement, storytelling, and early language development, where I have close to none.

When we work from our PPK, we behave in ways that are aligned with what we believe. **The common term used for these beliefs, values, and assumptions that underlie our behavior is** *mental models.*

Examples of mental models are

- Children socially construct their own knowledge
- Classroom management is a curriculum issue
- Students must learn to take personal responsibility for their own learning
- Teaching requires deep subject matter knowledge

No one will buy into change wholeheartedly if their ideas and life experiences **(PPK)** and their beliefs and values **(mental models)** have been ignored or undervalued. We have all seen people and their ideas dismissed openly, and we have also seen it done more subtly: "We have really listened to what you have said, but because of (waffle, waffle, waffle) we have decided to take another path."

Real listening is easy to spot. Patronizing people is also easy to see and hear.

We have often been called in to play a mediation role between warring factions. We begin by getting each person to write down, and then share, their mental models about the issue. As we publicly collect these, invariably there is amazement about the degree of agreement across factions. There are differences, but they are often minor. By working together out of the agreed mental models, progress can be made, and sources of disagreement often slowly dissolve.

Our PPK and our mental models drive our actions. So, the starting point in school change must be to tap these core resources to create a Shared Vision. We have found that this often puts teachers back in touch with their sense of vocation:

I have so enjoyed these two days; it reminded me why I wanted to become a teacher and refreshed my vision of myself as a teacher.

It was wonderful to see our vision emerge.

I cannot wait to get started and build the school which we have envisioned!

—Secondary School Teacher, Auckland, New Zealand

The last two days reminded me why I chose the teaching profession. We share a common goal in being passionate about our chosen profession.

It's interesting how differently I started this morning with kindergarten. Even though exhausted from yesterday I felt the passion for the children that I did when I entered the profession three years ago.

—Kindergarten Teacher, Sydney, Australia

Throughout, we will use quotes shared with us by the thousands of teachers who have taken a Shared Vision journey to become a school that delivers. These come from six countries: the United States, Australia, New Zealand, the United Kingdom, Sweden, and Norway, and cover all levels of schooling.

Not every teacher has a successful experience, nor does every school. We are continually learning about how to improve the processes we use. **Our processes will not be best for every school community.** We are happy to stand alongside the many other successful processes for school growth and development that exist internationally. Some share similar mental models to our processes and some come from a completely different mental model base.

As we have explored the best ways to create a genuine Shared Vision, we always come up against power structures. These can be formal structures; they can also be informal structures. Anyone who has worked inside any organization, not just a school, will know these well.

Often, we talk about power through the people who use or misuse it, and their associated behaviors. In our meaner moments, we refer to control freaks, bullies, micromanagers, naysayers, conservatives, cynics, radicals. In truth, they are each acting and responding from what their lives have taught them. They are trying to hold true to the PPK and mental models that have got them this far.

We each know in our heart how the real power structures in our school work, no matter what anyone may say. And most of us have learned to adjust our behavior to fit in.

Brené Brown (2010) expresses this situation well:

Fitting in is about assessing a situation and becoming who you need to be to be accepted. Belonging, on the other hand, doesn't require us to change who we are; it requires us to be who we are. (p. 25)

Laying bare dysfunctional power structures, and our collusion in them, is central to empowerment and self-determination. This does not come easily.

We began by asking people to use classic brainstorming to get out of their hearts and souls what they really wanted for their school. Immediately, we met a massive obstacle. In most schools, there are people who are used to speaking the loudest and the strongest. And they do so. In classic brainstorming we would hear:

"I think what she/he is *really* trying to say is . . ."

"Look, what do you really mean by that?"

"How can you be sure?"

"I think you are forgetting . . ."

You will recognize these voices.

How do you deal with this?

We chose to ban discussion.

We would explain before people started brainstorming: "We know that there are some people here who are good at discussion. Well, today discussion is banned. Discussion comes from a Latin root, *discutere*, which means to smash to pieces. And today we want all ideas to be heard. So, for those of you who are good at discussion we want you to imagine, just for today, that there are people in this room who can express exactly what they think without the benefit of your towering intellect to tell them what they are really thinking."

Sometimes there is a long silence, sometimes there is laughter, and sometimes there is applause. Almost always there is a massive sigh of relief.

> Wow! Can't believe what has been achieved in 2 days! As a facilitator I was anxious all weekend—but I have really enjoyed working through the process with a group—NO DISCUSSION! Love it!

Be clear, at the start of any effective change process there must be ground rules in place that allow voices to be heard. In this way, we can tap into the PPK and mental models of everyone involved. These are the bases for empowerment, respect, and genuine alignment.

THAT MAY WORK FOR INDIVIDUALS, BUT HOW ABOUT TEAMS?

Empowering individuals is central. But how do you empower teams? How does one achieve consensus and alignment in a school community if each person is expressing his or her own views?

As a young boy, I loved to read cowboy comic books and watch cowboy movies. I became enamoured of the image of the sheriffs or marshals or any "good guys" fearlessly walking down the dusty street. Shoulder to shoulder, hands hovering over their holsters, staring down the outlaws or "bad guys." That sight of committed people with good on their side facing you down, coming at you head-on, has stuck with me.

Everyone in a school can line up, shoulder to shoulder, and walk down that dusty street saying, "This is what we are about; this is what we will achieve together. Anyone who tries to get in our way will have to deal with all of us united together."

That would be an unstoppable force.

For a school to deliver, there must be a clear picture of what we will deliver, when we will deliver it, and how we will deliver it. Most people also want to know why. Our experience matches that of Simon Sinek (2009), when he argues that we should start with the why in everything we do. Do you know your why? What is the purpose, cause, or belief that inspires you to do what you do? For Sinek, knowing the "why" creates the buy-in.

We have visited few schools, companies, and sporting teams with a clearly owned and lived Shared Vision. Some have a vision on their wall; few have it in their heart or soul. When we have asked people about their vision-on-a-wall, many report, "That is what we say we do" and that the reality is very different. Such visions-on-a-wall are grist to the mill of the cynics in the school. As schools live their daily lives, there is a vision being lived out. It is composed of the beliefs, values, and assumptions that underlie every action, every decision, and every system that is in place. Seldom is this articulated at all or articulated clearly. But it is alive and well and the true driving force in the life of the school.

Turning our intentions into action and impact, often called "walking the talk," is crucial. To do this, we first have to be clear about what is the collective intention of those who make up our school community. There is rich literature available on organizational change and its challenges. At the top of this for us is the work of John Kotter from Harvard. We have great respect for Kotter's work and have learned much from it.

In his book *Leading Change* (1996), Kotter lists the eight common errors in organizational change efforts. The third of these relates to Underestimating the Power of Vision. His reporting on the aligning power of a Shared Vision matches our experience totally. He explains that without a vision to guide decision making, each and every choice employees face can dissolve into an interminable debate.

We can think of many staff meetings we have endured that resonate with this. How about you?

Our long experience has taught us that intrinsic motivation is where the real action lies. In Daniel Pink's book *Drive* (2009), he shares what he sees as the three elements of the new motivational operating system: Mastery, Autonomy, and Purpose.

> This era doesn't call for better management. It calls for a renaissance of self-direction. (p. 90)

From our experience, the secret is to help people tap into what they really believe, what they really want, what they would "crawl over broken glass" to deliver. Inside this collective resource are found the collective purpose and the bedrock of shared mastery to drive action. This chapter addresses our approach to tapping the power of purpose. Mastery runs strongly through the work of two major influences on our thinking, Peter Senge (1990) and Jon Saphier (Saphier et al., 2008). Personal mastery is one of Senge's five disciplines at the core of any Learning Organization. Saphier's continuing work on research for better teaching calls for focus on the professional repertoire of teachers as fundamental to quality teaching and learning.

The unique lived lives of those people who form a school community are the most powerful resource our children have. When all of this Personal Practical Knowledge (PPK) is respected and integrated, this is a resource of massive power for teaching and learning. Yet this is often buried beneath layers of doing and saying what is expected, years of working within a system with set parameters.

Brené Brown (2010) found from her research that our unexpressed ideas, opinions, and contributions don't just go away. They are likely to fester and eat away at our worthiness.

Our experience in schools is that years of being overloaded, and having insufficient space to stay in touch with what matters most deeply to us, slowly eats away at autonomy.

Any school can deliver if only this internal PPK is respected and aligned. Most schools need the rest of the world to get out of their way and let them become the school deeply embedded in their hearts and souls. They will ask for help if they need it and they will know who to ask.

Developing autonomy, both individual and collective, brings the sense of agency that builds individual and collective momentum. Giving everyone voice in designing our Shared Vision is a core element of autonomy and of schools that deliver.

As one teacher wrote to us:

> I had reached a stage of stalemate or dead-end with regards to my teaching. But I now see the light at the end of this tunnel, with renewed hope and sense of direction and balance to my life as a teacher. This new vision is most welcome and I am looking forward to it.

Many people ask us about the difference between a Mission Statement and a Shared Vision. For us, **a Mission Statement is a statement of overall purpose:** Why does this school exist? Often the Mission is set by the community, or the country, or the state, or the organization that founded the school. **The Shared Vision is a clear picture of how our school will deliver on that Mission.**

As Joel Barker (1990) puts it so succinctly,

> Vision without action is merely a dream. Action without vision just passes the time. Vision with action changes the world.

Vision is not limiting—it is full of air and light and life. It gives you an open world to travel into rather than closing you down from the beginning. This chapter provides a process that works for creating a Shared Vision together and turning this into action.

ALIGNMENT IN SCHOOLS AND IN LIFE

I was head of the science department in a large high school in Australia. At our heads of department meetings, we would each talk about what we were doing in our departments. Each of us was hard working, dedicated, committed, as were most of our staff. We had our plans and we were tightly focused on what we wanted. At one meeting, we had a discussion about homework. I had raised this issue for two reasons. One was what I saw as the unreasonable load on our students. The other was the unreasonable marking load on our staff. I did not mention the load on families. The head of languages said that his students had to compete in public examinations with students who had these languages as their

(Continued)

(Continued)

first language. So his students needed to do a lot of homework. When I questioned him about what would happen if we all set that amount of homework, he replied that he had to look after his responsibilities, and that I should look after mine. It occurred to me that we were like a bunch of skyrockets sitting in a bucket, all with enormous potential energy. But, when we were lit we each flew off at full speed in our own direction, all pulling in different directions. And the school as a whole went nowhere! Why do we not strap all of the individual and teaching team rockets together with duct tape? When they are lit, they would move off together with an enormous whoosh—all heading in the same direction, with all of the power heading the same way.

How does this experience relate with yours? Many organizations are constantly dealing with silos. The key is to know where the whole school is heading and how we can contribute together to the best outcome. What structures currently exist in your school to promote and ensure alignment?

An old crab catcher described a similar phenomenon to me. When he caught his crabs, he would tie them together with a piece of string. He would leave them on the beach while he searched for more. When he returned the crabs would still be there. They had each been trying to scuttle off in a different direction and together they had gone nowhere. If only those crabs had agreed on one direction in which to scuttle together, they would have been gone. Have a think about the crabs in your school and in which directions they scuttle at present.

EXPLANATORY POWER: TWO MODELS

As mentioned at the start of this chapter, having models that give explanatory power to what is happening is an essential element. What follows are two models, from the many we have tried and tested, that have proved invaluable for schools we have worked with.

The first of these models helped us see the importance of keeping a focus on the future and not bogging down in current reality and getting caught in the restrictions we can all see around us.

Mandates can be seen as restrictions. We learn about restrictions from the moment we are born. Babies spend nine months floating in a very safe, fluid environment. They emerge into a new reality. Let's face it, gravity is very restrictive! Babies do not lie around grumbling about this. They have an inner drive to learn their way forward, and they crawl, they walk, and then they run. This is the approach we see in schools that deliver—they focus on action, not grumbling. They take restrictions in their stride.

The best expression of this comes in **Robert Fritz's Model of Structural Tension (1987).**

Robert Fritz's Model of Structural Tension

Nick Zeniuk, through his work with Fred Simon (personal communication, 2015), introduced us to this powerful visual representation of Fritz's work (see Figure 1.1).

What Fritz has taught us is that between any vision we create and the current reality in which we live, there is always structural tension. This is normal, natural, healthy. So, when any new mandate arrives, welcome this new picture of the future. Then look at it from your context, your collective perspective, your current reality. Take your time.

You then have two choices in how to deal with this structural tension.

The first choice is to focus on the current reality. Poor us, they have dumped another mandate on us; we are still living through the troubles from the last mandate. Whining, moaning, groaning, wallowing. We have entered many schools who share with us this terrible state they are in. If we go back five years later, they are still whining, moaning, wallowing, and groaning—just about different things. They live in reactive tension. It is like walking through wet concrete. They are defeated. They have lost sight of their personal power. Their world is pushing them around, doing them over. And the world will readily supply such batterings regularly for anyone ready to sit around and wait for them. Breaking free from this is

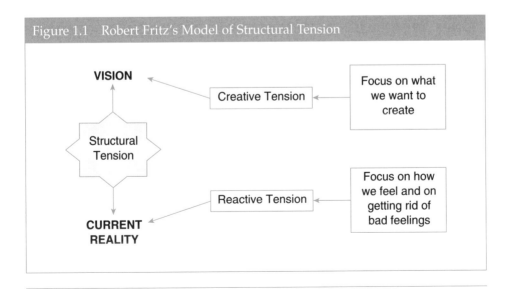

Figure 1.1   Robert Fritz's Model of Structural Tension

Source: Used with permission from Fred Simon.

liberating. As an elementary teacher from the south coast of New South Wales, Australia, put it,

> We are about to embark on a very exciting and inspirational journey with hopefully the results reflecting my longing of having an exceptional school with a shared belief. I'VE WAITED 28 YEARS FOR THIS!! Perhaps I have just wanted somebody, anybody, to encourage me (us) to take risks to do what we want, how we want.

This quote reflects the second choice: to focus on the vision, the future. A ferocious focus on the future leads to creative tension. Senge (1990) has found that mastery of creative tension brings out a capacity for perseverance and patience. We hope that you will know this delicious feeling, when you come to work filled with a mixture of calmness and confidence, matched with excitement and anticipation—working together with shared passion, shared commitment, on what really matters to you. This focus on the future drags the current reality forward; it transforms the reality into the future, the vision. This professional life is a joy.

A middle school teacher in Texas expresses this well:

> Our vision has excited and renewed me. I came from such a negative atmosphere that I feel in shock over our positive climate. Burnout and depression were so prevalent that I had even considered leaving the profession. Our vision is the answer to so many things I see wrong with education. I feel challenged to grow and take part in this endeavor.

Every school we work with lives inside a current reality filled with mandates of all shapes and sizes. Accept the mandates and get to work on your creative responses to them. Put your energies where they have influence; do not put your energy into areas of concern that you cannot influence but can complain about long and hard. Stephen R. Covey (2004) has found that proactive people put their energy into their Circle of Influence, generating impact. Reactive people put their energy into their Circle of Concern, with no impact.

As one high school teacher from Detroit, Michigan, wrote to his principal,

> As a parent of children in our school district I love our vision. I do want to share it. I do want to achieve it, but there is a problem. The problem is good old father time. The hours it will take to accomplish our vision are enormous. I teach, I coach, I counsel, I love our student body, I take care

of the people who mean the most in my life, my personal family. When am I going to have extra time to achieve our vision? In my teaching, our department has been bombarded with new state mandates. We must meet new standards. We have been thrust into teaching new curriculum we have no training for. In my coaching, I know it takes a full day on and off the field. As a result of my dedication, the workload between my students and my athletes is enormous. Sometimes I feel guilty and wonder what it would be like to be able to focus on only one area. I want to give more, but how much time for more is a major concern. Time is my worst enemy. I will help all I can. My time is yours. Help me to be able to give all I can.

Here is the cry for future focus. We are not suggesting that you should ignore your current reality. The issues this teacher raises are real, and they need to be addressed. This is the structural tension. But what we have learned is this: **only deal with the current reality through your future focus.** We do not put our initial energy into an analysis of the current reality. This is so seductive; people say to us, "How can we deal with the future if we do not know first where we are starting from?" You do not need to know this. This is a trap into which many fall. It will almost always bog you down in your present reality.

In our work, we start with the Future—the Shared Vision.

Once our Shared Vision is clear, we are ready to deal with the current reality, on our terms, using our strengths, our resources, our PPK. The current reality is addressed as we move powerfully forward toward our Shared Vision. There is no way we cannot deal with current reality. But, dealing with it from a future focus brings delivery not found in dealing with the current reality for its own sake. Five years from writing this plea, the teacher was a happy, fulfilled, energized member of a Blue Ribbon School in the state of Michigan.

This chapter takes you through our process for delivery. This will put you in touch with your collective power and with your collective creativity. Never again be daunted by mandates; embrace them. For many years, we have shared the joy of delivery in schools that have broken free from self-imposed chains and backed themselves and their rich inner resources. They have learned to balance autonomy and self-determination with accountability pressures by trusting themselves. This is seen by many as a dichotomy. In fact, autonomy and accountability coexist happily inside schools that deliver.

The second crucial explanatory model for us is **Daniel Kim's Levels of Perspective Model (2001).**

Daniel Kim's Levels of Perspective Model

Through his book *Organizing for Learning: Strategies for Knowledge Creation and Enduring Change* (2001), Kim introduced us to the Levels of Perspective (see Figure 1.2). This model has provided us with the most powerful lens we have ever found through which to view organizational life. The model allows us to view everything that happens at a school through each of the five perspectives.

Shared Vision. In this chapter, we share one effective process with a long track record for developing a Shared Vision. Our process draws on the mental models and PPK of the school community. Such a Shared Vision has a flavor of authenticity not found in a vision formed by hierarchy. Once the Shared Vision is formed, everything at the school can be viewed through this powerful lens.

Mental Models. As outlined earlier, mental models are our beliefs, values, and assumptions. Together they form what is often termed our *worldview*. Our mental models shape our actions and behavior. The mental models a teacher holds—even subconsciously—about teaching and learning drive their behavior. If I have a mental model of teaching as passing on information, then I might subscribe to a transmission model of pedagogy. On the other hand, if I hold a mental model of learning as understanding which is socially constructed, then I might subscribe to a more student-centered model of pedagogy.

Systemic Structures. Fritz (1987) suggests energy in organizations flows along a path of least resistance, like water across the landscape. We advocate that leaders at every level design and implement systems and structures to encourage energy to similarly flow toward realization of the vision. These are the enablers we put in place through which the desired mental models can be lived out. So, we see a classroom

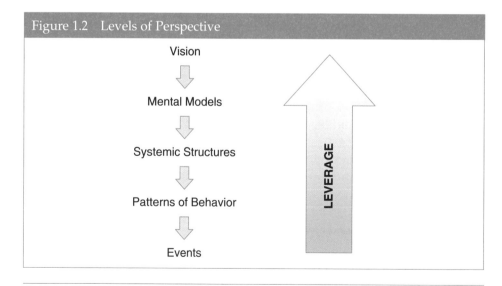

Figure 1.2   Levels of Perspective

Vision

Mental Models

Systemic Structures

Patterns of Behavior

Events

LEVERAGE

Source: Used with permission from Daniel Kim.

behavior system, a school attendance system, a department curriculum delivery system, a peer coaching system. We can see these systems and structures at work.

Patterns of Behavior. These are those things we see happening over and over again: a team meeting every month, the same child comes to school late every Friday, a newsletter goes out the same day each month, a teacher with a continuing classroom management issue. We see patterns in what is delivered.

Events. These are those single actions we see each day: an assembly, a parent conference, one lesson, a school excursion, a coaching session. Schools are filled with thousands of events. Patterns of behavior and events are indicators of the current reality and of where we are at in relation to the vision.

Kim's leverage arrow is significant. The higher up the Levels of Perspective you take action, the greater the impact or leverage.

- Taking action to build your Shared Vision is the most powerful action.
- Taking an action to embed a mental model into your culture so the Shared Vision will be realized is the next most powerful action to take.
- Designing a system or structure that supports living out a mental model to realize your Shared Vision is another powerful action to take.

When there is a clear Shared Vision, staff can be confident about the mental models that must be lived to reach the vision. So can parents and children. Where designed systems and structures support living out those mental models, you have alignment. You see the patterns of behavior and events you want to see. You see a school that delivers.

COLLABORATION AND CHALLENGE

In many schools, there is a high level of congeniality. People get along with each other; they share common interests. The staff room is a friendly and sociable place where staff can talk comfortably and happily with each other.

In other schools, there are high levels of cooperation. People are willing to help each other, to work together and support each other. There is teamwork here; staff are working for our mutual benefit.

Our experience is that these two characteristics are not enough. **To get the best from ourselves and from each other collaboration is needed.** Here staff are willing to challenge themselves and each other, to stretch themselves and each other, in working to achieve a Shared Vision. This is more than the intersection of common goals seen in cooperative ventures. There is a deep collective determination to achieve the Shared Vision. This often involves experiencing periods of individual and collective discomfort, and facing the inherent challenges. As James Kouzes and Barry Posner (2012, p. 135) found,

> Shared visions and values bind people together in collaborative pursuits.

Whenever we take on a learning opportunity, we take on a level of challenge; we also make decisions about the level of support we will need to respond to the opportunity. Each time a teacher hands a learning task to a child, that teacher also hands the student a designed challenge and a designed level of support. School leaders do the same with staff. Decisions about what are realistic levels of challenge and required levels of support will be determined by many factors. One of the key factors will be the mental models held about challenge and support.

Laurent Daloz (1986) provides a useful matrix for exploring challenge and support. His matrix suggests that

> High Challenge/High Support produces growth,
>
> Low Challenge/High Support produces confirmation,
>
> High Challenge/Low Support produces retreat, and
>
> Low Challenge/Low Support produces stasis (no change).

As we started to use this matrix inside organizations, we subjected it to the scrutiny of the PPK of the workforce, as we do with all models we use, including our own.

We have asked hundreds of people to map onto this matrix their most powerful learning experiences. The results of this process alerted us to something we had been missing. Coming from a background in teaching and education, we were strongly alert to the support needs of people while learning.

The pattern that emerges from collective experience is that the challenge axis is where the real action is. By far, the majority of powerful learning experiences are found in two quadrants: High Challenge/High Support and High Challenge/Low Support. Most people are hungering for challenge. Support is important, but challenge is the key to the deepest learning. Our data collection shows that many people are very busy but profoundly bored at work. Listening to the learning experiences of many people has added layers of meaning to Daloz's initial analysis.

High Challenge and High Support can indeed be a space for deep learning. Think of such times in your life: You are at the edge of your capability, fully stretched and being given all of the support you need. In my early career as an author I lived in such an environment for three years. I was working on Australia's first National Curriculum project: the Australian Science Education Project (ASEP). The work was highly challenging with tight deadlines. I had colleagues supporting me, a team leader supporting me, and other support staff including typists, data analysts, a laboratory assistant, editors, and illustrators. For me, it was exhilarating learning. Some of my fellow authors crumbled under the strain and left.

High Challenge and Low Support has been the most contentious area for us. Time in this quadrant can drive people into retreat. Most of us have experienced this. At the same time, most people report this is the quadrant for the deepest learning: lessons that are seared into us, succeeding against all odds. When I was a young researcher, I was invited by the OECD (Organisation for Economic Cooperation and Development) to head up a group at a major international conference in Paris on Learning to Think: Thinking to Learn. The stretch was massive and I was expected to deliver on my own (Edwards, 1991b). I still remember the daunting feelings and the thrill of what followed.

What we suggest for those exploring the balance of challenge and support is to see it individually, with no set rules.

One of New Zealand's top research scientists shared that Low Challenge/Low Support is the space he looks forward to: holidays where he lies on the beach with his fishing line tied around his toe, dozing. He explained that this is where the germs of many of his best research ideas work their way into his mind. He then goes back to work and frames up his grant application: High Challenge and Low Support. He gets the grant and is into High Challenge and High Support and cannot wait to get back to that beach.

High Challenge/High Support does produce growth; it can also be a space of high stress from high expectations and a space from which one may need a break. Low Challenge/High Support is a space that provides confirmation; it is also where many ask, "Am I missing something here?" or "Why all of this support, do they think I lack capability?"

Decisions about challenge and support are based on deeply held mental models. What is experienced as support for one person can be experienced by another person as being ignored, or by yet another person as unnecessary interference. The key is to be crystal clear about your mental models. Ensure that your challenge and support decisions are aligned with them.

Marcia Reynolds, in her 2014 book *The Discomfort Zone*, argues that for true shifts in thinking and behavior to occur, you must be willing to challenge a person's beliefs, interrupt his patterns, and short-circuit the conviction to his logic even when it feels uncomfortable.

Jim Butler and I developed the Learning Pit Model to introduce learners and teachers to the key understanding that learners get worse before they get better. This is outlined in detail in Provocation 2 in Chapter 2. **The learning pit shows that confusion, frustration, and challenge are essential elements in learning.** Many colleagues we have mentored have developed creative uses for our Learning Pit Model. For example, James Nottingham, in his book *Challenging Learning* (2010), explores the concept of challenge in learning. He has developed a Learning Challenge Model:

> my version of Butler's and Edwards's model and their concept of the pit. (p. 185)

What has emerged most powerfully for us and those we work with is this: **Challenge is the key to creating a collaborative workspace and learning space; support creates a cooperative workspace and learning space.**

Our work parallels the work of Kouzes and Posner (2012, p. 39):

> Opportunities to challenge the status quo and introduce change open the doors to doing one's best. Challenge is the motivating environment for excellence.

As you will see in our Shared Vision process, people are challenged to express their views openly, to vote openly, and to work collaboratively. Here are some typical responses to this way of working together:

> Thoroughly enjoyable two days. This has been a great experience as a whole staff. The process you use to obtain data and create the vision, and the whole research process, creates a sense of ownership for ALL staff members. There are few other ways to unify a staff so rapidly and to clarify where they are going so well.

> Whew! It's been humongous! To be able to finally take a full breath and be a voice amongst many. To be passionate about who I am and where I fit in, to have a go and see the roads we have taken together. It's great to be part of a team that has a vision to create an enormous change.

> Staff members are feeling inspired and have a sense of professionalism that has never been bestowed on them before. The strategies removed the ego and placed everyone on an equal playing field when it came to decision-making. We created a team of players that normally would not work together, producing a unified team with an integrated vision in its refining stage in less than two days. The organisation and clear decisive methods employed are so well structured that they appear resilient.

Challenge as fuel for collaboration is not easy to work with. It can be volatile. Team challenges as part of collaboration require particular team skills:

- Team members must be skilled in dialogue, not discussion (see Provocation 4 in Chapter 2).
- Trust must be present that allows the "un-discussables" to surface and breathe air.
- Negative and cynical voices must be respected, supported, and valued through this test of collaboration.
- Be clearly aware of your own idiosyncratic challenge and support needs and their effects on those around you.
- If challenge and support needs and patterns are misinterpreted or ignored, we can stifle the learning and growth of people, rather than enhancing it.
- The context of learning has a crucial impact on learning. Challenge and support is also contextual and should be explored in this way.

Effective teams know how to work their way through challenging periods. We see many teams and schools retreat under serious challenge. Instead they need to hold their nerve. The process described in the rest of this chapter is challenging. It has been tested against the lived realities of many leaders, teachers, and communities over twenty-five years. It is a PPK-Based Process, a practical process. It takes courage, commitment, and collaboration.

As one teacher expressed it,

> I loved the way you took on a strange, diverse bunch of lip-flappin' people and made them all look in one direction. And we feel good about it too!
> We appreciate how you have worked it down to us. Not like taking a strange philosophy home—makes a difficult bedfellow.

Those readers working in the area of social capital (Forsyth & Adams, 2004; Hargreaves & Fullan, 2012; Wellman, 2014) will see strong parallels with the way we work. Our Shared Vision process helps a school to mine its social capital through invitation, challenge, reflection, collaboration, active public recording, and a shared repertoire of strategies, tools, and protocols.

ALIGNMENT VERSUS AGREEMENT

Delivery requires disciplined aligned action. This continuously builds our momentum toward our agreed Shared Vision. If a staff member wants to move in a different direction, this becomes the focus for rich, respectful questioning, dialogue, and leadership action.

As one principal explained to me,

> Alignment is so elusive. The journey is strewn with obstacles and mysteries. Each person has gotten to this place on a personal, long and winding road. This reality makes leading alignment like herding cats. Every life is different. How in the world do you get them to go in the same direction? Once you figure this out you have found the holy grail of alignment.

It is important here to distinguish between alignment and agreement. So often the things that divide us are so small. Once we have alignment to a Shared Vision, this clarifies disagreements around how we may get there. These disagreements are healthy. What is not healthy is people undermining the agreed Shared Vision to get their own way. Some staff in schools we have worked with find it difficult to accept a genuine Shared Vision when they have dominated staff in the past and had their own way.

> What a process! I have to admit I was very skeptical (What! Two days and 80 odd people to come up with a VISION STATEMENT??). I thought that's what the executive did!!
>
> However, I am now totally sold on the incredible process of reaching consensus with a large group of notoriously, ad nauseously, argument-oriented people (teachers). Getting such a diverse group with so many different agendas and axes to grind to be heading in the same direction is nothing short of miraculous.

Alignment is of benefit to all people associated with the school. It means that we can all plan what we will do, knowing the direction will not change. For example, we know of school development coaches who prepare in detail for an initiative only to find out at the last moment that priorities have changed and all their work has been wasted. Knowing that there is sureness of purpose is a great gift.

Any school leader should think carefully before embarking on a Shared Vision journey. It takes courage and commitment for a principal to trust their school community to create the Shared Vision together. In our Shared Vision process, the principal does not vote, as you will read below. They trust their community to deliver the vision that is right for this context. **Never promise genuinely participative decision making if you are not willing to follow through.** Making such a promise of longed-for freedom for staff and then reneging on it leaves you much worse off than if you had done nothing.

A common challenge over time is turnover of staff. How does this affect a Shared Vision journey? Our experience is this:

- Schools that send their Shared Vision to applicants for positions have a strong start on alignment.
- Schools that run effective induction programs based around their Shared Vision, as lived in the school, build more alignment.
- Schools that listen to and respect what new staff and families bring have a base for checking alignment and enriching the journey with fresh insights.
- Many schools revisit their Shared Vision after three years. Some revisit annually. It depends on the progress on the Action Plan that emerges and on the turnover being experienced. These are contextual judgment calls.

As alignment to our Shared Vision emerges, there is a change of language and a change in the way people relate to each other.

WHEN VOICES ARE HEARD THAT ARE USUALLY STILLED

Our belief in alignment came from our strong, long experiences as young men in competitive sport. Anyone who has been a member of a great team operating together at the highest levels, and achieving success together, will never forget that exquisite feeling, that way of being. It is what Mihaly Csikszentmihalyi (1990) refers to as "flow." Many researchers tend to talk about this in a much more disembodied way. The feeling of powerful alignment is visceral and hard to put into words. You really "know it" when you are experiencing it!

John Kotter (1996) is clear about the power of Vision, as are many other researchers we respect deeply. Creating desired futures together is at the core of Senge's (1990) *Fifth Discipline* and his current writings (e.g., Senge et al., 2005, 2010). Senge is committed to people continually expanding their capacity to create the results they truly desire, where collective aspiration is set free and where people are continually learning to see the whole together. "Inspire a shared vision" is the second of Kouzes and Posner's (2012) Five Practices of Exemplary Leadership. Envisioning the future and enlisting others are the two commitments embedded in this practice. They argue that "shared visions and values bind people together in collaborative pursuits" (p. 135).

Our lives have taught us that people want to participate in the formation of the vision. When people have engaged with it, struggled with it together, challenged it, edited it, and written it, the power to act is already inherently theirs. Most people, in schools we work with, want to "own it," not be "sold it." Then they will fully commit, fully buy in. So, our work is posited on the fundamental belief that everyone should be involved in the creation of the Shared Vision. This is in stark contrast to the vision being bestowed from above and staff then being "empowered" to deliver it.

As a teacher at a school in Sweden shared with us,

> Det finns en växande Vi-känsla på vår skola.
>
> (There is an increasing feel of WE at our school.)

Our processes are intentionally designed to be open, transparent, and democratic. They create a Shared Vision that is openly shared. This works best in a school where trust levels are high and where people are listened to with respect. Such a culture is ripe for open dialogue and together creating a shared vision. But we have learned not to wait for this or to spend time trying to set this up. If this exists, that is a bonus.

The key is to get started and let the processes work on people. This taps into our current reality in a fresh way. This enables us to experience other ways of interacting and creating together. We learn about working productively together through our collective PPK and mental models—by actually doing it, not by talking about it. This is the well-known process of **acting your way into new ways of thinking rather than thinking your way into new ways of acting**.

As our colleague Sandra Russell (personal communication, 2015) expresses it,

> a process that listens to the participants and observes, dwells, and draws on the present context is always modern and up-to-date.

Here is one teacher's description of our process, after experiencing it for two days:

> What I enjoy is the fact that consensus p****s off people who dominate, and when voices are heard that are usually stilled.
>
> —Secondary School Teacher, Christchurch, New Zealand

INTRODUCTION TO SHARED VISIONING

What follows is a précis of our Shared Visioning Process. We have refined and refined this over the last twenty-five years, alongside teachers, school leaders, and school communities.

This is the first step to become a school that delivers. It is **a crystal clear picture of what you plan to deliver.** The process is normally spread over two days: the first day involves a process of deep respectful questioning, the Inquiry Probes Process. This draws the mental models and PPK from the Vision Creating Community. These form the first drafts of the Shared Vision. The second day involves writing the second draft of the Shared Vision. We can then identify the Core Values and the research themes: the areas that we must address to **get to where we want to be from where we are now.**

As mentioned earlier, this is not the only process for successfully creating the school you have always wanted. The process shared here is working in many school contexts across many countries. It also is working well inside business and elite sports contexts.

Underlying Mental Models for Shared Visioning

- A Shared Vision provides a base for alignment of everyone in the school.
- To be a genuine Shared Vision, everyone must be involved in the creation of the Shared Vision, knowing that their voice and their beliefs have been heard and respected equally with those of others.
- People who have been present and involved in the creation of the Shared Vision are usually willing to commit to its achievement, since it reflects their shared beliefs and values.

SHARED VISION CREATION PROCESS

Schools commonly start this process by committing two consecutive days to the eight steps of the first phase of the process. When this is not possible, many creative variations have been designed to complete the process in other time frames.

Here are the eight steps we follow in creating a Shared Vision. At the end of this list, we will discuss the steps in more detail:

1. Select the people who will be involved in the vision creation process.

2. Design a broad set of Inquiry Probes (key questions) each of which will tap the rich PPK of those who attend the vision creation day. **The probes should cover all of the key aspects in the life of your school.**

3. Select the best eight probes.

4. Put people into groups of six to eight people, each with a trained facilitator.

5. The facilitators take the groups through the Eight Inquiry Probes using two processes: **classic brainstorming and 10/4 voting**.

6. Once the top ideas from each group have been collated into a master list, each person gets a private vote from these top ideas.

7. Write a set of Shared Vision drafts using the top four responses from the final voting on each of the eight probes.

8. These drafts are given to the whole group for critique and feedback. Based on this feedback, a second draft is written. This process continues until a final version of the Shared Vision is agreed.

Step 1: Who to Invite

Some schools have invited just the teaching staff, others the full staff, others have invited parent representatives, board members, former students, current students, community or cultural leaders, and on we can go. The key is to have the voices that need to be heard in your school community. The choices you make will be determined by the relationships you have with your community. This is explored in detail in Chapter 6.

- Who would you invite?
- What message would you want the makeup of your list of invitees to send to your students, your staff, your parents, and your community?
- Be clear; your choices will send a message to your community!

Step 1 ensures that you have the best blend of people present at your Vision Creation Day.

Step 2: Designing the Inquiry Probes

Inquiry Probes are the questions we use to dig deeply into the beliefs, values, aspirations, and life experiences of those who attend the Vision Creation Day. Schools often find it helpful to have skilled outsiders help with creating a long list of possible Inquiry Probes. You can send these outsiders your latest documentation, which may include current vision; strategic plan; school newsletters; recent reports done on the school, or by the school, such as annual reports; or any other material that could provide ideas for probes. Or, you can have some respected skilled outsiders come in and observe the school and the way it functions and interview some staff, students, and parents, and from this design some possible Inquiry Probes.

First writing at least thirty diverse probes from which you choose your final eight gives much more powerful probes than just trying to write eight. It has been our experience that eight probes works best in forming a Shared Vision.

So, what do Inquiry Probes look like? Each school needs probes to fit its specific context, so no two sets are the same. Here are sample Inquiry Probes from a range of schools:

1. What capabilities must our teachers demonstrate so that our students have a love of lifelong learning?

2. How can we structure our school and programs so as to get the best performance from our teachers?

3. What benefits do we expect from parent and community involvement in our school?

4. In what ways do we promote higher-level thinking and deep learning by our students?

5. How can we best ensure balance in our lives and in the lives of our students?

6. What are the central characteristics of technological literacy that we will engender in our students?

7. How can we make our curriculum more challenging and relevant?

8. If we were to hear adults we respect talk about the graduates of our school, what would we most like to hear them saying?

9. How will we ensure that all voices in our school community are heard and respected?

10. What existing strengths in our school culture should we most celebrate and build on into the future?

The design of probes can be done completely internally. The fresh eyes of outsiders can help generate a wider set of probes. A blend of internally and externally generated probes is often best.

The Inquiry Probes for your Shared Vision process will be unique to you. There may be some that are the same or similar to those above. The best probes have that flavor of authenticity to the context that draws out powerful ideas from those who answer them. This requires attention to the language used and to the areas covered by the Probes. Over twenty-five years, we have helped schools develop thousands of Inquiry Probes. We have at times been asked to provide a "standardized list" for a school to choose from. We never accede to such a request; it misses the point. Probes must be owned and relevant to context.

Step 2 provides you with a rich list of possible Inquiry Probes.

Step 3: Choosing Your Final Eight Inquiry Probes

Whatever the generation process, the final set of Inquiry Probes must be chosen internally. This can be done by the leadership team or by the whole staff.

Trimming your draft list to your final eight can be done in many ways. You need to try out what look like your best ten to twelve probes on a small number of staff or leaders. What you want to ensure is that the probe produces rich data, and also that no two probes just give you the same data. Some probes can look great but give you mush when people respond to them. Some probes can look quite different, but when people respond to them, they just give the same responses. Ensure your probes give broad coverage of your key areas.

Step 3 provides you with your final eight Inquiry Probes.

Step 4: Set Up Groups With Trained Facilitators

Divide those attending into groups of six to eight people. We commonly recommend diverse groups. So, we spread non-teachers across the groups as well as mixing up the staff. Each group has a facilitator who knows the two key processes for completing Inquiry Probes. These processes are explained in detail in Appendix 1, which is a copy of the handout we provide to facilitators and group members.

For those not familiar with these two processes,

Classic brainstorming is an idea-generation process, where everyone shares their knowledge and insights;

and

10/4 voting is a powerful consensus-generating tool, used to trim a long creative list back to the chosen three or four priority ideas.

As well as being well trained and experienced in these processes, facilitators are chosen based on having strong credibility within the school community.

Step 4 ensures that you have your Inquiry Probe work groups in place, with their trained facilitators.

Step 5: Groups Complete the Inquiry Probes

The probes are worked on, in turn. It commonly takes 35 minutes to do the first probe, using the two processes. This settles to around 25 minutes once people become familiar with the processes. The eight probes commonly take around four hours to complete. As soon as each probe is completed the full list of responses is sent to the "Central Tally Room." The tallied votes and the priority items for each probe are identified clearly. Collation of these priority ideas for each probe is done in the tally room while the other probes are being completed in the groups.

My brain is fried. I wish this could be drip-fed to me over the period of a week or so. I really enjoyed the inquiry probe process as it almost totally eliminated ego-noise and blustering which is so common here.

Excellent to have our executive work in such a non-threatening way with us.

The principal does not participate in the Inquiry Probes process. He or she works in the Central Tally Room. This process is based on trusting the staff and community. A great benefit of not being involved in this part of the process for the principal is that if a staff member complains about "that vision of yours," the principal can reply, "How many votes did I have and how many did you have?" Diplomatic immunity! This process is about giving a voice to those one leads. You then lead the process to deliver on what the school community has envisioned for themselves, their children, and their families. This is commonly referred to as Servant Leadership. By giving away apparent power, real power emerges.

Giving us ownership of the project has already changed the minds of some reluctant people. It is a great new concept that I am excited about.

Commonly an "outsider" sits in the Central Tally Room with the principal and their top typist. Many staff report to us that they appreciate the feeling of openness and transparency created by this outside presence.

A master list of prioritized responses is prepared by the principal and those in the tally room, for each of the eight Inquiry Probes, by collating the top three ideas from each group. This involves combining ideas that are the same. This clear list of priority ideas for each probe can then be fed back to the whole community, as outlined in Step 6.

Mary Wilson is principal of Baverstock Oaks School, in New Zealand, which has had great success using this process. Wilson (personal communication, 2015) stresses the value of having "skilled outsiders" helping to facilitate:

The Principal has immunity and it doesn't appear 'rigged'. Outside eyes bring another perspective and can provide coaching of the Principal to lead the process.

Step 5 gives you a set of collated priority responses from each Inquiry Probe group in one master packet so that each person can make their final vote.

Step 6: The Final Vote

This master list of priority responses from each probe is given to each person at the end of the day. They allocate ten votes to their preferred ideas for each Inquiry Probe from the master lists of prioritized responses provided. They can allocate these in whatever spread they like. They do this voting privately. Groups then tally their votes. The group facilitator collects the tallies, brings them to the Central Tally Room, and helps to make the final collation of the votes for the whole group.

Step 6 provides the final votes from the Vision Creation Community on each Inquiry Probe, and it identifies the top four ideas this time from each Probe.

Step 7: Writing First Drafts of the Shared Vision

Once you have tallied the final votes for the preferred responses to each of the eight probes, you identify the top four responses from each probe. This provides around thirty-two key ideas and concepts. These ideas are then threaded together by Draft Vision Writers to make a series of paragraphs, to construct first drafts of the Shared Vision.

We commonly ask three writers or pairs of writers to create drafts of the Shared Vision on behalf of the whole school. These are commonly chosen from the best "wordsmiths" in the group. The drafts are prepared overnight. The Shared Vision fits on one page. It is written in the present tense. It is crucial that the writers of these drafts honor the language of those who provided these responses. As much as possible, they use the exact language as captured in the Inquiry Probes process.

Step 7 generates three first-draft versions of the Shared Vision.

Step 8: Forming the Final Shared Vision

These first drafts are shared with the Vision Creating Community, usually the next day, and members individually critique the drafts in detail. It is important in this process to remember that a Shared Vision is a clear picture of where we are heading. It is not a statement of where we are now.

Critiquing commonly involves highlighting sections (paragraphs, sentences, or words) they particularly like in each of the drafts and sections they do not like. They can also recommend new wordings, so long as these are to be found in the priority data generated by the groups through the probes. **This is not an opportunity to introduce fresh ideas.**

Based on these critiques, a writing team drafts one second draft of the Shared Vision, using the most highly rated sections from each draft. This writing team is commonly two or three skilled writers. These can be those who wrote the first drafts or new people. Writing a second draft commonly takes two to three hours and is a challenging process.

This second draft is read aloud to the group after lunch on the second day. We have found that this public affirmation of what the group has achieved together is commonly a deeply moving experience for those in attendance.

This draft then goes through further iterations over a period of weeks. The Vision Creating Community get the chance to do a critique of the new second draft. They have a copy of the priority ideas they generated and can ensure that the Shared Vision is true to their ideas. A third draft may need to be created and shared. Seldom does this process go beyond a third draft. By this stage, any suggestions are commonly minor editorial changes, which can be easily made. Remember that these new iterations must stay true to the data generated in the Inquiry Probes process. This is not an opportunity for any one voice to try to introduce new ideas and dominate others.

Step 8 generates the final Shared Vision of the future of your school.

Now the school is ready for aligned action!

Responses to the Shared Vision Process

From well over one hundred schools across six countries, here is a range of the typical responses to this Shared Vision process:

> I've been here a zillion years and I've never experienced the degree of consensus in a shared vision for this school as I have felt in the last two days.
>
> I must admit that I was somewhat cynical about these two days before we started. I LOATHE brainstorming sessions and Professional Development where we are required to do all the work and teach the facilitators. Thus I came into these sessions in a more negative frame of mind.
>
> I've also thought to myself 'I can't do research'. I haven't been to university.
>
> And with a downgrade of my qualification on the last pay-round I have felt undervalued.
>
> This experience has helped me to appreciate my colleagues more, to accept myself and my own Personal Practical Knowledge, which prior to this I dismissed as being somewhat irrelevant.
>
> *(Continued)*

(Continued)

I have an open mind towards the future—I genuinely feel 'profession-ally developed' and I am willing to give this a go as far as I am able.

I'm tired! But my mind is open and I have a feeling like a million things are possible.

I feel a bit like this has been an educational renewal, and I hope that I can stomp out all the skeptic in me.

Inspiring. It is nice to think we will be able to clean up the mess, get clarity and move forward. I feel like I've been treading water. I'm looking forward to the process. It is fantastic to have parents involved in a positive way.

Almost 100 percent of the feedback is positive after the two-day pro-cess. Two concerns arise for a small number of staff. The first is concern about their individual capacity to go through the changes that will be involved. Some are tired and unsure.

The second concern involves some having a lack of faith in their school leadership to push through any change:

It was an opportunity to re-discover what this group can do to make our school one of the best schools in the world if this plan actually takes place. I am concerned that what I heard at the end of the day from our leader may be an excuse for why things might not change!

They are right; leadership is crucial to any change process. We focus on leadership in schools that deliver in Chapter 3.

We have been asked about our choice of processes, particularly classic brainstorming. Our long experience with brainstorming has convinced us of its practical value in generating ideas. We accept that authors such as Susan Cain, in her book *Quiet* (2012), call into question its efficacy. She sees it promoting social loafing, production blocking, and evaluation appre-hension. Our overwhelming feedback from thousands of people is that in the context of Inquiry Probes, disciplined brainstorming works well. It promotes energy, excitement, creativity, and active involvement. We believe that **eliminating discussion is the key**. Not all agree. As one teacher in Varberg, Sweden, shared:

Det var nytt för mig att inte få lov att diskutera, men bra. Det var frustre-rande att rösta på en sak som du kände starkt för men som de andra inte röstade på. Många goda ideer kom kanske inte med. Men det är demokrati.

> (It was new for me to not be able to discuss but very good. That was frustrating, when you felt strongly for one thing and you voted for that but the others were not voting for the same. Many good ideas perhaps did not come along. But that's democracy.)

For those of you familiar with the work of Kouzes and Posner (2012), you will see that our process fits their three conditions for commitment:

> People are likely to become committed to a course of action when three conditions are present: when they experience a sense of choice about their decision, when their actions (choices) are made visible to others, and when their choices are difficult to back out of or revoke. (p. 226)

A YEAR OF "PREPARATION FOR ACTION"

From the Shared Vision, staff identify the key areas for "research" to shift the school to where it wants to be. We have used quotation marks here because many teachers like to tell us that they are not researchers. Teachers understand "preparation for action," and that is what this research really is.

In Appendix 2, we share four examples of Shared Visions from schools across four countries and show the associated research themes that they identified. In four examples, we cannot capture the full fascinating diversity in the Shared Visions we have seen. They are each matched to their particular context, as are their "preparation for action" themes. School size determines how many themes you can handle; small schools may have only three themes; larger schools can handle up to eight.

When staff search the world for best practices to bring back into their school, they have a passion for what they want to deliver. This drives right through any initial misgivings about being researchers. Often they find that the answers they are seeking are already inside the school. They can be at a school nearby or sometimes on the other side of the world.

> Being together was and is a fantastic experience—to share opinions/views/ideas in a 'safe non-threatening' environment where you felt that you were not judged for being who you are. It's amazing to work with a team who all are passionate about making our school truly a dream school where everyone loves to learn powerfully. There were no energy vampires, we are all sources of energy and we energise each other.

Those involved in the vision creation form teams to each explore one of these key theme areas on behalf of their school community. The teams are usually between three and twelve people, depending on the size of the school and the number of themes. People normally choose to join the team focusing on the theme about which they are most passionate or where they have particular skills and experience. Sometimes leaders ask some people to shift teams to ensure diversity and a balance of experience across the theme teams. This is a process of skilled negotiation so that each theme team is strong.

The teams take one year to do this research and trial ideas in their classes or across the school. Sometimes they visit other schools physically or across the Internet or invite visits from innovative teachers and schools they uncover. Sometimes the innovations needed are already in the school in nascent form. In the end, each team creates the recommendations that they believe will best move the school toward the Shared Vision in their theme area. Each recommendation will become part of the Long-Term School Development Plan.

Presentation of Action Recommendations: What a Day!

The day the school community comes together to see each Preparation for Action theme team present their recommendations is a special moment in time! There is no better way to spend time as a collaborative team. The day is spent observing the future of the school unfold before you. A future you have owned and created. Some recommendations take your breath away and bring you to tears because of their power. The recommendations are called *Task Descriptors*.

> This morning while I was writing my notes for my presentation, a wave of emotions came over me. The feelings of discovery in my class last year were so powerful. To me it wasn't about how flash I could present today, it was about sharing what I discovered in my class and spreading the news about how great it was to try something new and find success . . .
>
> This has been very empowering as it has clarified my thinking and enhanced my classroom practice. I was quite overwhelmed by how much I know and humbled by the children's willingness and enthusiasm. I love our shared vision; it empowers everyone.

Action design must be a part of any process that will deliver.

Each Task Descriptor is analyzed against a set of criteria following the formal presentations. Every voice is heard as the analysis is completed.

Appendix 3 outlines the process for moving from Task Descriptors to a plan.

Teachers respond well to initiatives that are well designed by their colleagues. In Kungsbacka, Sweden, a teacher shared this experience:

> Det är första gången i skolans historia som alla medarbetare ställde sig enade bakom en plan som den här handlingsplanen vi presenterade.
>
> (This was the first time in the history of this school that all staff, with one voice, said yes to a plan like this action plan we presented.)

DESIGNING THE LONG-TERM SCHOOL DEVELOPMENT PLAN

The ability to design a Long-Term School Development Plan is a crucial leadership skill. Our experience is that many leaders lack confidence and skill in this process. In Appendix 3 we provide design guidelines.

Following analysis, there will be a final set of Task Descriptors that the staff believe will result in the successful implementaion of the Shared Vision. These are then sequenced into a Long-Term School Development Action Plan. Excitement emerges as the community sees the Task Descriptors, which will begin the implementaion. The delivery journey toward their shared vision is begun!

There should be no hurry. The emergent action plan lines up what is to be achieved into a series of targets as defined by the Task Descriptors. Each is delivered with quality before the next target is addressed. Some teachers have confided to us "we never really finish anything properly." The joy and satisfaction that come from absolutely nailing an important agreed outcome together are infectious. In achieving one target, this commonly flows over to delivery on other targets at the same time. This sense of flow is one characteristic of the Performing Stage in the work of teams, as discussed in more detail in Leadership Challenge 1 in Chapter 3.

IDENTIFICATION OF CORE VALUES

Inside any Shared Vision is a set of Core Values. Core Values are statements of the mental models we are going to live together on our Shared Vision journey. Here are some sample Core Values:

- We value one another's time.
- We draw strength from our diversity.
- We continually think at the highest levels.
- We take personal responsibility for our performance.
- We respect every voice in our school.

To identify the school's Core Values, once again form groups of six to eight people. Each group uses classic brainstorming and 10/4 voting to identify the top three Core Values they see in the Shared Vision.

Once you get the top three Core Values from each group, form a priority list as you did for responses to the Inquiry Probes. Each person then has ten votes to allocate privately to that priority list. Adding up these votes will identify your top three or four Core Values for the whole group. Ways of working powerfully with Core Values is the focus of Chapter 5.

OUR SHARED VISION AS AN ALIGNMENT TOOL

The Shared Vision is an alignment tool. We use it to get everyone on the same page, speaking with one mind and one voice. Be clear that this does not mean agreement on everything. People are welcome to disagree and discuss things. However, **the Shared Vision clearly states where we are heading and that is not up for discussion.**

Once the Shared Vision is clear, we can identify the mental models that must be in place for our vision to be achieved. These include the Core Values. Ensuring that everyone lives the mental models necessary is key leadership work, as we discuss in detail in Chapter 3.

Once the mental models are clear, we can design the systems and structures that are needed to enable the mental models to be lived out. This is how the vision becomes a reality.

In New Zealand, they have an Educational Review Office (ERO), whose staff visits schools and observes and gathers data. They work with schools to report on progress. Here are excerpts from ERO reports on two schools using this Shared Vision process:

> There is a high degree of commitment to a recently developed vision, created by the staff, board, and community. This vision accurately reflects the school community's aspirations for high quality educational outcomes for its students.
>
> The review finds that the process of developing a Shared Vision has had a positive impact on teaching and learning strategies across the school. Staff and students share a commitment to learning and exploring ideas.

Freedom From Interference

In many schools, the lives of teachers and staff have a feeling of constant interruption. Blockages seem to appear to prevent learning and teaching from flowing at a natural healthy pace. Someone else often seems to think they know what we need, what extra things we can do. Teaching lives can become cluttered in ways that do not promote learning. Here is the power of a Shared Vision—it cuts through this clutter.

When a course of action is proposed, ask the following: Does this align to our Shared Vision?

If the answer is yes—then we get on with it.

If the answer is no—we will put this in the parking lot for another time.

Healthy education has a flow to it that is compelling for all involved.

Which Boundaries to Push?

An artist we know has spent time as a teacher. Her experience is interesting; it offers one "outside view." Her perception is that artists spend their time talking about how they can push the boundaries and teachers talk about how to keep things constant. This is one person's view, from limited experience. For us, it rings bells of recognition, not only in schools, but also in most organizations. Teachers do want to push boundaries; the challenge is to reach agreement about which boundaries. As we watch teams report back after a year of searching the world to find ways to enact their Shared Vision, boundaries are pushed everywhere. There is energy and there is excitement.

The Shared Vision gives us one way to create alignment around which boundaries we will push together and how we will go about this.

Tapping Personal Power

One of the major sources of stress in adult lives is having no real sense of personal power or efficacy. The feeling is that someone else is "pulling the strings" and that we are dancing on those strings. In many countries, large education departments have been pulling these strings for generations. Teachers can feel like marionettes in such a theater.

It is a joy to watch staff float out of school at the end of a day, where each has been respected and listened to at a deep level. At last, no one has interrupted to tell us what we are really thinking.

As one Swedish teacher explained,

> Jag insåg verkligen vikten av att jag hade en röst och att den hördes, som mycket uppfriskande. Att alla hade en röst, inte bara de som alltid tar över.
>
> (I really found the fact that I had a vote and that I could be heard very refreshing. That everyone had a voice, not just the people who always take command.)

Personal power leads to collective power inside our school and its community. Tapping this energizes our Shared Vision journey to deliver the education we all want.

The Shared Vision that emerges is genuinely ours.

Having worked in New Zealand for many years, our Māori friends and colleagues there have shared the alignment they see between our process and their culture.

There is a powerful Māori *whakatauki*, we share here with the deepest respect, that captures the spirit of what our process is about far more eloquently then either of us could:

Unuhia te rito o te harakeke kei whea te kōmako e kō?

Whakatairangitia—rere ki uta, rere ki tai;

Ui mai koe ki ahau he aha te mea nui o te ao,

Māku e kī atu he tangata, he tangata, he tangata!

(Remove the heart of the flax bush and where will the kōmako sing?

Proclaim it to the land, proclaim it to the sea;

Ask me, 'What is the greatest thing in the world?'

I will reply, 'It is the people, it is the people, it is the people!')

The flax bush in Māori folklore is a metaphor for the family. The outside older blades are the ancestors, the next layer in are the wider community elders, the next layer in are the current grandparents, the next layer in are the wider family (aunts, uncles, cousins), the next layer in are the parents and the innermost layer are the children, and finally the grandchildren to be born.

Our process, described in this chapter, ensures that all voices are heard and respected in forming the Shared Vision for a school community. It is indeed the people that matter. From the other side of the world, in the United States, Edgar Schein (2013) in his book *Humble Inquiry: The Gentle Art of Asking Instead of Telling* makes the same point from a different cultural base. Schein suggests a bias toward telling instead of asking because of what he sees as his country's pragmatic, problem-solving culture, in which knowing things and telling others what we know is valued:

Not only do we value *telling* more than *asking*, but we also value *doing* rather than *relating*, and thereby reduce our capacity and desire to form relationships. (p. 6)

Our Shared Vision process is based in asking, listening, and relationship from the start.

SUMMARY

Chapter 1 is about listening with respect to the voices of your school community. They will create together a Shared Vision for the school that is needed for their children, for their community. Such a Shared Vision provides ownership, relationship, and alignment. They will then deliver this vision with commitment and passion.

To do this requires a powerful enabling process. Chapter 1 describes in detail one such practical process. Here is a checklist for a process that works:

1. Choose a suitable time for creating the Shared Vision.

2. Decide who to invite to form the Vision Creating Community.

3. Create a set of Inquiry Probes: questions that will dig both deeply and broadly into the experiential richness of each person invited.

4. In groups, first generate broad creative responses to each probe, then achieve consensus on the top responses.

5. Use the priority ideas to write drafts of the Shared Vision and go through a critiquing process to get the Final Shared Vision.

6. Identify the Core Values in the Shared Vision and live them.

7. Clarify the areas that need to be researched to shift the school from its current reality toward the Shared Vision.

8. Form school community "Preparation for Action" teams and give each of them a year to research a different area and design action recommendations.

9. Based on whole staff critique of these recommendations, leaders create the Long-Term School Development Plan.

10. Implement the recommendations, live the Plan, work the Plan.

We have "road tested" this process. It has been refined and refined through implementation across many school community contexts in six countries. It is current. We were using it yesterday inside a school in Sweden.

In this chapter, we also share the ongoing blend of research and practice that characterizes this whole book. Our narrative is carried by the voices of real people delivering in real schools, backed by a rich tradition of research.

2

The Real Work

As the searchlight of our new Shared Vision falls onto our present reality, every aspect of life in our school community is seen afresh.

There are hidden aspects that have not had light shone on them for many years. Some of these will be what makes our school special, unique. And some of them will now be clearly seen as anachronistic, in need of change. Our special things are seen in this clear new light, our chest swells with pride; they are to be savored. Our anachronisms look a little grubbier. Hmmm, we should have addressed these long before now; time for a spring clean!

This is our focus in Chapter 2, to facilitate a new vision-driven clarity about what you do. In the collective minds of your school community,

What is the real work of your school?

and

What is not the real work of your school?

Answer these two questions and you can then deliver in sure steps.

Once we have a clear Shared Vision in place, there are two parallel targets for delivery. The first is this clarification of the real work needed to make the Shared Vision a lived reality right here in our school. The second target is to clarify and start living the Core Values that are inside our Shared Vision. This is the focus for Chapter 5. The leadership processes that underpin all of this delivery work are the focus for Chapter 3, for those who would like to go there first.

FRESH EYES

As authors writing this book, we do not, and cannot, know what your real work must be. Each school is deliciously unique, as is each community, child, teacher, and leader. What we offer in this chapter is a set of provocations. We have used them across many school communities to help them think afresh about their real work.

In schools, like in every organization where we work, much time is spent doing things that add little, if any, value. I spent so much time in my teaching career doing work that was not appreciated, gathering data that was never used, and doing administrivia that drove me and my colleagues crazy for no positive outcome.

> The school staff were asked to list all of the responsibilities and expectations a teacher had in the school. It came to fifty-seven. The staff developer commented, "You must be very, very, very tired." After the cheers died down, the staff were asked to identify how many of these actually contributed positively to student learning. It came to eight. The school began changing dramatically from that moment.

Many things done in schools are there because of habit or history. This archaeology needs to be examined. Moving energy from non-productive activities to high-leverage activities is a win for the school. This is where we have agreed we want our energy to be spent. This is what is in our hearts.

We learned from Ruth Gordon (personal communication, 1988), in Minnesota, three questions that are the key to examining current practice:

What are we doing now that we should continue to do?

What are we doing now that someone else should do?

What are we doing now that no one should do?

A teacher gave us a key fourth question:

And what will we do with the time and space we create?

We have helped many schools work through these questions, with powerful results. Honest answers tell us where time, energy, and resources should be invested. Schools that deliver are clear about this focus. They are also capable of searching to find the world's best practice to bring into their school. The community, the staff, and the students deserve nothing less. Bridging the gap from where you are to where you want to be requires

looking inward as well as looking outward. And these schools often introduce "razor gangs" who cut away the dead wood of outdated practices.
Creating freedom and space takes strength and clarity.

One of my favorite experiences with Bill is his courageous leadership
to create space for his staff. Here is the story of "The Herculean Task," in
his own words:

Teachers were frustrated. The sentence from the Shared Vision was
clear, "We will continuously think at the highest levels." They were trying hard to transform lesson plans from delivering the Texas Curriculum
into infusing thinking dispositions—Arthur Costa's Habits of Mind. "We
do not have enough time to teach thinking," became the battle cry to
block the way. We told our teachers we needed to complete a Herculean
task. Department chairpersons were asked to meet with their staff over
a month and divide the Texas Curriculum into three distinct stacks.
We made it clear. Each stack of curriculum needed to be of equal size.
A month later, the staff came to a staff meeting with the three equal
stacks. As principal, I asked them to place the stacks on a table in front of
me. Up to the stage they came. They placed the curriculum on the table
behind the label for each stack:

1. Need to Know

2. Nice to Know

And finally, the third stack!

3. Who Cares?

When the huge piles of curriculum were all in front of me, I picked
up the significant stack of "Who Cares" curriculum and ceremoniously
dumped it in a garbage bin. The staff roared. I looked at them and said,
"There. We will never teach this part of the curriculum ever again. Now,
we have time to teach thinking!" In the state that was the birthplace of
No Child Left Behind, we threw out one-third of the curriculum. The
ensuing results on our Academic Excellence Indicators were dramatic; we
delivered in a way that won our school a National Blue Ribbon Award.
Today I am often asked in our "curriculum-driven" world about the process each department used to categorize the curriculum. It was a simple
process. Trust the teachers!

We accept that having read this you may be feeling: Why bother reading on? That would never work for me—my situation is so different and
these writers do not understand. If you are feeling this, please reread that

last section and think through valid ways in which you could create the space you need for what really matters to you and your students.

We are not suggesting that each of you should throw out one-third of your curriculum. But it may be a great starting point! Leadership courage and decisive action are two keys to focusing on the real work.

> I particularly appreciate the concept of throwing out that which benefits no one, as teaching has become more and more paperwork/bureaucracy driven and therefore time consuming. A breath of fresh air.
>
> —Secondary School Teacher, Auckland, New Zealand

WHAT IS OUR "RETURN ON INVESTMENT" IN SCHOOLS?

The advice to leaders in the corporate world is mostly to focus on performance and on what adds to profits and earnings per share. This is their bottom line. The Pareto Principle is often cited: 20% of our effort delivers 80% of our productive outcomes. What company owners and shareholders want is clarity about who or what delivers and what is delivered. This is commonly referred to as Return on Investment, or ROI.

What is the ROI for schools? What is the real work of schools?

As a department head in a large secondary school, I watched with resignation the steady addition of new "flavors of the month" to our mandated curriculum. It just kept growing. Nothing was ever taken out of the curriculum.

So, who decides what should be taught? There is an old saying that "once you shut the door to your classroom, you are the curriculum." Of course, there is some truth in this. A critical awareness of who you are as a person, and as a teacher, is a healthy starting point. Teaching is an essentially human activity, and we bring our humanity to the way we teach.

We encourage school leaders to help staff be healthy, well-balanced people who live rich lives with joy. This personifies the person that we as parents want with our children each day. Long after our children forget most of the curriculum they are taught, they will remember their teachers. Can you remember your best and worst? Both of us definitely can. A good question for teachers to ponder is this: What will children remember about me when they look back?

Surely, one convincing measure of the ROI is what happens to our graduate children when they grow to be adults. What role has the school played in helping young people "be themselves" as their life trajectory unfolds? Is there anything we can learn from how our graduate adults live their lives? Our research in Australian business and industry reveals much about the products of our schooling (see, for example, Edwards, 2001). Chris Argyris (1991) has found similar results in the United States from over fifty years of research.

Every adult we work with is full of stories from school: of their learning, of teachers they remember with great clarity, of teachers who are thankfully only blurred memories, of their friends and life outside the classroom. Some have deeply felt appreciation of the benefits that have flowed from their schooling. Some are deeply scarred by the experience. Teaching is a noble profession that can burn deep into the lives of children and their families, into the lives of teachers and their families. This is high-stakes work!

We have found, for example, that most adults have a limited conscious repertoire of thinking skills and the crucial dispositions to activate these skills. We have found that many adults describe themselves as "I am just a . . . secretary or plumber or production line worker or . . . ." Some have been stereotyped from a young age and have bought into those stereotypes deeply. Some share with us that "I hate mathematics," or "I am no good at science," or "I cannot paint." Such experiences with adults have profoundly influenced the way both of us writers think about education and the real work of schools.

Schools are only one of many players in the development of a child. At the same time, their impact on self-confidence and skill in learning is highly significant. At their best, they help to produce self-confident, independent learners with a lifelong love of learning and the metacognitive skills and dispositions to go with that. We have worked with many such schools and enjoyed meeting their students and graduates. How many of these schools and teachers are aware of the magnificent impact they have had? **Teachers impact children now, in the present.** In designing for learning, it is important to balance this strong, initial formative influence with the slower developing, longer-term impact.

Argyris (1991) talks about the significant difficulties he had with teaching smart people how to learn. The very people he expected to be most open to their own learning proved not to be so. Such life experiences have deeply influenced Argyris's approaches to organizational and professional learning and growth. What have your life experiences taught you?

Anyone who has taught using student-centred methods knows the humbling power of what children can do if we give them the wherewithal and basically get out of their way. Whether we are working with children or with adults, central to the work that we do will always be a focus on the learner. This means respectfully attending to what their life has taught them. Our hand is a bridge across the divide to where they need to be. This inevitably bumps us up against what we should be teaching and why: the curriculum.

THE BASIS FOR THE CURRICULUM

One valuable dichotomy around curriculum is

> Culture-within curriculum

and

> Culture-without curriculum.

Culture-without proponents argue that there is an extant culture and the best of this culture must be passed on to our children through their schooling. So children need to learn the power and beauty of good literature, mathematics, physics, and so forth. They represent the best that our culture has to offer to young minds. It was the dominant belief for most of the 19th century that the mind is made up of faculties and that these should be trained in school. This concept has been remarkably resistant to criticism and still exists in various forms in our culture. That universities still have "faculties" is not an accident.

Culture-within proponents argue that children have a culture within them, the one they are living. So, here we study what the children are reading every day rather than the classics. We study the mathematics that helps our students deal with their everyday life realities. Learning has a strongly utilitarian flavor.

Research shows that the dominant culture routinely institutes a culture-without approach. In early days, this was seen as having a healthy "civilizing effect" on nations.

Dangerous Bases

At the end of the 19th century, the first brain theorists began voicing views on education. They talked about the links between physiology and psychology. This had obvious appeal to psychologists trying to acquire the respectability associated with being a science. Many are beguiled by what appear to be solid scientific bases for their teaching approaches. Often, these are merely metaphors. Faculties are but one example of this confusion between metaphor and fact.

The current fascination by many to use "brain theory" as a basis for approaches to teaching is concerning. I had a group of eminent brain researchers rip apart one of my early research papers. They explained that they were at the stage of the crudest of metaphors for how brains function. They were frankly tired of educators misquoting their work and extrapolating it to levels that were nonsensical. Their request to me was, *"John, any time that you are at a conference and a presenter says 'brain research shows' please stand up on behalf of all of us brain researchers and ask them 'What brain research? Please cite the paper.'"* They argued that you could find a brain theory to back up almost anything you want to do in schools. Indeed, Charles Hampden-Turner's 1981 book *Maps of the Mind* cited sixty possibilities that were alive and well at that time. We have come a very long way in the thirty-five years since then. So, when I read of "Brain-Compatible Schools," a wry smile crosses my lips.

The advice from the brain researchers to me was to stick to studying classrooms and teaching and leave the brain research to the brain researchers. At that time, I was researching with Perc Marland what students are thinking while teachers are teaching (e.g., Edwards & Marland, 1982). We were using a research technique called *stimulated recall*. We would video a lesson with one camera on the teacher and one on the students. At the end of the lesson, we would make rapid copies of the split-screen tape. These were then used in interviews with individual students. They would be asked to play the tape and stop it as often as they could to tell us what they were thinking. Their recall would be stimulated by the split-screen images. This gave us very detailed data. We analyzed the detailed data from this research with teachers and teachers in training. We learned that teachers who believe they know what the students are thinking in their classrooms during lessons are mostly sadly mistaken.

So, what are sound bases for deciding what is the real work of our school, our classroom, and our school community?

OUR LIFE LESSONS ABOUT THE REAL WORK OF SCHOOLS

We began designing this chapter by writing down "criterion" experiences in our lives that have deeply impacted the way we see the real work of schools. We ended up with twenty-four. Over time, we have distilled these back to eleven key "provocations" for you to consider as you decide what is the real work for you and your school. As you read through this chapter, we encourage you to stop regularly. Reflect on how these gentle provocations rub up against your current school practice.

Provocation 1: The Joy of Teaching

Many teachers feel they have lost sight of their passion for teaching. There is a whole book in dealing with this topic alone. What is it about teaching currently that can do this to teachers? Teaching is one of the noble professions. For many it is a vocation. Then, the reality steps in and over time can grind away at the passion that was there from the start. This can be turned around. Clarity about the real work brings confidence and excitement.

A teacher in Varberg, Sweden, felt strongly about this new way of working together:

> Jag hade tänkt att gå i pension nu efter nästan 40 år som lärare men efter dessa två dagar vill jag tänka över det igen eftersom visionen och skolans framtid ser så spännande ut.
>
> (I am supposed to retire after almost 40 years as a teacher, but after these two days I will think it over because the vision and future of the school excites me.)

One measure of a profession is how it looks after its own and also how it polices itself. Many professions are under strong challenge for being self-serving. There is a lot of altruism in education. Teachers will commonly do what is best for their students even at the expense of themselves. I well remember the challenges I felt as I tried to balance my role as a husband and father with my role as a fully committed teacher and head of department. One principal I worked under had the view that during term time "we were his" and during the holidays it was our time. For me, this completely misses the point. Compliance is no mind-set for quality in anything. Time freely given, in a way that is balanced for the person concerned, is where professionalism lies. This will shift as each teacher's life changes. How skilled are we at facing these phases in the life of a teacher and drawing the best from each phase?

Is this part of the real work of schools?

Provocation 2: The Learning Pit— Being Clear About How Learning Emerges

We always get worse before we get better when trying to learn any new skill. We learn the most when we are challenged. As Piaget (1964) explained to us, the mind must first be "dis-equilibrated" to create the need to learn. Life and good teaching can each give us intellectual itches that we have to scratch. Just as the body hungers for balance so the mind hungers for equilibrium. In his work, Piaget describes key processes for resolving the dis-equilibrations: assimilation and accommodation.

Our research in schools shows that confusion and frustration are essential elements in learning. They are to be celebrated and embraced, not avoided. The pathway from disequilibration to equilibration is littered with "mistakes." Argyris's (1991) research on "teaching smart people how to learn" showed him that many successful people have limited experience in learning from mistakes. They have made so few of them. Learning how to resolve mistakes is a valuable skill to learn early in life. This can provide a different perspective in classrooms and staffrooms.

Young Bill Martin's experience in the US schooling system is a perfect example. His teacher would say that the class was going to learn something new. The quick learners would struggle a little, get the message, and rocket up the steep learning curve. Bill and his slower-learning friends would just get more and more confused. They were trying to grasp the concept and climb the learning curve. Then the teacher would utter those fateful words: "Moving on!" You see, we have to get through the curriculum. We have to be at the Civil War by Thanksgiving!

What is really happening here?

When we are introduced to new ideas, new content, new ways of thinking, our minds are puzzled. This is commonly called *cognitive conflict* or *cognitive dissonance*. My colleague Jim Butler developed a powerful model for this process. We gave it the visceral name "The Pit" (see Figure 2.1). This model and its name had instant impact on both children and adult learners. Everyone is able to recognize learning pits they have known. It is reassuring to know that this is an essential part of the learning journey. Jim and I have been using this model powerfully since the early 1990s, in education, business, and elite sport (e.g., Edwards, 2001).

Whenever we start to learn anything, we first go into a period of confusion, frustration, and at times, angst. This is often uncomfortable for the inexperienced or unsure learner. As we struggle to master the new concept or idea, over time, we action learn our way deeper into the learning pit. This confusion is an essential part of the learning process.

After a period of intellectual struggle, the transformation begins. We start to grasp the new idea, the new way of thinking, and we start up what is often called the steep learning curve. *Steep* is the right word as most learning, in the end, rushes at us. Some call it the aha or the eureka moment. Here we experience growing understanding, clarity, and flow. Those of us who are skilled at learning, over time, learn to have confidence that we can get through learning pits. So that feeling of fear at the start of the learning journey becomes tinged with excitement.

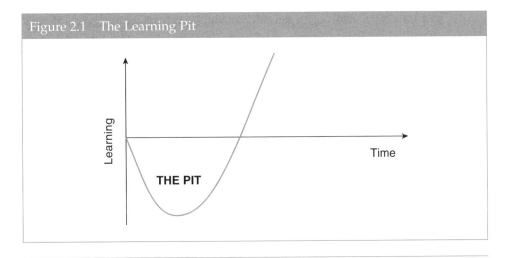

Figure 2.1   The Learning Pit

Source: Jim Butler and John Edwards.

However, Bill was one of thousands of children who spend their whole school career in a series of never-ending pits of confusion. There is little excitement for them. For such children, school remains a mystery that they never master. Their confidence in learning situations is deeply damaged, sometimes irreparably.

Some teachers believe that a key part of their role is to save students from confusion and frustration, the very elements that drive learning. Learning to be resilient and to be comfortable with being in the learning pit is an important disposition. This means accepting that frustration, fear, disappointment, and even despair are essential ingredients of learning. Effective teaching involves being clear about the learning pits into which children will be led and ensuring that these are of reasonable depth. Every child has the right to learn their way out of the learning pits we place them in, in some meaningful way for them as a learner. This is a lesson design challenge for any teacher. Watching outstanding teachers deliver such lessons, which cater to the personalized learning needs of all their learners, is a breathtaking experience.

The ongoing learning of staff provides an inspiring model of ongoing learning for children and their families. Jon Saphier, Mary Ann Haley-Speca, and Robert Gower, in *The Skillful Teacher* (2008) stress the absolutely fundamental importance of humility and constant learning for staff. Being clear about how little you know, as well as how much you know, establishes humility from the start.

We have learned to always triangulate our data: We look for three respected diverse sources. If they agree, we are comfortable. If not, we look more deeply. In relation to staff learning, we recommend three such sources:

1. In our experience, the existing Personal Practical Knowledge (PPK) of the staff, leadership, families, and broader community is the core essential triangulation source.

2. A well-established research knowledge base is a powerful second source for a rich triangulated understanding of individual and shared staff learning opportunities. Saphier's work is an excellent example of this. We cover this in more detail in Chapter 5. John Hattie's meta-analysis of educational research in *Visible Learning* (2009) is another such source.

3. Different schools and teachers have used a very rich variety of third triangulation sources. These include networking locally, nationally, and internationally; higher education study; action research done internally; observing learning in other professions; and forming mutually collaborative relationships with other organizations or schools.

Once we are clear that learning pits are normal, natural, and healthy, it can be quite liberating both for us as teachers and for our learners. Take a moment to think about pits you have known. What took you in, how long were you in, and what helped you out?

People have been counting my mistakes since I started school. I have made big bunches of them. Often I have been evaluated based on those mistakes. Yet, we know that challenge is an essential component of learning. As children move through these learning pits, is this the best time to evaluate them? Pits take time. The top of the learning curve is the best place for evaluation, after we have made all those mistakes and suffered through the learning pit. Mistakes are important when used to coach children and adults. They should not be counted.

This is the whole basis for **formative evaluation** as introduced by Michael Scriven in 1967. This is diagnostic evaluation, ongoing learning evaluation, an integral part of the learning process. It is the meat and potatoes of learning.

End-point evaluation is what Scriven calls **summative evaluation**. Final decisions and assessments do have to be made at key points. But what matters most is knowing what to do to help children get to where they need to be and want to be. Proving that they have reached that endpoint is important "after the fact."

Lorna Earl (2003, pp. 21–28) provides a different angle on this through her concept of assessment "of," "for," and "as" learning.

- "Assessment of learning" is essentially summative assessment.
- "Assessment for learning" is essentially formative in the sense of students and teachers regularly checking progress along the way.
- "Assessment as learning" is also formative; it is embedded inside the learning to actively assist students as they learn.

A school could declare, "We leave no child in the pit." We can agree that at least once a day or week, every child will experience the joy of learning as they rocket out of a pit. There would be no other school like it in the world!

An elementary teacher we worked with was very taken by the concept of "the learning pit" and told us that she would teach it to her students. She wanted them to understand what was happening to them through new learning situations. Pits became a part of the shared classroom language and this new understanding changed student behavior. Fast learners would roar up their steep learning curve. Then, they would ask if there were any students still in the pit who would like their help. One young lad in her class approached her and shared: "I spend a lot of time in those pits, Miss, don't I? And Tiger Woods, he went through one of those pits didn't he, Miss? So, it's OK to go through pits?" She reassured him. Shortly after this, she decided to move the class on to a new area of work. Up shot this lad's small arm: "Excuse me, Miss, I am still in the pit!"

Throughout the book we will refer to those involved in staff development in schools. We will use the generic term *instructional coach* for such people. Instructional coaches often have to skillfully address the generational differences of staff members. This can create inequalities of "pit time" among teachers. One prime example is anything related to technology. As one US instructional coach related,

> After a professional development session on a web-based data-tracking system, these two responses were both part of the feedback from the same session:
>
> "Great information, but moved a bit slowly for me."
>
> "Everything was presented so quickly. I need more time (with support) to process through."

Supporting both teachers and the groups they represent requires sensitivity to the different depth and timespan of the learning pits that you help people into or out of.

Learning pits are everywhere. We have found that workers in companies relate easily to the learning pit concept as do elite sportspeople. Leaders and coaches, as well as teachers, have to hold their nerve through pits. As Thomas Edison once explained, he was sad for the many potential inventors who pulled out at the very bottom of their "invention pits." Sadly, this was often just before they would have rocketed up that steep learning curve, as he had learned to do. We similarly find many companies abandon powerful change efforts just before they start to bear fruit. Building learning resilience in the face of the inevitable pits is a key life skill for all of us. Such "learning through failure" builds courage, tenacity, and an unstoppable learning disposition. As one teacher in Sweden shared,

> Jag ser fram emot de kommande åren där vi tar oss upp ur gropen och förhoppningsvis blir en enastående skola.
>
> (I'm looking forward to the years coming, crawling up out of the pit and eventually becoming an outstanding school.)

Some parents confide that they believe somehow frustration is bad for their child.

"You mean it is OK for him to be confused and frustrated?"

"Not permanently," we share with a smile.

"What a relief. I am going home to explain this to my struggling son."

Being clear about what happens when we try to learn something new is a powerful insight for learners, teachers, and parents.

Is this part of the real work of schools?

Provocation 3: There Are No Throwaway People

We must sustain hope for the future of every child who enters our school. They need this throughout their whole school career. Personal put-downs and rejection of others in a school environment must become obsolete. As Rita Pierson said so evocatively in her 2013 TED Talk, shortly before she died,

> Every child deserves a champion, an adult who will never give up on them.

In our careers we have met and observed many such inspirational teachers. Spending time in the classroom of Judi Hirsch, who worked in the Oakland School District with children that others believed to be uneducable, was an unforgettable experience. On one such occasion, a fresh graduate from Berkeley joined us to share with Judi's class members that he had once been where they were. Judi had an inextinguishable faith in every child, born of her years as a research assistant with Reuven Feuerstein. Parents of these children sent thanks to higher powers for the existence of Judi on this planet.

Teaching can be fulfilling and creative. It can also be grinding and destructive. Coaching provides an essential supportive structure in schools that deliver. For example, an instructional coach shared this with us:

> One teacher I worked with was hired as a middle school language arts teacher. She struggled with establishing classroom management routines and being consistent with expectations and consequences. During the second term of the school year, based on her request, she was assigned to teach a creative writing class to high schoolers. I sat in on a class when her students were engaging in a seminar discussion about how race and class affected their lives. They all passionately participated in examining issues that meant a lot to them. Afterward, the students said things like, "This is the only class where I can be who I really am." As a coach, I was able to engage in conversations with the teacher about how to transfer the things that were working in her high school class to the middle school classes. More importantly, this teacher who was viewed as ineffective as a middle school teacher was able to find her niche and passion with the older students.

I learned from watching Bill in his schools the powerful mental model "there are no throwaway people." Bill showed a lack of rushing to judgment and a patience and respect for his staff that I had not seen at that quantum level before. Staff that I would have happily throttled or helped on their way, Bill would hang in with. I know that on the current annual golf days he organizes, many of those in attendance are his old resisters.

I asked Bill how he became this way. While we have referred to this above, I will let him follow this through in his words:

> After thirteen years of schooling, I had no clear future or purpose in my life. The system set me up to fail, and I did. Fortunately, my skills at baseball confirmed for me that I had worth and allowed me to pursue education at a university. I chose to study teaching because I knew I could do that better than how my teachers did it to me. An injury destroyed my opportunity to play professional baseball. I left the university, devastated and out of hope. Over the next three years, I wandered from job to job, deeply depressed. As I did this, some of the people I worked with and the love of my life, Vicki, reignited hope by getting to know me, being kind, and giving me feedback on my worth. They helped me build a positive vision of my future. I determined that I would never sit in judgment of another person.

No child should ever be out of hope by the age of five, or seventeen. For a school to do this to children goes against all that we know. As teachers and principals, we are challenged to understand every child and every adult who move into our circle of influence.

Many schools we work with value such non-judgmental cultures and use a range of processes to establish this. At Lilydale District School in Tasmania, Australia, they have used Carl Rogers's (1956) concept of unconditional positive regard. Greg Morgan (personal communication, 2015) shared,

> The staff have adopted this over time, recognising that it lies at the heart of their Shared Vision. They have seen a gradual change in interactions between teachers and students, and in how teachers speak about students. This has confirmed for them the deep aspirational and transformative effect of this critical mental model. They have staff meetings in which they explore the huge challenges of truly being 'unconditional'. They are learning how to support each other in pursuit of this.

Everyone in a school has a right to feel valued: every child and every staff member. This requires teachers filled with joy, living balanced and rich lives. This models the productive and healthy human being that our children hope to become. Spending as much time caring for adults in schools as for children is not common. Selflessness is common in teachers. They often implement what is best for children, irrespective of its impact on themselves and their families. Pits abound. What structures do you have in place for supporting staff through what can be deeply personally challenging pits?

Is this part of the real work of schools?

Provocation 4: We Are in This Together

Each of us has our own personal strengths and weaknesses. The large high school I led created a small town of 2,300 people every day. It was vital to our collective well-being that we supported one another's weaknesses by understanding that everyone was doing their best. We can compensate for each other's weaknesses. It is also important to understand that in a "town" of that size, we cannot always get our own way. We share an individual and collective responsibility to make that big place work well. Often we must sacrifice some of our assumptions to do so. Some of the very small schools we work with have a different challenge. They have less diversity to draw on and less collective experience. At the same time, consensus is usually easier.

As I write, my wife, Vicki, and I have been married for 49 years. I learned about consensus the day after I got married. It was the day I woke up and realized I could not have my own way anymore. The most I could hope for was that together, Vicki and I would make better decisions than either of us could separately. That is what powerful consensus is all about.

Together, a school staff makes better decisions than any one member of staff can make. Consensus is when two or more people with different life experiences and mental models try to find common ground. A shared vision is even richer. It captures what is dear and close to the heart of each of those who contributed to it. In this way, there is far less compromise for the sake of harmony. There is excitement in pursuing shared goals or priorities together. Staff report to us that when a truly Shared Vision exists, there is a greater sense of "having my voice heard" than when they have to settle for compromise.

When we get into a hot argument, it often ends with "I don't like that person." What is really happening is a difference in mental models. Separate the person from his or her mental models and behavior. Differences in mental models can be discussed while still respecting the person. An "I must win and you must lose" culture can become bullying and toxic. Little good happens in such school communities.

Schools can instead choose to engage in dialogue. William Isaacs (1999) spells out detailed processes for dialogue, as does Chris Argyris. Peter Senge, Art Kleiner, Charlotte Roberts, Richard Ross, and Bryan Smith's *Fifth Discipline Fieldbook* (1994) is a rich source for dialogue processes through Argyris and Isaacs. Through the processes of inquiry and advocacy, around one another's mental models, shared meaning can be created. No winning, no losing, no smashing ideas to pieces. Skilled dialogue allows the richness of everyone's PPK to come to the surface. This is where the school finds the ideas that are better than any one person's. This is where challenging collaboration becomes powerful consensus. This is where a culture of trust is realized.

How do we work together across levels of education?

- Between different levels of education, what is the flow of information and insight into a child and his or her growth and learning?
- What do secondary schools do with the rich data from elementary schools? Sadly, much of it is ignored or binned.
- How do universities and other tertiary institutions build on data and learning about the individual learner from secondary schools?
- What would happen if detailed rich records were kept and followed the student through all levels of learning?

> The heads of science departments in the secondary schools in our city were invited to visit the local state university by the dean of science. When we met, he explained to us that they had to start afresh in teaching sciences to their first-year students. We expressed frustration at this. Our students had been well taught and achieved well and now had to experience the boredom of repeating all that we had done. His response was that they had students from all over the world and could not guarantee what preparation they would have had, so it was better to just start from scratch.

Imagine us all in this together, steadily building a corpus of knowledge and insight into how an individual child learns best. Real examples, real experiences. What a stunning resource. Imagine records of "Here is what happened when we tried this, when she tried that, when he tried the other, here is what helped, here is what hindered." We could create a map of learning over the twelve or thirteen years of a learner's life, as a start. It is *de rigeur* to talk about context these days. Here is context writ on a very large scale. It would allow us together to target the best learning context for every young learner, and promote the delivery of the best learning outcomes.

Is this part of the real work of schools?

Provocation 5: The Value of Practical Competence and Professional Mastery

Donald Schön (1991) from M.I.T. wrote powerfully about "the reflective practitioner" over decades. He not only had a profound influence on teaching and teacher development, but he impacted many professions.

He argued for the importance of paying attention to practical competence and professional mastery. You will hear his thinking, and that of his colleague Chris Argyris from Harvard, throughout this book. They have strongly influenced our thinking and our practice.

We have learned the value of professional know-how. We have deep respect for what teachers and school leaders know about their practice. We draw deeply from what families know about their children and from what communities know about their context. As you can see from Chapter 1, we also trust each school's ability to search out the innovations they need to shift their school to where they want it to be.

As Michael Polanyi's groundbreaking work on *Personal Knowledge* (1958) has taught us, professionals know more than they can say. Much of our most exquisite knowledge about teaching and learning cannot be put into words. We have all seen examples of this: how an experienced teacher intuitively pauses after a student responds to a question. This elicits a further response, which becomes an "aha" moment for that student. How did the teacher know to do this with that particular student at that particular time? Our research shows that questioning teachers, listening to them, provides insights for both them and us, about teaching at its best and worst. This is in alignment with a wide body of such classroom research.

For Schön, knowing-in-action is the basis for a rich professional tradition and knowledge base. This matches my experience as a researcher inside schools and classrooms. It also matches Bill's experience drawing the knowing-in-action from his staff and community. We see this rich knowledge "on the hoof" every time that we are in schools, and it is humbling. Personal Practical Knowledge is at the core of growing a school from within. School people know quality practice at all levels of a school when they see it. When articulated and shared across a school staff and community, it produces organizational learning seldom experienced. Most teachers would love to be clearer about what they actually do each day and its impact on their students.

> I am feeling that enthusiasm and wonderful sense of 'I wonder what will happen next?' for the first time in a long time! I absolutely want to be the best teacher I can be and I feel the tools, language, and opportunity to put my vision into practice.
>
> —Primary School Teacher, New Zealand

"Communities of practice" (Wenger, McDermott, & Snyder, 2002) have a rich history. They are groups of people who share a concern or a passion for something they do. They are practitioners who form their community through interacting regularly and learning together. They develop a shared repertoire of resources based on their PPK, their stories, and their own action research. Many such communities now exist online (Kirschner & Lai, 2007).

We argue for approaches to teaching and learning that draw on the rich lived experiences inside a school, its staff, and community. Our years of research into what children are thinking while teachers are teaching provide one such reality base (Edwards & Marland, 1982). This is very time-consuming research and sadly no one seems to be pursuing it at present. We need more detailed quality data on the reality of the mental life of both teachers and students inside classrooms, be it gathered by researchers or practitioners.

Is this part of the real work of schools?

Provocation 6: Working With Parents

> When working in schools, we are often asked if we will do a night with the parents. These nights are commonly well attended and it is difficult to stop and to leave. We often have people follow us to the parking lot. Parents are hungry to know about teaching and learning and about how they can play a more productive role.

Parents are so keen to help their children, and much of what they do to help is based on what they did when they were at school. When we have shared some of the latest research on learning and thinking with parents they are delighted, fascinated, and want to know more. A common comment from parents is "I wish I had learned this when I was at school." How can we tap this desire for learning among the wider community? Much of what most teachers take for granted can be a revelation for parents. Most parents also have their own skill areas that they can teach to their children.

> I was approached by a miner for advice about big problems he was having with his teenage son. The miner and I had become friends around a common interest in restoring antique furniture. He talked to me about constant fights.
>
> "What are they over?" I asked.
>
> "Bloody mathematics homework," he said. "I was never any good at it, and I'm still not."
>
> I shared with him that mathematics was a mystery to many adults. Most share with me that their enduring gift from school mathematics is knowing that they are bad at it. I suggested that it was the job of a trained mathematics teacher to teach math. "Why not take your son to your shed and share with him your love for old furniture and its restoration?" On my next visit to the company, I met a smiling man with a new insight into his "teaching" relationship with his son. What should we communicate about the role of parents in the education of their child?

Chapter 6 provides more detailed insight into the richness that flows between schools and their communities.

Is this part of the real work of schools?

Provocation 7: Opening Minds and Breaking Stereotypes

Here is an excerpt from a staff newsletter:

> Depending upon your viewpoint, attendance continues to be our number one nemesis. This problem is not unique to us. I personally believe it is a systems problem. We continue to view attendance as part of our behavior code of conduct. A new and fundamental solution would be to make it a curriculum and assessment issue instead. We really need to think outside the box on this one.
>
> Why don't we make work ethic, including attendance, a part of the curriculum we teach?
>
> I challenge each of us to make the commitment to create and implement a fundamental solution to attendance. Let's not continue to play this very tiring blame game.

The traditional mental models in schools are powerful. They worked for us; they should work for today's children. We need to think far beyond our fences.

Shifting attendance from being a behavioral issue that people complained about to being a curriculum issue that we taught was a major mental model shift.

We were in working-class Detroit! Parents understood the importance of getting to work on time. We started to teach work ethic as a key part of our curriculum. We applied this work ethic mental model to all aspects of our daily life together as a working community. Our attendance issue shifted dramatically.

We similarly worked together to shift our traditional secondary school teaching mental model away from the standard lecture. For years, we had been stuffing curriculum into heads by transmission. By shifting to block scheduling, teachers could not survive with the old lecturing mental model. One-hundred-and-ten-minute lectures kill even the best lecturers! Staff learned new mental models around social constructivism and the teaching skills to go with them. The change took three years. Few would want to go back.

Such mental model shifts profoundly influence the way we go about teaching and learning. Similarly the mental models we bring to looking at our students can have a massive impact on them. We always work to break stereotypes of ourselves and others. Respect comes from the Latin *respicere*—to look again, to re-spect, to see with fresh eyes. Who in your school community do you need to re-spect, to see with fresh eyes?

What mental models need fresh eyes to challenge them? What mental model shifts have you made around issues and people in your school community? What stereotypes need to be broken?

How does this mental reframing happen inside staff minds? Each of us has our range of ways to challenge our own mental models and those of others. Ask yourself this:

If I am doing this, what must it mean I believe?

And if I really believe this, then what would I be doing?

Try this on a lesson or an issue tomorrow and see how you feel. As a teacher in a Swedish school shared with us,

Våga ha ett öppet sinne!

(Dare to have a free mind.)

We often break our patterns of thinking using the lateral thinking processes of Edward de Bono (1992). As one example, his "define the problem" process forces us to question and requestion what we really think the problem is before we put time and energy into trying to solve it. What mental model shift should we really be working on?

So, is the real problem fifty-five-minute lectures? Or could it be

- Teachers love knowledge and passing on their love of that knowledge.
- Teachers do not stop often enough to allow students time to process what is being taught.
- Our concept of mastery is attached to knowledge, not to thinking.
- The structure of the school day is the real problem.
- Teachers are comfortable with the security that comes with controlling the lesson.

(We could go on to generate many more possibilities and challenge our thinking.)

Try de Bono's thinking strategies; they have profoundly influenced the way we think at home and in our work.

The dropout rate in the United States is declining but has persisted at the seven to fifteen percentage rate for decades.

One urban school system decided to approach this issue head on, rather than just shrugging its shoulders and accepting that some kids would consistently have higher dropout rates. The school system created a variety of alternative schools, designed to cater to such students, and then each school had the autonomy to decide exactly how best to serve its students. This involved increased funding for social services, bringing in drug counselors, creating partnerships with community colleges, and thinking outside the box in other ways. This school system posed the question: Why must we accept that poverty is an inescapable cycle?

—US Instructional Coach

By generating a wide range of problem definitions, then a wide range of possible solutions, a fresh angle on our old ways of thinking and working is often revealed. The secret is opening one's mind.

Martha Graham, the brilliant dancer and choreographer, gets to the nub of the issue in her widely quoted statement (as cited in de Mille, 1991):

There is a vitality, a life force, an energy, and quickening that is translated through you into action. Because there is only one of you in all of time this expression is unique. If you block it, it will never exist through any other medium and be lost. The world will not have it. It is not your business how good it is, or how valuable, nor how it compares with other expressions. It is your business to keep it yours clearly and directly, to keep the channel open—whether you choose to take an art class, keep a journal, record your dreams, dance your story or live each day from your own creative source. Above all—keep the channel open. (p. 264)

Is this part of the real work of schools?

Provocation 8: Be Wary of the Flavor of the Month and the Quick Fix

I met John at a conference—this changed my life. So, I am not against people attending conferences. What I am against is people continuously going to conferences and having Road to Damascus experiences—then wanting to change everything in the school to fit this new "flavor of the month." As mentioned above in Provocation 2, the real knowledge lies inside your school. No researcher, no author, has spent the time in your school that each of you have. They have to write for generalized audiences, not for your particular context, your particular school.

Having met John, I was excited and wary at the same time. We thought about, studied, investigated, and then started implementing some of his models and research. Years later, they were working powerfully for us, in our reality. Only then did we want to bring him to the United States to work with our school. My district was aghast at the cost: fly someone from Australia? I worked out that to bring John to do whole school staff development was actually cheaper than sending three staff to this conference, two to that conference, and slowly frittering away our funds on attendances that delivered nothing of real substance to our school. This is how the schools around me spent their staff development money. This is one argument I am glad that I won for our staff and community with our district office.

John spent three years with us. There are no quick fixes in education. There is a delay, a pit, sometimes up to two or three years, before a quality idea, strategy, or intervention produces the deepest learning. People expecting quick overnight miracles have little understanding of true quality.

A school in New Zealand had major issues with student behavior. They brought in a new behavior management program every year. None worked. There were six new programs in six years. Then, they spent a year researching student behavior. We will never forget the day they presented their research—memories of Shakespeare's *Macbeth*. In a large garbage can in the middle of the school hall, they ceremoniously dumped each behavior program they had tried, danced around them, and then burned them! "There," they said. "Now we will build our own program that will work for us!"

They stopped being a flavor-of-the-month school.

We know that one size does not fit all. We know that it takes time to get anything to work inside any school reality.

The changes that are experimented with in education are often "nibbling at the edges." Many staff plead with us to stop their principal attending conferences where they often find their next quick fix. A teacher in Varberg, Sweden, shared with us, after being part of finally working in an aligned way:

Till sist började jag verkligen tro på skolan, inte bara på vår skola.

(Finally I start to believe in School, not just our school.)

Holding one's nerve to see innovations through to their complete delivery is rare. Instructional coaches meet this challenge regularly:

Sometimes the focus of professional learning changes so fast, our heads spin. The intent is "a good one"; there is urgency to do so much, so quickly, to better serve our students, especially those who have traditionally been left behind. The Common Core State Standards (CCSS) in the United States were adopted by most states in 2010, and began to be implemented in 2012. Testing on the CCSS started in 2014–2015, and already there was a backlash. Many states have withdrawn. For a teacher, this meant getting acquainted with new standards, investigating how to teach to them, learning about the assessment and how best to prepare students, and then backing off, all within a four- or five-year span. It's no wonder that some veteran teachers' mantra is "This too shall pass."

—US Instructional Coach

Serious change involves changing the mental models of teachers, and this does not come quickly or easily.

If you chase two rabbits you will not catch either one.

—Russian Proverb

What "one thing" are you seeing right through to mastery at your school? Or are you racing from one flavor of the month to another? If it is transforming, it will take you time. It will not happen fast. Embedding new mental models over time creates a new culture.

Is this part of the real work of schools?

Provocation 9: Learning From Students Who Experienced Our School

I have been out of teaching for six years and am walking across an open-air shopping mall. A young man stops me and asks,

"Excuse me, but are you Mr. Edwards?"

"Yes."

"Remember me?"

As my mind starts sifting through its file, he reminds me who he is and shares that he was in the class when I delivered my first ever lesson.

It was a biology lesson and I had no training in biology. I was a metallurgist with no teacher training. I was doing a demonstration to test for the presence of sugars using Fehling's Solution. I had failed to note that it had to be heated. After an interminable wait for the expected red

(Continued)

(Continued)

precipitate in the deep blue solution, feeling the red blush growing on my face, and the snickers from students who knew that I should be heating the solution, I blurted out,

"This is why they call it Fehling's Solution—it never works."

There was no way they were going to laugh. They had me!

He reminded me of this unforgettable lesson, their absolute joy at the discomfort for their brand-new teacher, and the fun that we had together in following lessons as they accepted me as a fellow learner of year ten biology.

We had a few beers together and he shared with me wonderful stories of flow-ons for him and other students from their time with me. He also shared stories of disasters in the lives of some students that both he and I could have predicted.

Should one of our most valid feedback sources be our contribution to the lived lives of the students we worked with as a school and a staff?

One of my brightest students returned to visit me at school the year after he had graduated. He wanted to share with me how helpful the de Bono thinking strategies that I had taught him at school were for him now at university.

"But you never stopped complaining about those lessons," I reminded him.

"If you can't figure out why, then you're not as smart as I thought you were," he replied with a smile.

Then, after a short pause,

"I was the top dog in the system and put a lot of work in to get there. Then you come along with this new approach and some of the other students started to have smarter ideas, I didn't like that."

I learned not to expect our highest achieving students to love innovations in our teaching.

Many top schools ensure that every student is prepared for their next stage of life, whatever that may be. Each student has a personal adult advocate with whom they spend one lesson period every day in a vertical group. They give this pastoral care the same status as every academic subject. They also follow their progress for five years after leaving, to learn the lessons that are there.

> When you asked the seniors to write our visions and write our plans for that time and carry it with us, we gladly showed you our visions. With my goal, I dared to dream. I had written that I would be in the Goddard Honors Dormitory and that my novel would have a good start to it. I am there and I have begun my novel. You have shown us that dreams can come true.
>
> —US University Student

This book is made possible by us staying in touch with, and learning from, our "graduate schools." These are the schools we have worked with over years.

We can learn much by staying in touch with our graduates and by listening to them.

Is this part of the real work of schools?

Provocation 10: Measure What Matters

We watched the results flow in for the 2014 New Zealand National Election. In his victory speech, the continuing prime minister spoke about delivering what matters to the people of New Zealand. That is what he focused on and he believes this is what got him reelected. Schools are not so different.

I have never had a problem with national or state standards. Nations and states have the right to create the mission for schools and set the standards for success. My issue is when the standards become the sought-after product of education instead of children's learning. Producing test scores instead of quality learning in children is symbolic of this sadness in many places around the world.

In America, I was dealt a set of Academic Excellence Indicators as a secondary school's standards of excellence. Some indicators were National University Entrance Examination Results; State Test Scores in Reading, Writing, Math, Science; Annual Student Drop-Out Rate; Percentage of Students in Advanced Placement Courses; Student Success in Earning Course Credit; Number of Student Out-of-School Suspension Days; Number of Zero Tolerance Behavior Infractions; Percentage of Students Who Enrolled in Post Graduate Education Programs; and Average Daily Attendance Percentage.

When I arrived at a new school, **I would set up a database of Academic Excellence Indicators for that region. After that I would never worry about them!** All we did was dump the new numbers in each year. I knew the Shared Vision journey would change the numbers positively. The results were so powerful that twice we were recognized state and nationally. In one school, the results helped us secure a half-million-dollar government grant.

Below are results over time at Monroe High School.

Monroe High School, Michigan (Academic Excellence Indicator Growth Over Five Years)				

Michigan MEAP Test Scores

Math	Start:	57.6%	**Math**	After 5 years:	62.1%
Reading	Start:	46.9%	**Reading**	After 5 years:	67.0%
Writing	Start:	26.0%	**Writing**	After 5 years:	48.0%
Science	Start:	38.8%	**Science**	After 5 years:	52.1%

Student Behavior: Shifts Over 5 Years

75% reduction in out-of-school suspensions

25% reduction in zero tolerance infractions

School Attendance

Start:	89% ADA	After 5 years:	93% ADA

Annual Dropout Percentage

Start:	9%	After 5 years:	3%

Success in Earning Course Credit

Start:	68%	After 5 years:	89%

Not everything that is measured matters and not everything that matters can be measured. Essentially what is measured in most schools, as shared above, are lag indicators. They follow from getting the fundamentals right in your school.

Of course, these indicators are not the only ones we gather, but we do value and pay attention to where the state, government, and parents pay attention. Many of our colleagues share with us that "oppressive and universal standardized testing has run amok in this country and is on everyone's mind."

As one source for a triangulated view of learning and school effectiveness, standardized testing may have a place, but as *the* source, it is unwise.

The other measures we look at are measures that allow the decision makers in our school to make the decisions they have to make or want to make. The key is as follows:

What will honestly convince you, as the decision maker, one way or the other?

If the data will not lead to the making of powerful decisions, then why gather it, and take people's time and energy?

Think about your decision makers: students, teachers, school leaders, parents, district offices, school boards, education departments—each with different decisions to make and different data that will convince them. In turn, take each of these decision makers, or decision-making groups, and write down what you know will convince them one way or the other about the decisions they have to make or want to make. If you are not sure what would convince them, you could ask them. If I have to make a major presentation to convince a decision maker or group of decision makers, I will seek out people who have successfully influenced them before and find out how they did this.

Many people have important decisions to make in schools and to do this they need quality data to be gathered.

Is this the real work of schools?

Provocation 11: Delivering Results That Surprise and Delight

Here is part of a newsletter to staff after a parent night:

> The last parent who spoke to me Wednesday night thanked us for the outstanding education her senior daughter has received at MHS. She indicated that three years ago, she and her husband contemplated moving to Ann Arbor to ensure her daughter a "quality" high school education. She needed to tell me how grateful they were that decision was not finalized. She finished by saying what *we* know—the student who wants one, can get the best education offered anywhere in this country at this level right here.

Families deserve to know that our school is delivering. Sometimes, we do not tell that story. They need to know our school is passionate about the best practice of the profession. After a lifetime in schools, we see little deep change at a systemic level in what is seen as the real work of teachers. As has ever been the case, politicians and parents demand improvements "today." Our schools are often charged with failing a nation's children. What has changed? In America, my grandfather started school around 8:00 a.m. and finished around 4:00 p.m. He took six courses: English, mathematics, science, and history, and chose two electives, normally physical education and something else. That was 1915. My father did the same thing in 1938. I did it in the 1950s. My daughters did it in the 1980s. And now my grandchildren . . . . The forces of inertia are massive. Imagine if a doctor from 1915 was placed in a hospital today. Hospitals have changed significantly in the last century; why are schools so much the same?

Many parents get to believe that this is all there is; this is the way it will always be in our neck of the woods.

Our approach has always been to challenge this:

Help staff see what we can deliver.

and

Help parents see that we can have a world-class education for our children right here.

We know how to deliver this. We know what we need to be the "school of choice" in our community. The only question is "Do we have the will, passion and commitment to deliver it?"

Is this part of the real work of schools?

SO, WHAT DO YOU THINK IS YOUR REAL WORK?

We do not believe that our insights into what could be the real work are **the** answer. These are eleven provocations for you and your community. They are drawn from two lived lives. Working on all eleven would be enough to exhaust anyone. So this is no prescriptive set.

What we are asking for is a focus within a school community about what we believe individually and collectively is the real work for us. Where should we put our time, our energy, our passion, and our resources?

What is our real work?

and

What is not our real work?

In our experience, failure to address these questions is not an Achilles heel in education only; it besets many companies and sporting teams.

Getting this clear is one of the key starting points for a school that delivers.

Our Real Work: Spring Water, Not Bottled Water

Let us share one example with you from one of the schools we have worked with in New Zealand. They made a transforming decision for their school around what they saw as their real work.

From their Shared Vision surfaced a focus on helping their students to be thinkers of the highest quality. Over the following year, they explored the work of Edward de Bono and his CoRT Thinking Program (2009)—a thinking skills program. They also explored Arthur Costa and Bena Kallick's work on Habits of Mind (2008)—a thinking dispositions program. Students need both the thinking skills and the dispositions to be effective thinkers. Both of these programs are powerful, work well, and can be blended together.

However, as they explored these existing programs, they saw the potential to develop their own thinking program, based on local Māori stories and myths. These are stories and myths that are well known to the families and the community. So, what emerged are dispositions such as these:

Think carefully before you speak because your words reveal your heart.

Be like the *ururoa* [hammerhead shark] and persist even in the face of what seems like overwhelming adversity.

The bird that partakes of the miro berry reigns in the forest. The bird that partakes of the power of knowledge has access to the world.

These have a richness and flavor that we can never find in a more generalized program designed to suit students across the world. They are totally compelling. We asked the staff about the difference between their locally produced thinking program and the powerful international programs. Their response was that the "international" programs are "bottled water" and their program is "spring water." Some who have seen samples of this locally developed thinking program have been captivated by it. They ask for permission to use it in their schools. The response has been, "of course you can but why not develop your own?"

We have another school that has a very wide range of cultures represented by their students and families. In looking at teaching their students to think, they looked at the common elements across these many cultures. This brought them to the rich work of Carl Jung (1969). They are now developing a program for their students around the Jungian archetypes. I have never heard of such a program anywhere in the world. They have begun with the hero archetype. This exists in the stories of every culture in the school, as well as in movies such as *Star Wars*. Videos are being made of parents and children sharing the hero stories from each of their cultures. What a resource! This is valuing the diversity in the school and linking families through the alignment of their cultural stories.

Is this the real work of schools?

Implementing the Real Work

Getting to the real work usually involves change. There are many theoretical models of change in schools. These have power. Michael Fullan's magnificent body of research (from Fullan, 1993, to Fullan & Quinn, 2015) resonates very strongly with our research and practical experience in schools. Our favorite memory of a story from Fullan involves him visiting a school and being shown their stunning innovation. When he meets the principal, he decides to turn the conversation in a fresh direction. For many years he has been challenged as a researcher with, "This is very impressive but will it work in practice?" With a twinkle in his eye, Fullan asks, "This is very impressive but will it work in theory?"

Each school is unique; what works in one school may not work at all in another. At the same time, there is undoubted power in learning from the experience of others and from generalized experience. Fullan's early work (1993) provided us with a powerful set of guidelines for considering school change.

He advises that we do not presume that someone somewhere out there knows the answer—nobody knows the answer. For Fullan, productive change is the constant search for understanding, knowing there is no ultimate answer. Learning theory maps onto chaos theory. For him, those who will survive are those who are poised to learn.

Fullan (1993) argues that personal moral purpose and vision is the key.

He then offers the eight basic lessons of change:

1. You can't mandate what matters.

2. Change is a journey not a blueprint.

3. Problems are our friends.

4. Vision and strategic planning come later.

5. Individualism is underrated.

6. Neither centralization nor decentralization works.

7. Connection with the wider environment is critical for success.

8. Every person is a change agent.

In our early years, we used powerful research such as Fullan's to help schools change. However, a change has emerged for us. We now ask staff members to reflect on their personal experiences of organizational and personal change. We help staff to articulate and share their own PPK of change. We develop from this real, lived experience a model of change that will work for this group of staff born of their own shared life experiences. These are very different models. They are messier and they are complex in some ways. What they tap is what Fullan refers to at the start: Nobody knows the answer for you; the answers mostly lie inside.

Once a staff have developed their own model of change, it is informative to compare it with the work of researchers such as Fullan (1993, 2015) and John Kotter (1996). After we have checked off all of Fullan and Kotter's "keys" on the staff-developed list, we ask them, "What are all of these other things left on your list?" They reply, "These are the things that we know that they have not yet discovered." Amid the laughter, there is a glow of pride.

Is developing our own models of change part of the real work of schools?

This brings us to two core mental models that underlie all of "the real work" that we do: "The knowledge is in the room" and "bow to your data."

WHO KNOWS THE REAL WORK? SOCIAL CONSTRUCTIVISM

When we are in a room with a school staff, there are two of us and there are commonly between seven and two hundred of them. We share just over ninety years of educational experience: teaching, school leadership, and research experience. They commonly share between 100 and 3,000 years of educational experience.

Who would you trust?

We believe deeply that **the knowledge is in the room**, with all of us, not just with the two of us "at the front." There is no doubt that the people at the front are usually there because they can share provocations and new insights. They can think with us and bring fresh perspective. We are not suggesting that their role be devalued. At the same time, we regularly experience the collective pride when a group taps their PPK and delivers for themselves. It is inspiring and energizing to dare to think that we, as a group, have enormous agency over what we are seeking to achieve.

We spend much more time listening than most people in our role. Lev Vygotsky (cited in Moll, 2013) has taught us that most knowledge is socially constructed through rich interactions with other people and things. You will see throughout this book our commitment to social constructivism. **Working collaboratively, together with people, is a core part of the real work for us.**

STAYING HONEST TO THE REAL WORK: EVIDENCE-BASED DECISION MAKING

When you gather data in your school, or on your school, pay close attention to it. Do not be easily swayed away from your data. Evidence-based decision making is a strong bedrock. Of course, this is predicated on the skilled gathering of data:

- on skilled analysis of the data,
- on the use of triangulation to check the validity of data sources,
- on not confusing correlations with cause-effect statements, and
- on avoiding the many other traps that can lie inside data.

Dismissing data because it does not fit with our theory or with our preconception is a killer of organizational learning.

We have learned to not accept data as gospel, but to rigorously examine it, particularly when it appears counterintuitive. Try to triangulate it better, seeking additional data, to confirm the validity of what it is "saying" for our context.

Bruce Wellman and Laura Lipton (2012) use a helpful three-step approach to data:

1. Here's what! (i.e., the data),

2. So what? (i.e., What does it *really* mean?), and

3. Now what? (i.e., What are you going to do with it or about it?)

I remember clearly when the Australian Government gathered data from graduates on the effectiveness of teacher education programs. When the report on our university faculty was shared openly, the response was to challenge the validity of the data and the data-gathering techniques. When I said that maybe we should accept that our graduates are telling us that our degree program is not delivering, I was not popular with many of my colleagues.

If our data does not match what should be expected from research, we will question ourselves deeply. We will also question the research deeply. In the end, we must trust ourselves to read our own contexts. We need to gather the data that will convince us one way or the other, and find our own answers.

Once you have that quality data, **bow to your data.**

This honest open response to data, respecting it and bowing to it, forms an essential element in keeping us honest in our real work.

SUMMARY

In Chapter 2, our aim is to call into question where time, energy, and resources are used in a school. These are tough calls to make. Schools are commonly very busy places and the competition for attention can be fierce and constant. By making clear decisions about what the real work is, and what it is not, in your school, you enable everyone to focus and align.

We have used eleven provocations, rather than providing answers. The provocations are designed to stimulate your reflection on your priorities, your real work, and to dig deeply into your own experience. These provocations act in the same way as the Inquiry Probes used in our Shared Vision process in Chapter 1. They reinforce the value of internal questioning. The provocations can be addressed individually, in small teams, or as a whole staff. They can provide a focus for professional development days. The key is to probe for clarity so that time is spent on what is agreed as the real work of the school and not wasted on the many distractions calling for attention.

When your daily work is aligned strongly to an internally generated Shared Vision there is confidence in the value of the work. Focusing on the real work brings clarity, joy, simplicity, and decisiveness to learning environments.

3

Leadership

The interview process went well. I was asked to meet with the superintendent as the district's first choice to be its next high school principal. He stated that he expected me to work eighty hours per week. This dredged up years of bad memories. I told him I could give him a "smart" fifty hours each week.

I grew up in Western Pennsylvania as the steel industry was dying. It was an area where a good day's work was respected as the essence of life. Work hard for an hour and earn a good hour's wage. This work ethic became part of my soul. Even today, I do not have a picture of retirement in my head. I assume I will simply work until I drop dead.

I carried this strong work ethic into my first position as principal. I would tell my staff, "If nothing else, we will be renowned for our work ethic." As principal, I decided I needed to model work ethic for my school community every day. To do this, I would be the first person to work. At one of my high schools, the first teacher would get to work at 5:55 a.m. each morning. To beat that teacher to work, I would have to be there by 5:45 a.m. Not being the brightest cookie in the box, I decided if I did this in the morning, I would also need to be the last person staff saw as they went home! In an American high school, that is normally 7:00 p.m. or later. So much for a "smart" fifty hours!

(Continued)

(Continued)

For twelve years, I did this. One afternoon, John was engaging me in one of his insightful feedback sessions. My personal work schedule came up and he asked me why I was always first to arrive at school and last to leave. I explained how important modeling work ethic to my community was to me.

Then he asked me one of those questions where the answer haunts you forever. John asked, "Bill, how has that work ethic been for your family?"

I could feel the tears welling: "I have missed my three daughters growing up."

What is the reality of your approach to leadership? How does your vision for your leadership manifest itself in your life and in the lives of those close to you? Take your time, before you read on, to think through this. Who you are comes first. Jim Collins (2001) argues that it is more important to know who you are than where you are going, because where you are going will change as the world around you changes.

LEADERSHIP AS DISPOSITION OR POSITION?

Using distributed leadership and skilled delegation is one way to address leadership load. I learned this more deeply as I became more experienced. I learned to let go of control. This introduces a leadership dilemma.

On the one hand is the **dispositional mental model of leadership**. Here leadership is seen as a way of operating and delivering. Dispositional leadership focuses on the mental models that are brought to leadership, rather than on the position itself. Through this leadership mental model, leading and decision making are distributed. Everyone in the school is leading. Leaders are growing leaders at all levels. This is the model we have found over time to be most professionally and personally enriching and effective. We recommend this leadership mental model to others.

On the other hand is the **positional mental model of leadership**. Positional leadership places the leader as the key figure and initiator. This is deeply ingrained in most leaders. It is often what is required by context. Leaders are usually appointed because of their perceived expertise for the position. This recognizes their extensive PPK (Personal Practical Knowledge). They also have access to much information that is not shared with the rest of the staff or team. Some of this is confidential. This means that, for some decisions, they are the only person with the "big picture" view. In such situations, positional leadership is demanded by the situation.

For me this positional–dispositional tension was daily and healthy. We want you to look for, and feel, this tension in your leadership thinking and actions as this chapter unfolds.

On a line of tension between these two fundamental leadership mental models, where are you positioned at this stage?

There is a second fundamental line of tension that needs to be clarified when looking at leadership: Where is the balance between leadership and management?

LEADING VERSUS MANAGING

The Levels of Perspective Model (Kim, 2001) described in Chapter 1 has been invaluable for us as we look at the work of schools. We have blended this with our own work to create a powerful model, as seen in Figure 3.1, for understanding the difference between leadership and management. For us,

Leadership is working at the top three Levels of Perspective—vision work, mental model work, and the design of systems and structures.

Management is working at the bottom three Levels of Perspective—operating the systems and structures, patterns of behavior work, and events work.

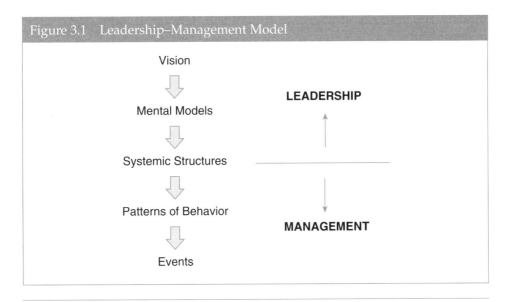

Figure 3.1   Leadership–Management Model

Source: John Edwards and Bill Martin, based on the work of Daniel Kim.

Please understand. This is not an either/or proposition. **Schools must be both led and managed.** It becomes a matter of degree. If you spend all of your time managing, there will be very little growth.

There is a need for leaders to manage. Management ensures the smooth operation of systemic structures, positive patterns of behavior, and impactful events. It ensures that valuable resources are used to their best capacity.

Leading involves the constant struggle to figure out how to balance this leadership–management tension line. In my leadership, I fought non-stop for more leadership time. It is seldom given to leaders.

In our experience, **more management means slow change; more leadership equals quicker, deeper change.**

We are continually moving up and down the Levels of Perspective. Leaders move in and out of each level throughout the school day. Leadership requires us to know which level is impacting our leadership at any given moment. Leaders can feel good about their use of time if they see they are working at the upper Levels of Perspective. If they are involved with an event or pattern of behavior, they need to be thinking about how they can move these moments into the upper levels.

Fred Simon (personal communication, 2015), who brings long experience in applying the levels in business settings, shared with us how often he found that his people could better access the levels of perspective at the systems level: "What structures do we need to have in place to facilitate reaching the vision?" and then asking "What mental models do we need to have to enable the structure we want?"

Our experience is that **you must always know the mental models that will take you to your vision.** The relationship between vision, mental models, and systemic structures must be clear. This is the complex dynamic of leadership.

> As a school leader for some sixteen years, I had only been shown the generic style of leadership using inspirational words and sayings such as 'be a democratic leader' and how to organise and manage my school. Sadly, I was never shown what to lead and what to use to educationally lead my school. Yes I had become just like my brilliant colleagues—I was an exceptional administrator and manager but in truth I was not an educational leader. I did not know the way. I was a big events manager and knew the predictable patterns of behaviour of students, teachers, and parents. I even knew my own patterns of behaviour so well. But nothing ever changed and we all drove our own agendas.
>
> —Principal, New South Wales, Australia

Shifting an activity from the events level to higher levels is an important leadership skill. For example, a child arrives late. As a leader, you could deal with this event. With many children arriving late you could be very busy. Add staff arriving late and that is a full-time job at the start of each day! You could wait to see if a pattern of behavior emerges. If the child or teacher never arrives late again you have saved valuable time and energy. If a pattern emerges, you can draw this to their attention and deal with it. An even higher leverage way to deal with lateness is to design a system or structure to deal with lateness of students or staff. A well-designed system means that anyone who arrives late knows exactly what is expected. All staff, children, parents, and office staff also know. So lateness is dealt with skillfully and consistently. This systems design work is leadership work. Operating the system is management work.

But what is the basis for the system? Your mental models! If you have a mental model that all staff are professional and will deal ethically with any lateness, you would design a system based on individual integrity. If you have a mental model that arriving late is disrespectful to the whole school community, then you would design a different system. Every system shouts its mental models to a school community. Clarifying these mental models is high leverage leadership work. Many leaders agree with us but say they are so busy with events they have no time to clarify mental models and design systems. They are stuck in management and have no time to lead.

The combined mental models form the vision. Ensuring that mental models are clarified and aligned to the Shared Vision is high-leverage leadership.

It is inevitable that differing opinions, based on a variety of mental models, will arise whenever an important decision needs to be made in a school.

In one school, a decision about the best way to serve high school students who were below grade level in reading was a complex and multilayered one.

- The principal considered budget implications,
- the counselors considered impacts on the rate at which students were earning required credits towards graduation,
- the teachers considered motivational factors, and
- the instructional coach considered which practices showed the most promise in comparable settings.

Ultimately, all stakeholders went back to the school's vision and mental models to prioritize considerations. While not everyone agreed with the ultimate decision, they could all understand and explain why it had been made.

—US Instructional Coach

A significant part of the work of leaders is communication—conversation, dialogue, and each instance of this is an event. Leadership writer Susan Scott (2011), in *Fierce Leadership*, suggests an organization moves forward one conversation at a time. Leaders have opportunities to mentor, model, coach, and advise with each event where they interact with others. Over time, this can strengthen desired patterns of behavior, and evolve into a systemic structure. And behind every conversation are the mental models of the participants, either transparent or hidden.

> In fact on arrival to school yesterday morning, most of my staff was gathered in the staff room debriefing from the evening—the sharing in those moments was deep and truthful—we all ended up crying again. . . . My staff has been moved beyond any force or energy that I have ever witnessed before. The opening has begun . . . just magnificent . . . The minute I walked into the school, I felt empowered for the first time in my educational life. I have a crystal clear vision as to where we are going; I have a clarity on how to do this and, at last, the understanding of why I need to do what I need to do.
>
> —Principal, New South Wales, Australia

John Kotter (1996) says that most organizations are overmanaged and underled. He goes on to say that more than 80 percent of what goes on inside organizations is management work.

From our experience, management helps you get through the day; running the systems and structures which ensure efficiency and effectiveness. Management involves such activities as organizing the classroom, hiring staff, setting up coaching meetings, budgeting, and problem solving. It can keep us deep in what we call "the foxhole of busy-ness." We can be very, very busy working away on the answers and the improvements being demanded of us right now.

As one school leader in Sweden shared with us,

> Jag är trött på att förvalta—jag vill leda skolan.
>
> (I'm tired of managing—I want to lead.)

Leadership builds tomorrow; it focuses on the long term, on developing culture and shared vision. Leadership helps people align themselves with the vision and inspires people to make it happen. We know that our people and the lives they have lived are our most powerful resources. So leading involves trusting that the mental models and PPK inside people are the fundamental source of delivery. This can mean resisting other sources which commonly lay claim to legitimacy. There are always many outside the school who are sure they know what is best for us. Through ensuring that every one of our voices is heard, leading can tap the full potential inside the school.

> I have gradually changed my role to more leadership functions, e.g., vision (where we are going together), mental models (what we are thinking, believing, and valuing), and systemic structures (how we are organising) and less management functions, which I have found that teachers and other staff are doing with far greater skill and far better results than I could have achieved. No doubt I still have more to learn in doing this.
>
> —Principal, Queensland, Australia

From reflecting back on our lives in leading, in coaching leaders, and in listening to and observing leaders, many leadership challenges emerge. We have held these up against the practice of the many leaders we have worked with and are still working with. Here are what we collectively believe are the top eight leadership challenges in a school that delivers.

As you work through these challenges, please go back occasionally to those two tension lines:

Position–Disposition,

and

Leadership–Management

Check how you see your positioning on those tension lines as you explore leadership more deeply.

THE EIGHT LEADERSHIP CHALLENGES

Leadership Challenge 1: Hold Your Nerve During Storms

School communities are made up of people. Each person is living a unique life; no individual "signature path" will mirror another. So, everyone brings her or his own experience, knowledge base, and practice. All of these unique lives are combined in a school. In this respect, schools are alive. There is no other school like ours in the world. The reason is simple. No other school has the same complexity born of the "lived lives" of the individuals who make up our community.

Our inability to understand this reality is a problem across the globe. Many nations, states, and regions believe all schools should be doing the same things. For example, the national curriculum taught will be the same from school to school. This is impossible. Through the uniqueness of each school community, the curriculum is interpreted and taught differently. This "school as living organism" reality is at the root of many failed mandates!

A key role of the principal is to help the staff understand a school's healthy life cycle, and that storms are a natural part of that. In many respects, storms are collective pits, and we know how valuable they are!

Dr. Bruce Tuckman (1965) researched the development and evolution of groups. His work articulated an explanation of team development and behavior through four phases: Forming, Storming, Norming, and Performing. We first learned about Tuckman's work through Peter Block's 1993 book, *Stewardship: Choosing Service Over Self-Interest*. We have found that Tuckman's phases make a good umbrella for what we have observed as the stages of life in a healthy school. Of course, our PPK is different from Tuckman's. So, our descriptions of the four phases are markedly different from his. At the same time, we want to acknowledge that Tuckman's phases provided a powerful basic structure for us to better understand the evolutionary processes schools and their staff experience. The two major differences for us are in the forming and the storming stages as outlined below.

For example, Tuckman sees forming as a phase where conflict is avoided and not much gets done; people focus on keeping busy with routines.

On the other hand, **during forming, we drive strong action through the formation of a Shared Vision, a time where every voice is heard**. We create a safe container for people to open up about what they really want. This enables people to surface, and face together in the open, what may have been otherwise hard to say in public.

> I thought I was getting towards the end of my teaching career and envied our newly trained staff members who are so lucky and privileged to be able to start their journey with this exciting project that will mould their teaching and their lives for years to come. But, I have also changed my thinking. I still have a lot to give, a lot to learn, and would also be privileged to be part of this ongoing process, so there are plenty of reasons to rethink an 'ending date' for my teaching life.
>
> —Teacher, Sydney, Australia

And, in storming, Tuckman sees a phase where there is a strong directive role for the "supervisor."

On the other hand, **during storming, we trust groups to face up to, and work through, the inevitable challenges themselves.** These experiences are healthy and growth producing. We invite leaders to explore being more a "servant" than a supervisor. Staff are trusted to research the future of the school. They will disagree and over time find alignment. In this way, they each have a shared role in school leadership.

Here are Tuckman's four phases as we have experienced them through our own teaching, leading, and research in schools.

Forming: Agreeing to Do Something Together

- Intellectual collaboration
- Taking the risk to trust others
- Uncertainty
- Negotiation
- Skilled consensus
- Excitement
- Creating the Shared Vision

Storming: The Struggle to Break Free From Current Reality

- Moving from fixed mind-sets to growth mind-sets
- Potential confrontations
- Surfacing of ego and factions
- Use and abuse of power and politics
- Collective awareness
- Clarifying professional development needs
- Action learning
- Developing focus and commitment

Norming: New Systemic Structures and Mental Models Are Embedded

- Fundamental systemic change
- New shared mental models emerge
- Performance norms established
- Alignment
- Team learning
- Confidence that the vision is achievable
- The emergence of a long-term plan

Performing: The Enjoyment of Doing Our Work

- Continuous cycles of learning and improvement
- Synergy
- Fine tuning
- Dramatic shifts in skill acquisition
- Collective sense of achievement and satisfaction
- "This is the way we do things around here"
- Sharing a state of "flow"

Leaders at every level must hold their nerve during storms. Storms are essential for learning. We learn and change when challenged. Storms are a natural phase in a school's healthy life cycle. Effective leaders have a deep understanding of the behaviors in storms. They know them well and embrace them with confidence and good humor. They have developed the expertise of working with others to navigate through everything from eddies to hurricanes. Collins (2001) in his research into good-to-great organizations found that the most effective leaders had "inner wiring" such that the worst circumstances bring out their best. They are unflappable. When challenged, they become clear headed and focused.

Most schools we have observed enjoy starting something new, the Forming Stage. It feels good. It is exciting.

This quickly moves the school into the Storming Stage. We begin to see uncomfortable behaviors show up. People are not getting along so well. Resistance begins. This feels unpleasant. We decide to get rid of these uncomfortable behaviors. We stop working on the new initiative.

There is almost always a tempting new innovation waiting for us. These are found at conferences, from our reading, from colleagues, from mandates, wherever. We form up again. It feels good. We are excited. Then we go into another storm. The uncomfortable behaviors show up. We do not like them. We quit again. And guess what is waiting for us? Another tempting offering. We form and start again . . .

So many schools tell us this is the pattern of behavior throughout their school history: forming, storming, back to forming, then storming, back to forming. . . . They have never followed any innovation to a completely satisfying end; they have never "nailed it." This is a killer of staff goodwill and a drainer of energy and passion.

Storms are natural and essential to a healthy school. They are also natural to a healthy classroom and a healthy coaching relationship. The storm is critical to creating alignment. The disagreements that cause the troublesome behaviors must happen. Alignment is the product. The Promised Land is the Norming Stage leading to the joy of Performing. You must hold your nerve to get there. Schools that spend most of their time in the Performing Stage are inspiring places to be. We have had the honor of experiencing this many times. It is hard to put into words what you feel. Here are some of the words that come to our minds:

- calmness
- creativity
- energy
- freedom
- strength
- positivity
- openness, and
- confidence in their ability to deliver under any circumstance

There has been a fair amount of 'pit work' in that time. I once again find myself diving headfirst back into the 'pit', wallowing around in the new learning. The journey we have started has set a fire under me, and comes with new flames. When your arse gets burned you cannot sit still, and you have to be up rushing around. I enjoy this feeling (metaphorically) and look forward to the new flames, and I really can't wait until the flames become a blaze! I feel that we have come together as a staff and are a far more cohesive unit. This has come through us working together. Everyone is now included and I believe we are all now valued. It has been hard but enjoyable work. I now feel able to openly say how I feel and will be listened to.

—Australian Primary School Teacher

In my thirty-six years in schools, I only spent seven years in the absolute joy of Performing. The majority of my teaching career was spent Forming and Storming. When I became a principal, I realized I would have to lead my schools through Forming and Storming to get to Norming. Twice, once for three years and another time for four years, I experienced the exquisite feeling of Performing. *I would not give these years up for anything!* They are what teaching is about. Every teacher deserves to spend most of his or her career in this Performing Phase—it is a key target for schools that deliver.

Leadership Challenge 2: Designing Mental Model Action

Greg Morgan (personal communication, 2015), a principal in Tasmania, Australia, shared his experience with us:

I find in most situations with angry, aggressive parents, that if I listen hard for their mental models, I will soon find common ground to work with—we go down into a pit but the shared mental models bring us back up. I don't know how many times (e.g., when accused of being unfair for suspending a child) I have said to a parent, 'You know, we're on the same side of the fence—we want the same for young James: a good education, happy at school, good friends, learning how to get along with people. Right at this point, we don't have full agreement on how we should each respond to this current incident. In fact, *there is no fence!* Young James is at the centre of what we both want. We'll get through this and he will continue learning positive, respectful behaviour . . . '.

As the chief steward of the vision, my loyalty is to it, rather than to a party in a dispute. As I draw on my own deep values, it will guide me through every potential pit. Has not failed me yet!

We believe leadership is about mental model transformation, such as the shift to "there is no fence." This involves engaging people in becoming clear about the mental models needed to drive the delivery challenge they face:

- A principal helps staff clarify the mental models in their shared vision.
- A teacher helps children identify their mental model targets for learning.
- An instructional coach helps teachers clarify their mental model strengths to leverage, and their dysfunctional mental models which need work.

Leading supports learners to stay true to the mental models they have chosen to enact. A strong professional adult learning culture is the fuel for mental model shifts.

Through leading you see people's mental models driving their behavior. Everyone's mental models are resistant to change and so they should be. Our mental models have led us to our current life, so they should not be lightly changed. We often hold conflicting, inconsistent, and dysfunctional mental models. I have clashes between my mental model of valuing fine wine and fine food and my mental model of a healthy body.

Leadership requires the design, co-design, and support of actions that, over time, embed new mental models into the school culture. In this way, aligned actions and events at every level of the school drive the realization of the Shared Vision.

For Morgan (2013),

The real leverage for leadership and tapping human potential resides in aligning the key mental models of all stakeholders in a co-constructed vision. (p. 103)

Morgan has found that

When stakeholders are genuinely engaged at the level of their mental models, the vision is theirs; when their mental models are also skilfully engaged enormous leverage can ensue from the single-minded, common purpose that can emerge when key mental models of stakeholders are aligned. (p. 111)

He concludes:

A hermeneutical consideration of leading suggests that seeking the answer (to what is good leadership) from beyond ourselves is flawed; that "understanding" about leading can only ever be arrived at by interpreting its lived experience. (p. 111)

This action learning experience of leadership is common across many leaders of schools that deliver.

Leadership requires the design of actions that meet two mental model challenges:

Firstly, influencing new mental models aligned to student achievement;

Secondly, influencing every person in the school to live the school's Core Values.

The details of this challenge are the subject of Chapter 5.

We cannot command or coerce anyone to transform a mental model. Influencing mental model shifts is about designing deliberate actions that enable someone to design and take personal actions. When we choose to implement these personal actions, we can begin to build robust new mental models.

Mental model shifts do not happen with a snap of the fingers. This is why the one-shot professional development event seldom has impact. Leadership involves being strong and smart in the face of mandates and top-down requirements. These are always deemed essential and are often stressful and at times distracting for those of us who have to implement them. The leadership key is to not allow them to derail the aligned work of the school.

It commonly takes three years for new mental models to become deeply embedded in practice. Change will begin immediately, and results will start to emerge. The secret is to stick with the work and allow its full richness to emerge.

> As mentioned earlier, I met John at a thinking conference. It was in 1988. As a new principal, I had just come to the mind-bending conclusion that my school's success would be dependent upon adults changing. Even more frightening, I would have to be the catalyst of those changes as leader. That's why, when John presented "The Model of Human Action and Change," I hung on every word. It is now the Butler Model named after John's friend and long-time research colleague, Dr. Jim Butler. Immediately, the essence of the Butler Model (in Edwards, Butler, Hill, & Russell, 1997) made sense to me. It was the blueprint for action to transform mental models.
>
> As a model for action it has never failed me.

There are six key elements in the model (see Figure 3.2):

Public information is information which is available in the public domain through observing, reading, professional development programs, lectures, the Internet, and the media in general. This is external to the self.

Current Practice is the way you currently do things. This is external to the self. You can observe a person's practice.

Personal Practical Knowledge (PPK) comes from your lived experience and your reflections on that experience. This is true knowledge; **it drives action** and is internal to the self.

Mental Models (or Worldview) come from culture, traditions, and life experience and are made up of beliefs, values, and assumptions. These are internal to the self.

Reflection is looking inside yourself to make meaning. It usually involves careful or long consideration.

Generation is the design or creation of new ideas and insights (see, e.g., Edwards, 1996).

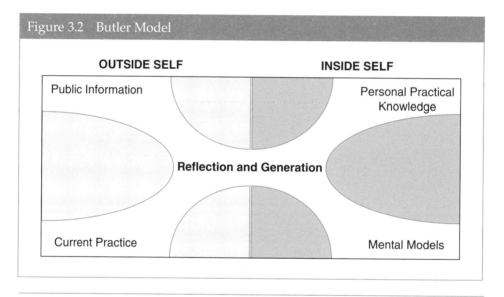

Figure 3.2   Butler Model

OUTSIDE SELF   INSIDE SELF

Public Information   Personal Practical Knowledge

Reflection and Generation

Current Practice   Mental Models

Source: Adapted from Butler (1994).

The Butler Model is a model of human agency. It highlights the constructs and relationships to consider when exploring human action. Reflection and generation are at the center of the model. They provide the communication channel between the inside of our self and the social context, external to the self, in which we live and work. We use the model to inform all of our work on individual and organizational change. It provides a structure to enable us to keep track of our thinking and ensure that we are considering all four key elements and giving quality time to reflection and generation processes.

The Butler Model can be taught to learners as a tool to shift behaviors and mental models. My experience has taught me that applying the Butler Model significantly reduces resistance to change. Any time leaders look at an issue or challenge, it can be addressed by first applying the four key elements of the model:

1. What quality public information is out there that we can access and study?
2. What do we currently do; what is our current practice around this issue?
3. What does our life experience tell us; what is our PPK?
4. What are our current mental models?

We can then reflect skillfully together around these core elements and generate insights, plans, and actions. So we

- design actions and implement them,
- collect data on the actions taken and their outcomes, and
- this data becomes a key source of new Public Information which can help generate the next action phase.

Over time, by taking continuous action around the Butler Model (Edwards, 2001), mental model shifts are influenced. This model provided a "lesson plan" structure for me as a principal to lead my staff through designing actions to transform mental models. We use a range of other strategies for mental model work. These are discussed in Chapter 4.

What mental model shifts will take your school to where you all want to go together? What learning designs do you use as a leader to influence these mental model shifts in your staff?

Leadership Challenge 3: Creating and Maintaining Alignment

Chapter 1 focuses on alignment. Here we want to explore its implication for leadership. Leaders initiate, create the conditions, and monitor this never-ending process to deliver the Shared Vision together.

> Thoroughly enjoyable two days. This has been a great experience as a whole staff. The process used to obtain data and create the vision, and the whole research process, creates a sense of ownership for ALL staff members. There are few other ways to unify a staff so rapidly and to clarify where they are going so well.
>
> —Secondary School Teacher, Christchurch, New Zealand

> I was stunned by the amount of enthusiasm generated. I can now see that we have created the motivation and commitment to move forwards together, with everyone contributing to the growth, development and success of our school.
>
> —Head Teacher, UK

The Shared Vision becomes the heart of alignment for a leader. Seth Godin (2008) brings a fresh perspective to leadership when he talks about tribes. For him, a tribe is a group of people connected to one another, connected to a leader, and connected to an idea. For us, the key in Godin's work is around the centrality of connectedness. Brené Brown (2012) makes the same point about the power of connection in her work. Our process helps people to connect through the formation of their Shared Vision and through the collaboration and challenge that are inherent in moving that vision to reality. Godin found that intent matters, and that it is not about money or status, but about a mission.

Two common questions in our personal coaching are the following:

How does this align with your Personal Vision?

and

How does this align with your Shared Vision?

These are questions of real power.

Think about it. When people truly share a vision they are connected, bound together by a common aspiration and common mental models. This creates a sense of alignment in approaching their current reality.

Similarly, alignment to a Personal Vision keeps people honest to themselves.

In coaching, by drawing people back to their vision, this ensures that their actions are aligned to who they say they are.

Leading Through Disagreements

People find energy and comfort as they align. Decisions on how to best move forward are constant and disagreements are natural. They create storms of varying strengths.

Without alignment, disagreements can push us anywhere and bog us down in endless debates, lurching this way and that. Usually, the powerful win and the rest of us lose. Disagreements can burrow underground, destroy the foundations, and topple the whole structure. Leadership involves asking questions to reveal and clarify the mental model differences behind the disagreement. Once the protagonists can see that the matter is not about who they are or their personalities, the disagreement is depersonalized. They can then resolve the mental model difference amicably and skillfully.

One Mind, One Voice

We certainly hope your leadership group is a congenial lot! That always makes for better Friday afternoons. But congeniality doesn't bring much to the transformation table. Collaboration is what is needed for change. And, at the heart of leadership team collaborations are those brutally frank and honest conversations that go on behind closed doors. Before opening the doors, the team agrees on those issues they must align to. When they are out with the people they lead, **the leadership team speaks with one mind, one voice.**

Jon Saphier (personal communication, 2015) recommends building Instructional Leadership Teams:

> Each member of the leadership team influences the quality of teaching and learning through their individual conversations with teachers and through their participation in meetings of teachers. In the same way, at the heart of leadership are those complex, difficult and honest conversations the leader must have with their leadership team members.

A lack of such crucial alignment impacts everyone.

> When leadership are unhappy with other leadership members, do not relay this to staff—it undermines and makes staff jumpy and unsure. Feedback needs to begin at that level—be received and worked through, so it does not have a chance to unravel the rest of us.
>
> —Primary School Teacher, Auckland, New Zealand

If you are not of one mind, one voice, the cynics will find the weak link and drive a Mack truck through the hole. Cynics on leadership teams are especially dangerous. We cannot allow those closest to us to be such destructive Mack trucks because they can destroy our efforts instantly.

Never ignore leadership team cynics.

Leaders support leadership team cynics in making the personal choice of commitment. *We have a right to ask for that commitment.* Leaders continually invite cynics to make a commitment. After time, if the data proves they are not willing to commit, leaders help them to leave. Nothing less can be accepted.

Collins (2001) argues that an effective leader gets the right people on the bus, the wrong people off the bus, and the right people in the right seats. Collins found that great vision without great people is irrelevant. Indeed, he suggests that an organization should limit its growth based on its ability to attract enough of the right people. Tom Rath and Barry Conchie (2008) provide a powerful perspective based on over twenty-five years of Gallup interviews with thousands of executive teams. They found that effective leaders surround themselves with the right people; they understand that while the best leaders are not necessarily well rounded, the best teams are. Ensuring a strong leadership team of the right people, living one mind and one voice, is core leadership work.

Alignment's Friend: Resistance

As soon as we choose to lead, a friend for life hops up on our shoulders and whispers in our ears, "You are a leader and I am now your friend for life. My name is resistance!"

As Niccolò Machiavelli suggests in *The Prince* (1532/1961),

> There is nothing more difficult to take in hand, more perilous to conduct, or more uncertain in its success than to take the lead in the introduction of a new order of things, because the innovator has for enemies all those who have done well under the old conditions, and lukewarm defenders in those who may do well under the new.

Within every school there is a solid core of staff and community members who think, "This too shall pass." Left to their own devices, they can destroy any initiative. These people have a name. They are our resisters. Can you see your resisters? Do you know who they are?

When I first became a principal, resisters were my biggest surprise. They can come in all sizes and shapes and can be anybody. Sometimes, all I needed to do to see a resister was look in a mirror!

Leading in the face of resistance critically involves designing: **a process to deal, and live comfortably, with resisters.**

To deal with resisters requires understanding their source of power:

- Our school has been down this path before.
- Our school may be committed, but the state and regional offices are not.
- Prove to me that the leadership team supports this.
- Why would I want to do this when you might leave?

Resisters are often good people worn down by the past. History supports them. Sometimes they are the voices of our own doubts! They have the data to prove that other attempts to change the school have passed in the night.

Leading means running to our resisters as fast as our legs can carry us. We ignore them at our own peril. Unattended, resisters can destroy us. Run to them fast. When you get there, what do you do with your new friend?

- **Never argue.** Our natural response to resistance is to argue. We want to persuade the resister that where we are going together is special. Arguing doesn't work for a reason. There is some truth to what they say and believe: "This is the fourth Shared Vision we have done in this school and nothing good has ever happened." Arguing makes them dig in, even more committed to their position.

- **Never coerce.** We cannot coerce resisters. They must make their own choices. Leading involves listening to the resister's reality. Leading replaces coercion with an invitation: "Come along with us on this new journey."

- **Engage resisters in Facilitative Questioning.** Seek to understand resisters. Facilitative Questioning is a powerful tool for doing so. It involves questioning to help both you and the resister to understand the resister's mental models. Often, this reveals paths toward new awareness. This process is outlined in detail in Chapter 4.

- **Share information.** People often resist because they do not have the right information or necessary communication. Supplying this removes resistance remarkably easily. Once they know what they need to know, they relax and come on board.

- **Keep going back to resisters.** I would visit and revisit our resisters. After questioning them, I would share that I was going on our Shared Vision journey and invite them to do the same and then leave. Then, I would go back the next week. "How is your resistance today?" More questioning, more genuine attempts to understand. Through these very regular visits over time, some of my resisters became good friends and still are. Some have confided that "the twentieth time I saw you coming down that hallway toward me, I gave in and came on board."

Godin (2008) reports similar experience. He sees part of leadership as being the ability to stick with dreams for a long time—long enough that the critics realize that you are going to get there one way or the other, so they follow.

- **Keep your eye out for enemies.** Rarely, over time, I realized I was facing an enemy. It took me a long time to learn to recognize the difference between a resister and an enemy.

I can count on one hand the enemies I eventually saw clearly in my long career. These are people who are seriously intent on damaging you, the school, or both. Once I reached this realization, I moved into a totally different mode: "Here is what you will do, and here are the consequences of not doing it." With such "enemies," I would be happy to have a completely new conversation. John says it best:

> All of us need to be clear about the concept of a salary. No one is paid to come to work and undermine their employer. Some people need to be reminded of this.

For such staff, helping them to find a school that is aligned with where they want to go is a good use of mutual energy. Most schools and school systems have clear processes in place for helping people to find other employment more suited to them and their belief structures.

How does this process for working with resisters compare to yours? It is a significant leadership achievement when a resister accepts the invitation to commit. Resisters who commit often become great allies. Leading involves ensuring alignment of every member of the team in some way that is valid for them and valid for the whole team.

Leadership Challenge 4: Using Time Wisely

All of this complexity is faced with time as a daily devil trying to distract you. As a principal, I would wake and not be able to return to sleep. I was often thinking of the hundreds of people passing through my life, demanding time and expecting answers. There are two opposing forces in our work. They constantly arm wrestle each other: **the joy of leading and the weight of responsibility of leading.**

Modern leadership faces a particular ever-present demand for speed. Hurry! People will tell you—hurry, do everything at once, deliver the quick fix. You must produce student achievement now, if not yesterday.

As schools look at the tasks they must accomplish, they commonly assume they can do more than is realistic. This is a dysfunctional mental model we observe in national school system after national school system. Why do we cave in to this mentality? The fast, energy-draining pace seems to be the norm in schools. Our most valuable resource is the well-balanced human being working alongside us. If leaders take care of those individuals, they will produce great learning.

> I was asked to take on another two roles outside my school . . . up came this little voice and asked 'does this take me closer to our vision or further away' . . . for the first time I said no . . . I do not want to be an EVENTS manager anymore.
>
> —Principal, New South Wales, Australia

We believe leadership serenity is found in "less is more" and "slower is faster." Changing adult behaviors is complex and time-consuming. If a staff member changes a mental model for the better, tremendous synergy drives you forward. That is why we must be careful about our strategic planning. If we fall into the events trap, we waste valuable time and resources. This diverts us from embedding new mental models into our school.

Time can control you. That is one mental model about time that leaders can have. There is another: Wise leaders take control of time. As James Kouzes and Barry Posner (2012) report,

> Time is the truest test of what the leader really thinks is important.
> (p. 202)

We introduced Ruth Gordon's (personal communication, 1988) powerful questions early in Chapter 2. They make for a tremendous opportunity to reclaim quality time:

What are we doing now that we should continue to do?

What are we doing now that someone else should do?

What are we doing now that no one should do?

Where would this example fit with Ruth Gordon's questions?

> Tuesday morning of this week, we were all looking at each other saying, "It's been a long week!" That's when you know things are going to be a bit rough.
>
> We're entering major testing season at my schools. Testing is out of control: 11th graders will spend 21 hours in standardized tests over the next 8 weeks or so. Crazy.
>
> Yet I have to convince teachers it's at least somewhat worthwhile so they can convince kids it's at least somewhat worthwhile, even if none of us believe it.
>
> —US Instructional Coach

There is a dedicated timeframe for a school day. We see this in every country where we work. Effective school leadership involves controlling time for four central outcomes:

student and staff learning,

and

student and staff well-being.

Leadership involves removing obstacles to this core work. We have fond memories of loud cheers in schools when the leader announces, *"No more time in this school will ever be spent on this activity!"*

To be a school that delivers, time aligned to the Shared Vision is needed for

- Instruction to be sacred and uninterrupted
- Quality teaching and learning experiences
- All staff to be together to collaborate and make decisions
- Staff and children to give and receive quality feedback
- Quality research, action learning, and planning
- Sustained conversations everywhere in the community

What daily choices are you making around your collective use of time?

Every moment a team is together must be a quality moment. Leaders understand that their team has only so many hours together. They need to be times of deep thinking and reflection; to give and receive rich, quality feedback; and to enable participatory decision making. They also need to be times for personal and collective celebrations.

Leaders do not allow negativity to dominate in public. Team members who want to continually whine and moan can come and talk to the leader privately.

The principal told us that he had four bullies on staff. Their negativity would drive every staff meeting. They would jump up and speak first and loudest, and they worked as a controlling team. These were "old hands," and this was their school. They claimed to speak for all staff and tolerated no disagreement. They crushed the young new principal. Staff would leave meetings frustrated and unhappy. We asked why he allowed them to do this. We shared with him the mental model: No bully should be allowed to dominate a public forum. At the next staff meeting, the principal organized the staff to work in groups with each group collaborating to put one idea forward. The four bullies attached themselves to the same group. When it was time to present ideas, the principal chose their table in the middle of the reporting sequence. One positive idea after another was heard. Then, the "bully table" said their one negative idea. Other positive ideas followed. The bullies' collective voice was now in correct proportion, softened to one voice among many. The positive ideas drowned them out. So, at the next meeting, the bullies decided to spread themselves out to four different groups. They could not get even one idea up! The staff had found their own power, their own voice. **Never allow bullies to dominate the floor.** Just allow them an equal voice and ensure all voices are heard and respected.

Leaders tell us that much of the time they do have is consumed by administrative duties and meetings. Compartmentalized meetings continue to fuel the mental model of the school as a series of silos, always separated from each other. Effective administrative systems and structures are best designed to be in alignment with the agreed mental models in the school.

It is an "If-then" process:

"If" we believe this mental model, "then" this is the system to deliver the mental model.

For example,

if we believe in staff personal responsibility,

then our appraisal system will be staff driven rather than leadership driven.

Leadership Challenge 5:
Accountability Based on Personal Responsibility

Successful school change relies on personal and collective responsibility. Leading in this context means enabling staff and students to find this inside themselves.

Leaders share with us that most of their people want to be responsible. They want to be a successful team. They want clarity around what their responsibilities are. Valuing personal responsibility means engaging staff in partnership conversations. These clarify the nexus between personal responsibilities and organizational responsibilities.

Quality leadership addresses four elements fundamental to accountability:

1. Ensuring that the real work is done.

In relation to leadership, this means ensuring that everyone commits to the real work:

- We are clear about the behavior changes and the mental models we commit to live.
- Forces of conservatism can challenge this focus, and leadership ensures that these are resisted.
- Distractions are everywhere, and leadership means ensuring no diversions.

This allows clarity around the data that must be gathered by each person to promote their learning and inform their personal actions. Evidence-based decision making using valid data provides consistency and confidence. Regular iterations are essential to ensure we keep our minds constantly open to new learning from experience and not getting stuck in one place.

2. Developing the Skills and Dispositions
for Reflection on Individual Work and Behavior

To be accountable for our behavior and performance, we must first be able to see it clearly. In relation to leadership, this means ensuring that personal and collective reflection are an essence of the school culture. Space and time must be created for constant reflection-in-action, reflection-on-action, and reflection-to-action. These are fundamental to personal responsibility.

This often involves leadership in promoting the following:

- Development of the necessary skills and dispositions for skilled reflection
- Rich conversations flowing from deep individual and shared reflection
- Clear personal systems and structures for reflection, for sharing, and recording the actions
- Intrinsic motivation, which drives taking chances, questioning established policies and practices, and exploring the territory that lies beyond the vision

3. Developing Listening, Questioning, and Conversation Skills

To have the crucial conversations mentioned above, people need skills in processes that get to root causes. Such processes include Facilitative Questioning, dialogue, and double loop learning as covered in Chapter 4. Modeling and articulating these practices through skilled staff who already have these skills is a powerful teacher for the whole school community. Probing and asking follow-up questions is a skill needed to help yourself and others get down to root causes and mental models.

Chris Argyris (1998) recommends two powerful questions as a strong base for promoting empowerment and personal responsibility:

How long have you known about this?

and

What have you done about this?

The intonation is important here. These are gentle supportive inquiries, redirecting responsibility to where it needs to be. Addressed accusingly or punitively they will backfire.

Many leaders have found these questions to be key circuit breakers for dependencies they have set up. Initial responses to the Argyris questions are commonly not so positive. **If you have been able to get your leader to do much of your work, you may not like having to take your own responsibility.**

If a person's first thought when faced with an issue is to come to you as their leader, these questions encourage them to take personal responsibility first. If your first thought as a leader is to respond to such questions, to save time or to help, then you could be setting up dependencies. Simon Sinek (2009) argues for personal responsibility. For him, a leader's job is not to do the work of others; it is to help people figure things out for themselves, get things done, and succeed beyond what they thought was possible.

Having well-developed dialogue skills enables staff to use advocacy and inquiry. This promotes a culture of skilled openness in which personal responsibility will flourish. We need to be questioned to help us each become aware of our own defenses. These are so skilled and automatic. Most of us see defensiveness easily in others and are slow to see it in ourselves.

4. Leadership and Culture

Argyris (1994) suggests that a culture of personal responsibility is one where people are helped to figure out

- why they live with problems for years on end,
- why they cover up those problems,
- why they cover up the coverup, and
- why they are so good at pointing to the responsibility of others and so slow to focus on their own.

> A colleague principal confided her shock at discovering that the annual whole-school beach excursion was past its use-by date. She had believed it was a much-loved feature of the school's calendar. It was a tradition since before her appointment and she happily kept it going. Her leadership team dutifully went along with it. But all secretly felt it was an artificial attempt at whole-school cordiality. They thought that a series of smaller grade-based excursions might be better and more economical. It was several years into her role that a chance conversation with an experienced senior teacher revealed the truth. She was surprised to learn that they thought it was what she wanted. Not one of them had initiated a conversation about it.

Our culture must encourage people to get said what needs to be said. There is a clear leadership role here. Leaders ensure that the necessary organizational systems and structures are in place to support openness and honesty, without recriminations. Such cultures are liberating to work in, and we have seen them across all countries where we work.

One such structure we have seen in action is "The Staff Open Forum." The rationale behind this is . . . "So that we can live our Shared Vision in an authentic manner, we will surface honestly any barriers to achieving our collective goal. Staff open forum is that place to collaboratively gain consensus on a way forward with shared ownership and responsibility. It is an opportunity to view an issue/concern through a number of different perspectives."

At one school, a number of perspectives were raised about the annual staff retreat (a 3–4-day off-site staff time to focus and align to the journey ahead). The interesting issue was not the value held for the learning and collaboration these days created, but that the need to "sleep over" created some major childcare issues for some staff. With all views aired and respectfully listened to, a decision was made to trial a "non-sleepover" three-day retreat. The finish on the final day would include a family picnic to celebrate our team. The great thing was people felt comfortable to openly share their points of view and listen respectfully to others. They voiced a strong commitment and value for starting the year this way together.

Leadership Challenge 6:
Growing Leaders and Leadership

Leadership is something we choose to do. Principals influence an environment that encourages everyone, staff, students, and other community members, to choose leadership.

A young New Zealand teacher told us she became fascinated by the Levels of Perspective. She had also read a poem written by John's wife, Sandra Russell (1996), "The Things We Steal from Children." The teacher wondered what she was stealing from the children in her classroom. She wanted to choose more leadership and help her children do the same. One day she went into class and told them, "Today is an 'I can do that, Miss' day. If you see me doing anything today that you think you can do, tap me on the shoulder and say 'I can do that, Miss' and I will let you do it." Can you guess how many taps she got? 57—she got 57 taps. She was amazed how much she was stealing from students. Later, the students independently operated the first two hours of the day. This freed her up to do more quality one-on-one work with children.

Growing leaders requires focus on delegation and on responsibility structures.

Delegation

Trusting people to lead is the starting point. Delegation is the vehicle that drives building leadership capacity. As we discussed in "Leading Versus Managing," leaders spend their time at vision, mental models, and designing systems and structures. They must minimize time dealing with patterns of behaviors and events. Leaders delegate these to other staff. The beauty of delegating patterns of behaviors and events is that they can provide a leadership growth opportunity to others with no previous formal leadership experience.

Once we have done something many times it can become automatic for us. What used to require challenging mental model work for us can become automatic, event-like behavior. We delegate this skillfully to a person new to it. They then have to explore their mental models, try to make sense of the systems and structures, and make their own meaning. This is leadership work for them.

A basic mantra for us is this: **If you can do a job in your sleep, why are you still doing it?**

A deputy principal we worked with explained how he ran the weekly Monday Morning Information Meeting for all staff. We asked why it was he who always ran it and how long he had done so. As he explained in detail to us, we observed the rolled eyes of the other members of the leadership team. He explained that he was the only one who had all of the necessary information. You can guess our question. When we returned to the school the following year, he rushed up to us. "I no longer run the Monday Meeting," he shared with pride. "I delegated it to two of our young up-and-coming leaders." "And everyone enjoys it much more," laughed his colleagues. "But it took two of them to replace me," he smiled. Shortly after this, his wife approached us at a conference. She thanked us for returning Sundays to their family after so many years. This man could run those meetings in his sleep. For him, it had become boring management work; for the two up-and-coming leaders it was exciting leadership work.

Unfortunately, delegation is often seen as "dumping" onto someone else. For someone feeling already overloaded, getting a delegation offer is no thrill. We often accept the offer, fearing that to refuse may be a "career limiting" move. On top of this, while completing the job, how often has the delegator interrupted to explain that we are not doing the job right? They take over and "manage" the next steps. Often, we finish the job to the best quality we can, only to have those in authority tell us the job has not been done correctly. We feel "dumped on" and frustrated.

The "dumping" mental model can be mitigated through delegation:

A Solid Delegation Process

Effective delegation begins with a meeting. The leader meets with the team member to whom they want to delegate a responsibility. The leader presents the purpose of the task to be delegated. The leader invites the team member to take on the job: "I feel you are the best person to do this vital job. You are my first choice. So, I am asking you to keep this meeting confidential if you do not want to take it. Because if it is not for you, I want to provide this leadership opportunity to someone else."

Both participate in deciding what the final product will look like. In our experience, this is the "missing link" in delegation. Without a shared vision of the end product, the person being delegated to is left in never-never land. They try to guess what the picture looks like inside the leader's head. The team member can do a brilliant job of designing his or her own picture. But if it does not look exactly like the picture inside the leader's head, it will be deemed less than a quality effort.

Following the agreement of the shared picture, the conversation continues using several steps that are part of the process:

- The leader and team member agree on the resources they will have to lead this responsibility. Resources include human resources as well as economic resources. They also include time.
- The leader and team member agree on the support they will receive throughout the responsibility.
- The leader and team member agree on a timeline for the completion of the responsibility, including appropriate checkpoints.

Once you have delegated a responsibility to a team member, never interrupt them as they are practicing leadership. We have observed many "mother hen" behaviors in leadership. These involve keeping control, not trusting anyone to do a better job than you can. How many times have you watched this mother hen mental model alive and well at conferences? The age of technology makes this easy to see. Cell phones and iPads are on fire during the day as many leaders constantly check back with the school. The school can't survive without them!

Think for a moment about this: How long are you able to be away from your school without checking in?

We watch leadership emerge in the team research projects described in Chapter 1. Often individuals and research teams drive the implementation of innovative recommendations. As Kouzes and Posner (2012) found,

Leaders seek out projects that will increase the discretionary range of their team and provide greater decision-making authority and responsibility. (p. 176)

Trusting the staff to define the school's future through best practice research is a powerful structure to grow leadership.

> We were working with a principal in a school at the top of the South island of New Zealand. We asked him about various aspects of his school. On a number of occasions, he called in other leaders in his school saying, for example, "I only have an overview brief on that, Greg has the detailed responsibility and understanding; I will call him in." He openly admitted that he was not the master of everything in his school. He delegates and trusts and is a relaxed leader. This is refreshing.

When I observed Bill leading his schools, he was a master delegator. The only thing he told me that he would never delegate was the budget. There is a growing point for Bill.

Responsibility Structures

It is reassuring to be with a leader who has set aside the real time needed to meet well with you. There is calmness and a quality to the dialogue you experience. You will then feel this across the leadership team, the staff, and the children. The leader makes time for them, just as she has made it for you.

> I watched Bill meet with a young enthusiastic delegation of students who wanted his permission to run a new event they felt the school needed. As they started to justify, Bill said, "You have my support, now what do you need from me to help?" They stood there stunned; this was not the same critter as their previous principal. Bill helped set up a responsibility structure with these students and they floated out of his office.

Most schools have a clear list of staff responsibilities. For people to take personal responsibility, they must first know clearly where their responsibilities start and finish. So their role must be clearly and openly negotiated with their leaders and colleagues, leaving no confusion. What is my work and what is the work of others? This will obviously be linked to the Personal Vision of the person and to the Shared Vision of the organization or team.

This settles the fundamental question—responsible for what?

Leadership Challenge 7: Paying Attention

Leadership is about paying attention to what is important. Anyone who takes the time to watch closely will see what matters to you as a leader.

What principals attend to often influences what staff attend to, and this flows through to what children attend to. Edgar Schein (2004) has found that being systematic in paying attention to certain things becomes a powerful way of communicating a message, especially if the leader is consistent in their behavior.

This demands that, as school leaders, we must be clearly aware of where we direct attention. At times leading can become so busy that this crucial self-awareness is lost or ignored. At times like this, leaders rely on a strong leadership team willing to tell them hard truths.

> The school's Core Values have always been a priority for attention for me. Once, our drama club was putting on a production in our auditorium. One thousand people were watching. The play was scheduled to end at the same time as our last lunch period of the day. I saw that the play would run over time and feared the chaos that might result from unsupervised students roaming the halls during class. I had the play stopped just as it was reaching the climactic scene. The drama director and students had worked on the play for months. One of our Core Values was "We are fair to one another." After suffering through the anger of the next hour, my leadership team called me to an emergency meeting. In no uncertain terms, they asked me to explain how my power play was an example of living our Core Value. I had no answer.

There is no shortage of experts on where schools should focus their energy, where leaders should attend. Everyone is an expert. "They" know what school leaders should pay attention to.

Reality checking is fundamental to our credibility as leaders and people. Getting feedback from trusted colleagues, and refocusing, is a good use of leadership attention.

What are your filters for identifying what you will pay attention to? My own filters were born from my life experiences and personal study of organizations and leadership when I was named a school principal for the first time.

> When I was named to my first principalship, I had decided that if schools were going to improve, those improvements would not happen solely through the discipline of education. Rather, it would come from a broader study of organizations and business and leadership. From my home in Houston, I called a good friend. He owned a small vacation chalet in the deep woods of Northern Michigan on a small lake. I asked if he would allow me to spend a week in reflection and planning in that serene

environment. When he asked me my purpose, I explained I was going to figure out how to create the most magnificent school in the world ever conceived by man. Peals of laughter crossed the space between Texas and Michigan! I traveled to Michigan. I would read, study, reflect, and take notes from 8:00 a.m. until 3:00 p.m. every day. I still have the seventy-five pages of original notes from the experience. On our last day together, we were in Ed's rowboat and he asked what I had accomplished. I explained, "I've done it. I know how to create the most magnificent school ever conceived!" He argued that would never be possible and rolled me out of the rowboat into the water at my audacity.

What I learned during that "hermit" experience was my version of the "best practice" of organization transformation. My early "pay attention to" filters were born at that time. They have served me well. Here is a summary, as I do not want to inflict on you those whole seventy-five pages:

Create and sustain a Shared Vision journey.

- Facilitate the creation of the Shared Vision.
- Engage in solid planning.
- Develop the action plan.
- Create pilots and safe practice fields without disturbing the whole school vision journey.
- Provide opportunities for staff and students to make independent decisions.
- Constantly innovate.
- Free your champions.

Explain the school's Core Values incessantly.

- Model, articulate, and teach the Core Values.
- Develop a shared language.
- Manage your symbols.

Successful customers are our students.

- Embed best practice mental models of teaching and learning.
- Ensure authentic student voice.
- Everyone must crave feedback: adults and children.

Express personal interest in staff and children.

- Listen.
- Sustain conversations.
- Get people to believe in themselves.

(Continued)

(Continued)

- Generate continuous learning.
- Lead by wandering around; be visible.
- Stimulate quality of engagement.

Be culture maker.

- Live with fun, zest, enthusiasm.
- Stir things up.
- Get rid of your excuses.
- Generate incentives.
- See the complaint as an unparalleled opportunity.

Sense outside changes and adapt to them in the school.

- Deal with political mandates.

These filters grew from synthesizing the work of over fifty researchers at that time. You will see throughout this book the new researchers who are currently influencing our practice. Balancing research and practice brings another healthy tension to the way each of us thinks about our leadership. Perhaps you could make this a third leadership tension line for reflection.

Passion, energy, and time are essential. What really moves you, makes you emotional? What fills you with such passion you must shout it to the rooftops? What are you willing to fight for in your school? I mean the "I'll put my job on the line" fights. In your answers to questions like these, you will find the real leadership work you must pay attention to.

A challenge for all of us is paying attention to the balance between home life and work life. It is impossible to categorize our life as either work or home; they feed each other. Michael Fullan explains that the only way to separate work life and home life is to not be a person at work. The boundaries between home and work need clarity and protection, particularly in this digital age. Nicholas Carr's powerful writing in *The Shallows* (2011) and, more recently, *The Glass Cage* (2015), are provocative resources for reflection on the boundaries and balances we are currently building for ourselves. These are crucial areas for both staff and leadership attention.

> I am still growing and learning each day, but with new vigor and much broader perspective. My own family has seen the changes!
>
> —US Mathematics Teacher

Close attention to detail can be a straitjacket if used for judgment. If used for growth and development, it brings the type of fine grain that sharpens even the best of us. As we work together, and with other colleagues, we watch each other closely and give each other fine-grained feedback.

Leaders who keep the Shared Vision in their hearts all day, every day, find success. It becomes their protective armor. For me, it was also my crap deflector. If what we were asked to consider would not move us to our vision, we would not spend time, energy, or resources on it.

What do you pay attention to? Those you lead are watching!

Leadership Challenge 8: Strength of Character

Being a principal is both gratifying and stressful. The many voices around you are never silent. They foster a shrill presence in the life of every school leader. Principals are the "middle" managers. In large systems, this is a tricky space. Forces above and below often collide, making the principal the shock absorber. This can be the same for a leader at any level. Teachers can be caught between children and school administration. Instructional coaches can be caught between the person they coach and the administrator who evaluates the same person.

Strength of character is essential in this environment. As Kouzes and Posner (2012) found,

> modeling the way is how leaders make their visions tangible. (p. 190)

Rath and Conchie's (2008) extensive research showed that

> without an awareness of your strengths, it's almost impossible for you to lead effectively. (p. 10)

Over my professional life, I have worked in the institution of education across ten countries. Interestingly, all of these places have one overriding similarity. They are all top-down systems. This is just the truth. This isn't bad. This isn't good. It is simply the way education is structured internationally. New initiatives start at the top and slowly dribble down to those below.

All of these systems have evaluation processes to rate the quality of their staff. I have never received a poor formal evaluation. Still, twice I was threatened with termination of my contract. Why? I had a reputation for not obeying the people at the top. And it was well earned.

When I look at the pattern of behavior of most school systems, the school principal is one of the professionals most at risk of criticism. Often, education systems believe the best way to improve a school is to change principals. They are right in only one way. Changing principals will change schools. The simple fact is that the new principal will have different mental models than the old principal. Changes can go in any direction as the school mirrors the new mental models.

Autonomy is powerful. If I am the person at risk as principal, then I want autonomy. No one ever guaranteed me autonomy as a principal. I am happy to live or die on my personal decision making, not on what dribbles down from above.

Strength of character is needed to stand and fight for autonomy within controlling systems. Over time, I learned to match this with hard-won political astuteness. Without this blend, I would probably have been terminated from my contract on a number of occasions. Keeping detailed journal notes and working with a skilled personal coach both helped me develop my character and political awareness. Seeking advice from respected colleagues was, and still is, another great source of such development for me.

All top-down systems have ceilings. These ceilings are set by nation, state, and regional mandates, laws, and regulations. They are set by the system's CEO. They are set by the cultural context of the community. The school is an integral part of that larger system. Schools are expected to work within the parameters of that system. Success means that you always perform within the system's ceiling.

A leadership strategy is to locate the ceiling. Then, move to it and push hard. Over time, with luck and determination, the leader has a higher ceiling. Smart leaders move into the system and look for that ceiling. The ceiling determines how much growth and change the system will tolerate. As a leader, you have to gauge how long it will take you to hit the ceiling and when it is time to leave.

Our observations are that conformity and politics are often the drivers of top-down systems. Children will not maximize their achievement through conformity and politics. Education needs creativity that leads to innovation. Being "different" requires strength of character.

It is in "the try" to meet these leadership challenges where you find successful leaders and schools that deliver.

Leadership is threaded through every chapter in this book. For your ease of reference as our reader, this chapter has pulled together the key challenges involved in leading a school that delivers. The models included are those that we live ourselves and that have worked for our many leadership colleagues. The evolution of our leadership covers forty years across education, business, and elite sport, and it continues. Where we are specifically talking about principal leadership, we have said so.

To be principal of a school is serious work. My twenty years of school leadership were rich professional years. The experience was multifaceted, to say the least:

I was the chief crap deflector.

I was the builder and caretaker of culture.

I was the lightning rod for all of the school's storms.

I was the architect of the future.

I was micromanaged in private.

I was given credit I did not deserve.

I was given blame I did not deserve.

It is a complex role. While many of these responsibilities are shared with others, the buck usually stops with the principal.

During our combined years, the two of us have worked at most levels of leadership in a school:

Principal

Deputy principal

Department chair

Team leader

Teacher coach

Principal coach

Staff developer

Consultant to schools

Between us, we have been researchers, curriculum designers, teacher trainers, and authors for national and international curriculum projects. We have also led, and served on, committees and task forces at many levels, locally, nationally, and internationally. We have been led by a wide variety of leaders. And we have a significant number of children who have recently lived, and grandchildren currently living, the experience of being led in schools. So we come loaded with PPK and defining experiences of leadership to share from two rich, full lives. We are under no illusion that these lives are typical or exemplary.

Leading a school is not for everyone. You will know stress. There is never any closure. If you are unable to detach from your school life, the stressors will suck you in and drain you mercilessly. Be clear. For me, there was a level of professional satisfaction that few of my colleagues in other professions experienced. At the same time, I had a clear picture of the harsh realities of leadership. This wasn't me being negative. It was simply my reality as a principal.

THE JOY OF LEADERSHIP

I loved being a principal. My class was made up of our community and everyone in it. I had the most challenging class in the school, and the largest class size as well. I never forgot that **being principal meant that I was still a teacher—the lead teacher and lead learner.** I thrived on leading the creation of the learning culture. This established the challenges for children and adults to continuously grow, learn, and achieve.

There is a story written by Margery Williams (1922), perhaps you have read, that contains a wonderful conversation that defines the joy I felt as a principal. The story is *The Velveteen Rabbit*. The conversation takes place between two toy animals in the nursery—a new rabbit and an old skin horse. They are talking about what it means to be real:

> "What is real?" asked the Rabbit one day as they were laying side by side in the nursery. "Does it mean having things inside and a stick-out handle?"
>
> "Real isn't how you're made," said the Skin Horse. "It's a thing that happens to you. When a child loves you for a long, long time, not just to play with, but *really* loves you, then you become real."
>
> "Does it hurt?" asked the Rabbit.
>
> "Sometimes," the Horse replied, for he was always truthful. "When you are real, though, you don't mind being hurt once in a while."
>
> "Does it happen all at once, like being wound up bit by bit?"
>
> "It doesn't happen all at once. You *become*. It takes a long time— that's why it doesn't happen to people who break easily or have sharp edges or have to be carefully kept. Generally, by the time you are real, most of your hair has been loved off, and your eyes may drop out, and you get loose in the joints and very shabby. But, these things don't matter at all because once you are real, you can't be ugly, except to people who don't understand."

The greatest gift a principal can give their community is herself or himself. Becoming real is central to this.

SUMMARY

In Chapter 3 we focus on the three key lines of tension in leadership:

the tension line between leadership as disposition and leadership as position,

the tension line between leadership and management, and

the tension line between research and practice.

These are all healthy tensions to be savored by all involved in leadership. We encourage you to constantly refer back to these tension lines in your daily practice, and as you read this book. They have held us honest in our own leadership, and have done the same for the many leaders we have coached and are currently coaching.

Our aim is to open up the reality of school leadership and to focus your thinking on leading and leadership delivery through eight leadership challenges:

1. Holding your nerve through the inevitable storms faced while leading.

2. Designing and delivering mental model change, which is at the root of growth in any school.

3. Creating and maintaining alignment to our shared commitments.

4. Using time wisely.

5. Delivering accountability based on personal responsibility.

6. Growing leaders and leadership at all levels of the school.

7. Paying attention to what really matters.

8. Modeling strength of character.

4

Authentic Action

This chapter is about action. Schools that deliver are places of positive energy, with that refreshing feeling of action and delivery. Taking staff and a community on an action learning journey demands authenticity from all of us. Ongoing delivery on our promises creates trust and confidence. Personal accountability for delivery has two edges: being careful what we promise in the first place and then ensuring that we are action oriented. Nothing feeds momentum more than authentic delivery—the shared satisfaction of together nailing things that really matter to us.

ACTION IS WHAT MATTERS

Many teachers report to us that their lives are filled with administration, documents, constant interruptions, and other distractions, which take them away from delivery of what they most value, teaching their students. What we are interested in is what promotes action and, even better, aligned action. Inaction on what we care about deeply is what saps our energy and often our spirit.

It is continuing action, well evaluated and documented action, which is behind delivery. This takes not only a strong action skill set, but it also requires perseverance and resilience. The more that this delivery is aligned to who we say we are, and believe we are, the more fulfilling our professional life.

Our positive intentions are not always so evident to others in our actions. **We tend to judge others by their actions and ourselves by**

our intentions. Most of us assume a match between our intentions and what we actually do. This will definitely not be how all others see it.

There are five key understandings behind authentic action. These form the basis for this chapter:

- The knowledge base for action
- Openness to learning and confidence to learn
- Being clear about the "me" I present to others
- Credibility and the credibility killers
- The high-leverage drivers of action

Children have a strong in-built sense of justice and fairness. Many adults retain that. When they experience people not delivering on their promises, it feeds into this sense of injustice, sometimes very strongly. This can breed and feed cynicism. Schools often experience very clever people mired in cynicism. It is so easy to see others not walking their talk. It is not so easy to recognize when we fall short ourselves.

Gandhi was asked to help a child break a habit of eating too much sugar by the child's father. He sent him away, saying that he couldn't help him that week and asking him to come back the following week. This happened a couple of times but then he agreed to talk to the child. When the father asked him why it had taken him a number of weeks to agree to speak to the child, he replied that he himself had a habit of eating too much sugar. He had spent some time breaking that habit before feeling he could in good heart address the issue with the child. Authenticity!

Let us take you through our five bases for authentic action in detail.

THE KNOWLEDGE BASE FOR ACTION

Actions are driven from our mental models and our knowledge base. Mental models have already been covered in detail. What about the knowledge base?

If we read about something, hear about something, see something in action, we can take that information and share it with others. We can put it into our own words. We may be able to make some links to our previous knowledge. **We cannot yet live it; we cannot drive performance from it. We can only talk about it. In this respect, information is passive.**

If we take something that we see, hear, or read and try it out in our lives, we stand a chance of turning this into **actionable knowledge**. This is what Jim Butler (1994) refers to as **Personal Practical Knowledge (PPK).** As we outlined in Chapter 1, it is personal because it is ours, it is practical because we can drive behavior from it, and it is true knowledge. For Butler, PPK is the answer to Montaigne's famous question: "After all that I have thought about and participated in, what do I know?"

The differentiation between information and knowledge is crucial.

Information does affect our practice. When you are cooking off recipes, off the information in the book, or on the packet, you get one type of cooking.

Knowledge is derived from experience. When you are working off thoughtfully lived experience and PPK, you get a very different type of cooking. Diners can tell the difference. So can teachers when listening to their leaders and children when listening to their teachers. The ability to deliver quality results is based largely on deeply held actionable knowledge.

I was invited to a secondary school recognized for using Edward de Bono's thinking skills. Because of my research in this area, they wanted me to meet with the teachers who were teaching these skills. My first question was to ask them about their experiences of using the skills in their own lives. Not a peep! No one was using them. I described some of the powerful ways I used them in my life and asked the obvious question:

"Why would you be teaching them to your students, if you are not able to use them powerfully in your own lives?"

They pointed toward their deputy principal and said, "We are teaching them because he told us to."

While there is a light-hearted side to this, there is also a deadly serious side. These teachers were working out of information. They had no deeply lived experience (PPK) of de Bono's strategies.

Teaching what we have lived and experienced at a deep, personal level has an authenticity that is one crucial element of first-class teaching. Such teaching taps into our intrinsic motivation as a teacher and our passion. As a student, I well remember the absolute joy of having a knowledgeable and passionate teacher.

So, how do we develop this Personal Practical Knowledge?

We develop PPK through the ongoing iterations of action learning.

Action Learning

Both of us were taught early in our lives that learning is not a spectator sport. We knew that to really learn we had to get off our backsides and do something. My life as a child outside school in Australia was filled with action, learning by doing. This was a strong part of our culture. In the United States, Bill developed a similar love of the outdoors and sport as places to chew into life and learn through direct experience. Both cultures highly respect delivery.

My research inside classrooms and inside business and industry reinforces this concept. The "doers" stand out from the "talkers." They earn respect. Students warm to teachers who deliver, just as workers respond to bosses who deliver. As I watched Bill lead, I saw that **his staff paid close attention to the way he lived his leadership, his walk**. Some confided in me at the pub that they did not particularly agree with Bill on many things, but they all told me that they respected him. "You get a handshake agreement from Bill and you can bank your life on it."

His parent body shared with me: "You never want to talk with Mr. Martin at the gas station; he never stops talking about that vision!"

When their working-class Detroit school won their Blue Ribbon Award (Toporek, 1999); they all wanted to talk about that vision (see Figure 4.1).

Figure 4.1   When a Shared Vision Is Delivered

MHS is a Blue Ribbon school

By Sheila Toporek
Staff Writer

MONROE — There is only one way to be recognized as an elite school in the United States, and Monroe High School is well on its way.

The Michigan Department of Education announced this week that the school is one of the top 14 schools in the state and will go on to the national level to compete for the honor of being chosen as a National Blue Ribbon School.

The best learning model we have found, that encapsulates what we have learned from our lives, comes from Reg Revans (2011). Revans learned similar lessons to us from such experiences as working with British coal miners. His concept of action learning involves driving oneself through ongoing loops of ACT—Gather Data—Reflect—Design—NEW ACTION as a start to a new loop (see Figure 4.2).

Figure 4.2   Action Learning

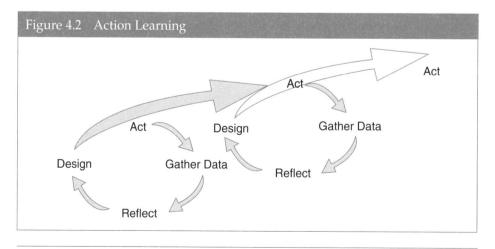

Source: Adapted from Revans (2011).

So, for example, if I want to learn a new way of managing student behavior in my classroom, I can start my action learning:

Iteration 1

Act–1. Do what I normally do. (Try to speak firmly to students and keep them in their places.)

Gather Data–1. Collect the best data I can on how I currently manage behavior and the effectiveness of my strategies by shooting some video of my classroom.

Reflect–1. Reflect deeply on what the data tells me about my current practice in classroom management.

Design–1. Based on this reflection on my data about the effectiveness of my current actions, I design what I think will be an improved process.

Iteration 2

Act–2. I now act on my new design. (Learning all student names and having them question each other to come up with the elements of a classroom management agreement, which I will help them implement.)

Gather Data–2. I gather data on how our new approach is working for all of us.

Reflect–2. I set up reflection time for myself and the class together: to look at what has emerged and what impact it has had on how well we all work together. As part of this, they question the validity of my data.

Design–2. Based on this reflection, I design my next action learning iteration. This time I bring in a respected colleague to mentor me. She is also well respected by the students.

Iteration 3

Act–3. With my colleague, I share with the class what the data showed us about the last iteration. We ask them to give feedback on what they would change, based on the data. Together we create a new action plan.

Gather Data–3. Since the students challenged the validity of my data set, we agree that they will gather data this time, as well as me. At the same time, we agree on what would be convincing data for all of us.

Reflect–3. Once again the class and I reflect on the full new data set.

Design–3. I and two students selected by their classmates come up with a new design based on the data and our shared reflections and processing of the data.

Iteration 4

We will stop here with this example. Action learning is ongoing. We keep iterating and keep learning.

Learning is not linear, as is often suggested in schoolrooms, going from not knowing to knowing. Real learning involves these iterative loops, constantly revisiting and redefining where one is going, and constantly seeing the links between the phases in the loop. Some refer to these loops as cycles of continuous improvement. Action is the driving force for learning. The skilled gathering of data provides the input for skilled reflection. Reflecting on data not only provides a basis for design, it also provides insight into better ways to gather data in the next iteration. So, each of the four action learning steps can be continuously improved and drive deeper learning.

All of our work is based on action learning (e.g., Balatti, Edwards, & Andrew, 1997; Edwards, 2001). Iteration after iteration, a constant movement toward improvement, is a strong driver of delivery. What these iterations keep delivering is new PPK, ready to be rechallenged to continue the action learning. Many teachers will be familiar with this approach through action research or "practitioner research."

The Power of Reflection

Throughout this chapter, we will refer to the ground-breaking action science research of Chris Argyris and Donald Schön. We also draw on the practical experience of leaders and authors such as Arie de Geus, based on his successful career with Shell. While this work is mostly from the 1990s, we find it deep, relevant, and powerful for the schools and organizations with whom we are currently working. We use it daily and recommend it to you as our reader. Like all of the best research, it has a timeless quality. We blend it with our own current action research and that of more contemporary researchers and authors.

As discussed briefly in Provocation 5 in Chapter 2, Donald Schön in his seminal book *The Reflective Practitioner* (1991) explored how professionals think in action.

In his preface Schön laments,

> I have become convinced that universities are not devoted to the production and distribution of fundamental knowledge in general. They are institutions committed, for the most part, to a particular epistemology, a view of knowledge that fosters selective inattention to practical competence and professional mastery. (p. vii)

In our work, our concern is with the epistemology of practice—with professional knowing—as it is lived out in daily practice. It is through deep reflection on daily practice that the evolving pathway to a Shared Vision is revealed.

Schön describes two types of reflection: reflection-in-action and reflection-on-action.

Reflection-in-action involves thinking about something while you are in the process of doing it. It helps us deliver with better quality. It enables us to reshape what we are working on, while we are working on it. He refers to common phrases such as "thinking on your feet," or "keeping your wits about you." He uses examples revealed in skillful performance, such as baseball pitchers "learning to adjust once you are out there" and jazz musicians improvising on their feet.

While living our everyday professional lives, we show ourselves to be knowledgeable. This can be hard to describe or explain as our knowing is buried deep in our action. This **knowing-in-action is central to under-standing professional practice.**

Reflection-on-action is much more widely known. Ruminating on what one has done, why, and how we could have done it differently or better is a commonly talked-about process. For Schön, we reflect-on-action in order to reveal how our knowing-in-action has contributed to the out-comes that have emerged. This process encourages us to take our time to think through what we may do differently next time.

We also explore **reflection-to-action as a process that leads to the skilled design of new actions** through reflective practice. This is the start of a new action learning iteration.

Developing a rich repertoire of reflection strategies is one powerful way to improve our ability to deliver at depth. To do so requires getting to root causes, what Argyris (1991) refers to as double loop learning.

Professional Knowing

Our experience has taught us six keys to professional knowing:

1. We know more than we can say.

2. We have knowing-in-action.

3. We are contextually skilled.

4. Our professional learning is our own professional responsibility.

5. Individual learning and team learning are both central.

6. Professional learning is a journey, not a race.

Let us compare these mental models with the common understanding of the knowledge base of a profession. The systematic knowledge base of a profession is seen as having four essential elements:

*   It is specialized.
*   It is firmly bounded.
*   It is scientific.
*   It is standardized.

Professionals apply standardized knowledge to solve concrete problems.

Edgar Schein (cited in Schön, 1991, p. 24), articulates this Technical Rationality Model of Professional Knowledge, which has dominated professional education.

First, there is the underlying discipline, the "basic science."

Based on this is the "applied science": the day-to-day procedures and problem-solving processes.

Once these two are clear, one can develop the skills and attitudes of application to the real-world problems of practice.

Most professional degrees are based on this model.

I was part of such a model for eighteen years, preparing teachers. Our teachers-in-training learned the basic disciplines of education, then the applied science of teaching, and finally they had a practicum. Despite attempts by some colleagues and me, we could not shake this model from within.

Nineteen years ago, I left the university to live a different way. Like Schön and others, my life had taught me that knowing-in-action is what matters. This is a slippery concept. Most professionals with whom I work recognize that there are things they "just know." As Schön explains, they are commonly fuzzy about how they learned these things; they simply find themselves doing them. They are usually unable to describe clearly the knowing which their action reveals. At the same time, there is deep satisfaction in exploring and understanding this knowledge-in-action. Tapping this PPK brings power and confidence to individuals and to teams.

When knowing-in-action is articulated, captured, and shared, it has a power not found in standardized knowledge. Knowing-in-action comes from reflecting-in-action. When you reflect-in-action, Schön suggests that you become a researcher of yourself. You are not dependent on theory. **You are constructing a new theory about your unique case.**

Our colleague Mike Gillatt (2013), principal of Hutt Intermediate School in New Zealand, describes his self-construction as a leader. He took control of his leadership growth and became a researcher of himself. This journey took him from dutiful deputy principal, to a principal delivering winning performance, to a principal in serious doubt, to a principal who "changed the waters in which he swam":

> The inherent busyness of school life meant I worked incredibly hard on a daily basis. I was never daunted by my long "to-do" list. I was prepared for this, having witnessed it first-hand and been told by my role models; this was the typical day-to-day life of a leader. A problem arose, I fixed it. Even better, the more problems I fixed the more staff trusted my leadership. I was entrusted to fix their issues by providing expert advice and solving problems

wisely. It was affirming that they saw me as a good leader and wanted my help. (p. 37)

Gillatt became aware of the dependencies he was creating and felt trapped in a role that was no longer satisfying. That set him on a journey to "let go of deeply ingrained patterns of thinking." He drew inspiration on this journey from a quote from Schön (1987), which sums up the fear that many leaders and teachers have of the complexity, ambiguity, paradox, organic growth, and uncertainty that accompanies a real learning journey:

> The master craftsman says "I can tell you that there is something you need to know, and with my help you may be able to learn it. But I cannot tell you what it is in a way you can now understand. I can only arrange for you to have those experiences yourself. You must be willing, therefore, to have those experiences. Then you will be able to make an informed choice about whether you wish to continue. If you are unwilling to step into this new experience without knowing ahead of time what it will be like, I cannot help you." (p. 93)

The growth of instructional coaching across the world is strong evidence for the benefits of this mode of learning. Coaches work alongside teachers in their classrooms, observing their knowing-in-action and promoting reflection-in-action and reflection-on-action. This is authentic learning that creates breakthrough opportunities.

One secondary social studies teacher I worked with wanted to support students in improving their writing through the revision process. To that end, she put in place the structure of writing conferences. After a couple of months, she shared with me her frustration that the writing conferences weren't working. As I observed her one-on-one conferences, I noted that she read to each student her written comments on the paper and then dismissed the student. In a reflecting conversation, I posed questions around the purpose of the conference. In what ways was the purpose different from the written feedback? What types of feedback did she want to provide students that would support students' growth as writers? We then had the opportunity to confer with students together, pausing to collaborate on feedback when needed. As a result, her conferences with students became much more intentional and involved more dialogue and specific, targeted feedback.

—US Instructional Coach

This fits our practice exactly and is what differentiates the way we work from many other approaches to professional and school development. **Our belief is that schools, their staff, and community know what they need to be doing. When unsure, they can work together to action learn their way to the breakthrough insights they need.**

Despite examples such as these, for Schön (1991), the reality is that

> because professionalism is still mainly identified with technical expertise, reflection-in-action is not generally accepted—even by those who do it—as a legitimate form of professional knowing. (p. 69)

There are strong parallels between Schön's concept of knowing-in-action and our concept of Personal Practical Knowledge. PPK drives growth, learning, and delivery.

Balancing this approach is the experience of Jon Saphier, John Hattie (2009), and others. They have each clarified a "research base for teaching." Saphier shows how teachers choose from their repertoire a response that meets the needs of the child or the situation. So, building such repertoires and knowing how to make wise choices, is one sound base for better teaching. This forms the foundation for the valuable book *The Skillful Teacher* (Saphier, Haley-Speca, & Gower, 2008).

For us, this exemplifies the shift:

> **from information**, research they have read, and practices they have been trained in

> **to PPK** that comes from thoughtful repeated cycles of action learning.

Often these cycles involve mediation from a coach or colleagues or a leader.

How do you see reflecting-in-action and knowing-in-action as being lived in your school culture?

OPENNESS TO LEARNING AND CONFIDENCE TO LEARN

Nobody walks their talk. It is simply not possible. But some sure get closer than others!

Argyris (1993) talks about this difference between

> our "espoused theories," what we say that we do, or "the talk,"

and

> our "theories-in-use," what we actually deliver, or "the walk."

He argues that there is coherence in the ways we act. It is not just that we do not walk our talk, but we consistently do not walk our talk. We are consistently inconsistent. This is because our behavior is driven off deeply held mental models—these serve to help us act consistently. Our PPK, what our life has taught us experientially, equally drives this consistently inconsistent behavior.

The problem is that we are usually not aware of the walk-talk mismatch and no one will tell us. Many people are afraid to give feedback—I might hurt the person, they might give me some feedback I do not want in return, or I might go into their little black book. So we do not tell the person about their inconsistencies. We do, however, often tell others. Most people live in a feedback vacuum. Most of us are starved of the very feedback we need to be able to look clearly at our theories-in-use, and these drive our behavior.

One aspect of our ongoing action research in schools, and in organizations, involves teaching people how to skillfully give and receive feedback and how to act on it. This involves a major mental model shift in the way we conceptualize feedback. The results are profound. Most people ask us "Why were we not taught these things when we were younger?"

Argyris (1991) has much to report about the lives of adults in the workplace. By projecting back from these we can gain some insights into approaches that may be helpful during schooling. After a lifetime of research, he concludes:

> Those members of the organization that many assume to be the best at learning are, in fact, not very good at it. I am talking about the well-educated, highly powered, high-commitment professionals who occupy key leadership positions in the modern corporation. (p. 4)

> If learning is to persist, managers and employees must also look inward. They need to reflect critically on their own behavior, identify the ways they often inadvertently contribute to the organization's problems, and then change how they act. (p. 4)

> Teaching people how to reason about their behavior in new and more effective ways breaks down the defenses that block learning. (p. 5)

However, the skill of reflection is not widely used by most adults in the workplace. We have found from our research that most workers, be they managers or operators, seldom switch on their reflection (e.g., Edwards, 1994). Most claim to be too busy, and many see the process as slowing them down or as avoiding "real work." Australian workers believe that managers have high IQs and work with their heads while operators have low IQs and work with their hands. We have been told that operators "hang their brain on the gate" when they enter their workplaces and just do as they are told all day. They then leave work and use all of their creativity in their sport and leisure activities.

This is a powerful example of what Carol Dweck (2010) calls a fixed mind-set, where people believe that traits such as intelligence, creativity, and ability to learn are fixed. She argues for growth mind-sets where people believe that they can grow and develop these traits through learning and effort. The action research shared in this book shows the impact on teachers and their communities when they are trusted to grow themselves.

One New Zealand principal shared with us earlier this year his passion for our process and

> your message about the amazing *mahi* (work) that a team of ordinary people can achieve together.

Another principal expressed it differently:

> I hear the value you place on the human resource, as opposed to simply being teachers (as a job). We need to value ourselves beyond the school gate. We need to revisit a 'vision' and ensure it's a 'shared vision'. We need to value the expertise we have within our schools.

Over many years our research has shown the impact of opening people to their ability to think differently and grow cognitively. In a series of research studies (Edwards, 1991a) we showed the positive impact on student achievement and attitude from the direct teaching of thinking skills. The work of Lisa Blackwell, Kali Trzesniewski, and Dweck (2007) with New York City students over their Grade 7 to 9 years showed similar results to ours. Students with growth mind-sets significantly outperformed students with fixed mind-sets.

We have also shown that workers at all levels of companies can deliver significant innovations through action learning projects (e.g., Edwards, 2001; Hill, 1994). This results in organizational learning seldom experienced. In a manufacturing company we worked with, we had a quiet operator on a production line begin by designing a way to prevent back injuries for herself and her colleagues. This work resulted in an award. She then went on to redesign a significant section of the production line with similar outstanding results. Once she plugged with confidence into her ability to grow and learn, there was no stopping her. One of her colleagues shared with all of us that she had known this woman at school and she was amazed that "someone like her" could do such high-quality work.

What roots do these mind-sets have in our schools? What modeling do teachers provide of being open to feedback and learning on the job themselves, in real time? What opportunities are students given to challenge the stereotypes that are attached to them early in life?

Argyris (1994) has found that workers and managers collude to let the managers have all of the responsibility and workers have none. He has also found that most people reason defensively: they are afraid of being wrong or being seen to be wrong.

At what age do we learn to feel that being wrong can so hurt us? Where do we learn such narrow hierarchical, comparative, and competitive views of human functioning? People also fear the gathering of data on their performance and fear feedback. How does this relate to school environments and the life lessons learned there?

Being Clear About the "Me" I Present to Others

In this chapter so far, we have looked at how we each make our own meaning and how we action learn our way to our unique set of Personal Practical Knowledge. How our behavior flows from this base, and how others interpret that behavior led us to the research of Chris Argyris (1993).

Argyris suggests that the mental models that most of us work out of when making meaning and interacting with others are

- What I observe are the facts
- What I know is the truth
- Any reasonable person would see what I see and know the truth as I know it

From our experience, most people recognize these well, particularly in others. On reflection, most of us can see serious flaws in such mental models as a basis for quality communication. Argyris's antidote to this thinking is to use the metaphor: the ladder of inference.

The Ladder of Inference

The Ladder of Inference (Argyris, 1993) is a model for understanding how our minds move from perception to action (see Figure 4.3).

Argyris argues that we each construct our own world based on our mental models. To work effectively in teams requires us to know ourselves and how we make our meanings and to respect that others can make meaning in totally different, equally valid, ways.

All that we normally have access to is our observation of a situation and the person's actions in that situation (the top and bottom of the ladder). The rest is hidden inside people's heads, and we have no real access to that. Argyris's Ladder is a useful model for understanding and articulating the steps we make in our minds.

Given the crucial nature of these intervening steps, particularly in the teaching profession, exploring ladders is a fruitful use of time. They provide a means of teasing out the mental steps taken from our perceptions to our actions.

We start from the bottom rung of the ladder, the situation as a video camera would catch it.

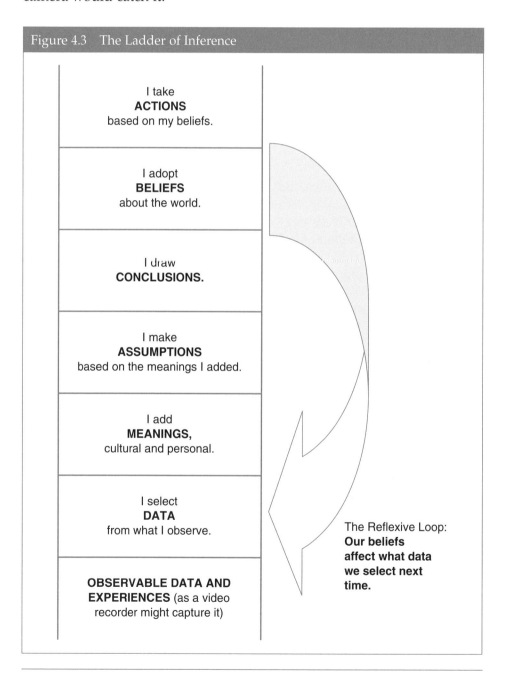

Figure 4.3   The Ladder of Inference

I take
ACTIONS
based on my beliefs.

I adopt
BELIEFS
about the world.

I draw
CONCLUSIONS.

I make
ASSUMPTIONS
based on the meanings I added.

I add
MEANINGS,
cultural and personal.

I select
DATA
from what I observe.

OBSERVABLE DATA AND EXPERIENCES (as a video recorder might capture it)

The Reflexive Loop:
**Our beliefs
affect what data
we select next
time.**

Source: Adapted from Senge, Kleiner, Roberts, Ross, & Smith (1994, p. 243).

Step 1: Our mind selects data from the situation.

This is determined both by what is there to be observed and the beliefs (mental models) we bring to observing. Depending on your attitude toward the Dalai Lama, you see and hear very different things as you observe his behavior. Let us thread a teaching example through this explanation:

Year 7 teacher Richard McGrath enters his classroom early in the morning after a week's absence due to illness. When he phoned in sick, he was told, despite his protests about her ineffectiveness, that the school would have to ask Alison Vermay to cover his class. He scans the room and notices the furniture is less tidy than he would have left it; there are noticeable graffiti on some desktops. Clearly, the work the class had been doing is different to what he had started, and the remote to the air conditioner is broken. He notices also what appears to be a hastily scrawled note sitting under the stapler on his desk.

What Richard sees is what Richard sees. Anyone else entering that classroom at that moment would "see" his or her own version. Some of this may cohere with what Richard sees and some of it will be completely different from what Richard notices.

Moving up the ladder to the next rung.

Step 2: We immediately make meaning.

Our minds are meaning-making minds and we instantly make meaning from the data we have selected. **This meaning is our meaning, unique to us**, and others will easily make a slightly or completely different meaning. Even if we were to look again at the same situation our own meaning may change.

Richard fumes at the disappointing state of the room and sighs at how it is just not worth the mess you come back to, to take days off. It is just as he had feared. Alison has yet again let down him, the children, and the school. "I can just imagine the pathetic excuses she has written in that note!"

Other teachers on staff who know Alison differently would see this situation differently. The meanings they make of her actions are very different from those Richard makes. This is what we all do.

Step 3: Attached to our meaning are a whole set of assumptions that are inside us, from our upbringing, our life, our PPK.

Once again, these will vary significantly from person to person.

Richard thinks it is no wonder Alison is at the bottom of our list of substitute teachers. There's no way the room would be in this state had he been here. She clearly did not follow his teaching program, and her lax supervision allowed a remote to be destroyed under her watch. This is also yet another case of school leadership not listening to common sense from staff.

Step 4: Based on the meaning and the assumptions, we draw a conclusion.

In any situation, the conclusions we draw are the tops of our ladders of inference. Inside our heads, we have climbed these steps to get to our conclusion. There is, for each of us, a sound basis for our conclusions.

Alison has clearly not followed the detailed plans Richard has provided. Richard concludes that he needs to take this further. It will not be an easy conversation with the assistant principal, but it must be had. Richard feels vindicated in his belief that Alison is incompetent. He had warned the school this sort of thing would happen but they didn't listen. And as for little Joey Sutton, he's always trying to get his hands on that remote and use it as a baseball bat. *Just wait till I see him!*

Step 5: This conclusion then is matched against our mental models, usually reinforcing them, but occasionally challenging them.

And this mental model will then help to determine the data one will select from the next situation. Our mental models are built over time, through rich experience.

Richard is very clear that this sort of unprofessional conduct on Alison's part gives the teaching profession a bad name, sets back children's learning, unnecessarily consumes valuable resources in repairing damage, and creates more work for him and his colleagues. It is Richard's ethical duty to do something about this.

Step 6: Based on our conclusion and our mental models, we then decide on the action to take.

Our action decisions are based on our best assessments of any situation. We seldom ask for anyone to question these, or check on them, before we spring into action. Too often, these action decisions are private. How widely we canvass action options before moving varies from person to person and context to context. A sage piece of advice we have learned from an experienced leader is this: You can act quickly with reversible decisions; but move much more slowly with irreversible decisions. Of course, if you find you are reversing a lot of decisions, even if they are reversible, you might want to question the way you make decisions.

Richard walks out and heads toward the office. Unfortunately, one piece of data he did not scrutinize was the handwritten note sitting under the stapler on his desk. Had he read it, he would have seen it was written by an old buddy of his, Rick James, who has returned to teaching after several years' absence. He had been called when Alison Vermay had herself been unavailable on one of the days due to her own illness. Rick had left detailed notes about the work the class did, apologizing that he could not follow Richard's program due to the assistant principal having mislaid the information. Richard also apologized for the damage to the remote, which he himself inadvertently caused, when it bore the full weight of his chair. He was personally looking into a replacement. As Richard heads into the office he spots Alison Vermay chatting with a couple of colleagues. He also spots the assistant principal, standing on his own. He takes a breath and heads straight toward him to do what he knows needs to be done.

(We thank our colleague Greg Morgan for sharing this powerful teaching example.)

We are up ladders about everyone and every situation. What few of us consciously realize is that the view we see from up these ladders is a view of our own making. It reveals just as much about us as about what we "see." The old saying "seeing is believing" is probably back to front. "Believing is seeing" is probably closer to reality.

Everyone's ladders are driven by their own mental models, and we have no control over the mental models of others. Their mental models determine the data they select, which drives their meaning making, and their associated assumptions, which lead to their conclusions then their actions.

What we can control is the actions we deliver.

By our actions we either starve ladders or feed ladders.

I coached an introverted senior executive. In meetings, he would regularly "go inside himself" to think through what was transpiring. The feedback I received from his colleagues was that they thought he felt superior, and that once he had his say, he was not interested in what others said. When I asked him about this behavior, he was totally unaware of it. When I shared the observation, he said, "That is what I need to do, go inside myself

(Continued)

(Continued)

and figure out what I really think." After much probing, he finally suggested that maybe he could make some brief notes for later thought and stay present in the meeting. His colleagues reported an instant reaction to this changed behavior. Like all of us, he found it tough to stick with the new behavior. People were very used to the old behavior and would quickly spot the slightest reversion. He was slowly starving the old ladders. This is not easy when one has a long history with a pattern of behavior. Shortly afterwards, he gained a new position in another organization. This gave him the perfect opportunity to establish new ladders from the start. He did so with great success.

We are all being observed by people who know what we have promised, know what we have said we will do and how we will do it. They also know our regular habits. Seeking open feedback on how our actions match our promises from colleagues, students, families, and our community provides one convincing source of data for learning and change.

Spending our days moving comfortably up well-worn ladders seldom helps. Similarly, not being vigilant on what matters most to our self can condemn us to being stereotyped and just accepting the ladders people are up about us.

Each of us can focus on being clear about what ladders we want to starve in others about us or our school or whatever, and what ladders we will feed.

Focusing on clarity around ladders people want to feed and starve, and then helping people hold themselves to this, is one of my most powerful coaching strategies. I watch this closely in myself; it takes self-discipline and it takes people around me to help me keep myself honest. When I first left the university to set up my own company, this drew a singular focus from me. My advisers told me that it would take five years of such focus to establish a successful company. I was still espousing balance and family first and my practice was initially miles from that. Luckily, I have a wife and children, and some dear colleagues, who helped me see the gap between my words and my actions. When faced with competing mental models around an issue, it is time to seek feedback and take time to reflect on priorities.

Language and Self-Discipline

Self-discipline with the language we use is central to "talking our walk." Our language reveals us, and the discipline to use language that accurately represents our thinking is a critical skill. Language feeds ladders.

When writing about *Planning as Learning*, Arie de Geus (1988) concluded:

> And here we come to the most important aspect of institutional learning: . . . the institutional learning process is a process of language development. As the implicit knowledge of each learner becomes explicit, his or her mental model becomes a building block of the institutional model. How much and how fast this model changes will depend on the culture and structure of the organization. Teams that have to cope with rigid procedures and information systems will learn more slowly than those with flexible, open communication channels. (p. 74)

In our current work, we listen with interest as new language emerges in schools undergoing transformation. In schools embarking on the direct teaching of thinking, we hear the language of thinking emerge and see the new clarity it delivers. Inside workplaces, we often hear the language of "ladders" emerge as people shift to new ways of dialoguing and respecting each other's views. Our experience matches that of de Geus in that school culture significantly impacts how change and new language emerge.

At the same time, be wary; new language can be exclusionary. If change starts with a leadership group, or a small group of enthusiasts, for a period they are likely to use new language. We have heard such groups described as the "secret squirrels" or the "chosen ones." Only they know and use the new language; they are the "in group" and the rest of us are the "out group." This needs to be watched for in any change process. Ensure that everyone is brought on board with new concepts and new terminology in a way that respects and encourages involvement.

New language can signal fresh new approaches that we all agree on and commit to. People enjoy new language if it signals change for which they hunger. Some people will always classify new language as unnecessary jargon—they simply do not like it. For example, I had a senior international sports coach challenge me about using the term *mental model*.

"Why not just call them beliefs?" he asked.

"Go home tonight and look up *beliefs* on the Web and see what you get, then look up *mental models* and see what you get," I replied.

You can try this for yourself. *Mental model* takes you to a more specific area and specific literature. *Belief* takes you to a much broader area.

Accuracy of language makes a big difference.

We have both experienced how using particular language has at times led us to the people and the conversations we needed to join.

CREDIBILITY AND THE CREDIBILITY KILLERS

Our credibility is important to each of us. It takes time and consistency to establish credibility with any person or group. Over time, trust grows.

The Competence Component of Trust

Delivering on what we say we will do is fundamental to trust in ways that few understand deeply. Most people believe that trust is about character. If I am a good person, with laudable qualities, I will be trusted. There is no doubt that character is one key component of trust. Our experience is that most people do not seem as aware of the other component of trust: competence. I may be a great person, but if I do not deliver I will lose trust. It is sad to see good people confused about being no longer trusted. Often no one is willing to give us the skilled feedback that our continuing lack of delivery, our letting others down, has eroded the trust levels. The competence component must be attended to.

How do you check your competence, your delivery, for those around you?

Defensive Reasoning

We have found, like Argyris (1991), that

> the master program that most people use is profoundly defensive. Defensive reasoning encourages individuals to keep private the premises, inferences, and conclusions that shape their behavior and to avoid testing them in a truly independent, objective fashion. Because the attributions that go into defensive reasoning are never really tested, it is a closed loop, remarkably impervious to conflicting points of view.

Defensive reasoning is the number one credibility killer. We learn the technique early in life to protect ourselves from hurt. Once we have a healthily formed ego, and sense of who we are, we can let go of this. Many people do not, it becomes their common mode of response, and this steadily erodes their credibility.

Children and adults need rich and effective feedback to learn. Feedback is the working business of how to improve oneself. Students need the language, confidence, and skill to give helpful feedback to their fellow students and their teachers. Most students and adults lack strategies for combating the temptation to use defensive reasoning. They lack strategies for productive reasoning. The research of Argyris is a powerful source for this, as is our own research in Australia (e.g., Edwards, 2001). Edward de Bono, in books such as *Teach Yourself to Think* (2010), provides a range of practical productive reasoning tools. *Cognitive Coaching* (Costa & Garmston, 2002) helps people develop powerful repertoires for their own growth.

The skills for giving and receiving feedback are learnable. Our results show that you can have a profound effect on the atmosphere and efficiency of a workplace through introducing these skills as a part of everyday work life.

Principals send a strong message when they invite people to hold them accountable and give them feedback. Acting on feedback themselves adds power and authenticity to their requests for others to do the same.

Think about your own responses to feedback. Do you recognize the commonly felt need to defend yourself when you are questioned closely? The message that defensive reasoning sends to the recipient is "do not give me feedback again." And they will not. This withers one of the crucial avenues for reflection and growth.

A fellow credibility killer is "taking offense." This is one of the great controlling strategies. Somebody says something and the other person chooses to be offended. They go quiet, stony faced, and drop their eyes or gaze ahead. The "offender" then is expected to plead for forgiveness or to play "guess the grievance."

"What have I done to offend you? Is it this . . . ?"

"No."

"Is it that?"

"No," as they keep good mental records of all of the "tender spots" being revealed by the supposed offender, for later use.

People are sensitive, and we do get hurt at times in the flow of relationships and interactions. Knowing how to negotiate such impact is an important skillset in any team, on any staff. Rushing to take offense is not part of that skill set. It is an absolute killer of collaboration and teamwork.

THE HIGH-LEVERAGE DRIVERS OF AUTHENTIC ACTION

We would like to finish this chapter by sharing what ourselves and our colleagues have found to be the five highest-leverage drivers of aligned action. Together these ensure authenticity:

Personal Vision

One key to walking the talk is to know what talk we should walk.

Some people who I have coached seemed content to drift along in life serendipitously, letting the waves of life wash them this way and that. I encourage them to create a Personal Vision for where they want to be in their life.

They can then use this to hold themselves accountable. As their coach, I can also use this to **help them hold themselves accountable**.

If staff are going to commit to helping the school achieve its Shared Vision, an honorable school will do the same in return.

One of the top principals we have worked with had a classic example of this. One of her staff had in her Personal Vision to spend some time working overseas on Super Yachts. To achieve this she needed to attend a preparatory course. Unfortunately, all such courses were in school term time. The principal gladly agreed to give this teacher that precious time. So, the young lady did the course and left on her Overseas Experience. When she returned from overseas, we think you can guess which school she was dying to return to. This outstanding young teacher is now a totally committed staff member back in the school. The school helped her achieve her Personal Vision and she is helping the school achieve its Shared Vision.

How would you handle such a request? What do you see as the relationship between Shared Vision and Personal Vision?

The use of a Personal Vision can be powerful, and it can be a personal and cultural minefield. Let us explore this for a moment. Whenever anything personal comes up, so does the issue of privacy, as it should. A Personal Vision is very private to many of us, and work is not an all-consuming mission for some of us. Most of us like space between who we are and what we do at times, breathing room. Some staff say to us that they do not want to share such personal information with their principal.

The whole power dynamic that begins to play out if a leader is "holding" someone to their Personal Vision can be damaging. Our approach involves each person holding themselves accountable. They design and seek the feedback they need to do so.

The use of Personal Visions as part of staff development requires strong trusting relationships, leadership skill, and experience. Where they are used well, the effect is positive and dramatic.

Here is one example of a Personal Vision. It is shared with permission by a person I am coaching. **A Personal Vision is normally one page and written in the present tense.** It captures the future as the individual would like it to be and will endeavor to make it be. The individual chooses the time frame for their Personal Vision. In this case, it is five years. So this is a picture of how this person sees his life in five years' time:

I am living free of mental burdens, happy with what I am doing and inspired and challenged by what I am creating. I am in love and grateful with my kids and my wife. I am close to a few friends. I speak my truth and pause before I speak. I am free of outbursts and anger, learning constantly and an expert in a very exciting field in a community or sport context. I spend quality time with music and outdoor pursuits, doing these with my kids. I give where I can of my time and my creativity.

I am surrounded by space: space to mentally think, to feel my emotions, accept them, and do the right thing. Space around me to walk, breathe, and explore. Space in my schedule to play with my kids, learn with my kids, and participate in my kids' life. Space to be with my wife alone, to communicate, sit together, and grow together. I am a good teacher and role model to my kids; I am a loving caring, open, proud husband to my wife. As a family, we have open chats about our learning, our successful and less successful attempts and efforts.

I work on challenging projects, and work with a coach. I travel for work periodically, and it does not consume me. I have very specific useful expertise in learning and leadership, and work at a strategic and leadership level. Our team is strong and productive; we do amazing things together and I add value to this. I am an entrepreneur. I enjoy growing my skill base in learning, creativity, and productive invention.

I have found my own groove and live in this groove, caring less what I look like and what people think. I have uncovered the true skills inside me and am less self-conscious of the thoughts and criticism of others. Financially, we run our finances effectively rather than it run us; we have dialed into a financial rhythm.

We are off the grid, on a small plot in the mountains, with space and a bit of land. We are an active part of the community we live in. I have natural connections to our land, our food on the table, and nature and I continue to explore adventure, yoga, and meditation. I have hobbies that include woodwork and home handy work. I have grown up, matured; I am free of fear and anger; I speak truthfully, honestly, and with integrity and empathy. Life is full and rich in where we are, what we are doing; and how we are together. I have a sense of purpose and mission and I am on the road I have chosen to pursue. I am leading my own destiny.

My life is full of love and simplicity.

In every school, early in my time as principal, we would have a Professional Development Day of Personal Visioning where we could create a Personal Vision or polish and refine the one already there. The Personal Visions were a vehicle to talk with staff about their lives.

Thank you for helping me have the courage to pursue my personal vision. Your support and guidance was the nucleus to my new beginning (at 42 that is hard to do—start anew!). I am truly enjoying my counseling classes.

—US Music Teacher

In Appendix 4, we share Personal Visions from three different staff in schools. These Personal Visions are part of a process where each staff member designs a Personal Vision for the upcoming year and beyond. So, they are to a much tighter time frame than the Personal Vision above, which has a five-year time frame. The staff use these Personal Visions to work with their principal on what they envision as the work for themselves in the coming year. They also signal longer-term goals that each year are broken down into "next steps." This enables them to work collaboratively with the principal to keep themselves aligned and to take valuable steps toward their longer-term goals. These are revisited every year to enable everyone to hold themselves accountable and clear about their desired future. The impact on professional growth in the school has been significant and is in some cases described by those involved as life changing.

> I was struggling with this. . . . mostly thinking others needed to change! The (Personal Vision) probes really challenged me and at times I wanted to give up. Thank you for encouraging me to persevere. I don't think I have ever been so clear about the road ahead and the steps to get there aren't so scary.
>
> —Primary Teacher, New Zealand

In a personal professional coaching relationship, the power structure is different from that between a principal as coach and a staff member. It is important to be crystal clear about roles and to stick to those roles in a disciplined way. Breaking roles can damage trust and the coaching relationship. For example, if a leadership team member is the coach, there must be clear delineation between this coaching role and the role in formal staff performance reviews.

Our colleague Brendan Spillane uses the evocative metaphor of the campfire as the shared space lit by the Shared Vision. He was recently asked, "Can the campfire be too hot to sit at for some people?" What a conversation follows from such a magnificent question.

As Spillane (personal communication, 2015) puts it,

> We need to be wary of the evangelical fervour that can be associated with vision—it can force people away or to stay unfaithfully, acting to survive. The vision has to be hot enough to warm people, to draw them into the circle. No vision and they will light their own fires for warmth somewhere else. But if the leadership is constantly throwing more wood into a fire that's already burning well, it's a furnace not a fire. Less wood is more!

The challenge here is how can anyone help you work toward your Personal Vision if he or she does not know your Vision? This obviously fits within the trust framework that exists between people. Ideally, a school has a culture of trust where all adults are open and trusting with each other. This makes it easier to also have trusting relationships between adults and children.

Peter Senge and colleagues (Senge, Kleiner, Roberts, Ross, & Smith, 1994), teach us that clear Personal Visions and democratic Shared Visions will always be in alignment.

We have developed a powerful process for forming a Personal Vision (Edwards, Martin, & Russell, 2009) and there are many other personal visioning processes available internationally. They are worth exploring to find one that suits your context.

Getting to Root Causes

If we are getting outcomes we do not want or like, we can simply change the actions or behaviors that caused those outcomes. Argyris (1992) calls this single loop learning. It is also sometimes called "a Band-Aid fix." It gets us by. If my lesson does not go as planned, I can simply tweak the design for next time: change the seating, use a different example, do it after lunch rather than before, call on different students.

However, to get to root causes, we must get back to the mental models that drove the actions that delivered the results. Learning to look deeper, question deeper, to find the underlying mental model, is double loop learning. If my lesson did not go as planned, I can go back and look at my design. What mental models am I working off? What assumptions am I making about the students and the conceptual leaps they can make? How do I look at the differentiation among my students? How do I use them to help each other construct meaning? How much direct experience do I believe they need? What is my belief about the pace and the conceptual load? All of these double loop questions are taking me back to my underlying mental models. This provides much deeper double loop learning (see Figure 4.4).

Fred Simon (personal communication, 2015) found that the following questions helped his workforce get to the double loop level:

What did I actually observe that led me to believe what I think happened?

What did I think would happen?

What assumptions or beliefs do I have that led me to think that?

What are the assumptions I can make that are consistent with what happened?

Under those assumptions, what would or should I do differently to get the results I truly want?

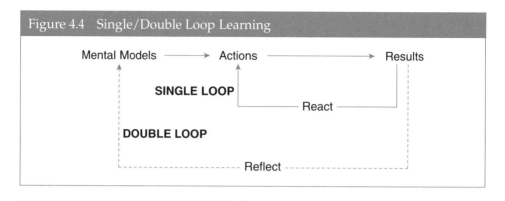

Figure 4.4   Single/Double Loop Learning

Source: Based on Argyris (1993).

For Simon, the most dangerous mental models for teachers dealing with complex issues are

There is always one correct answer.

I know the correct answer—the truth.

If I tell them the truth they will learn it.

To avoid such single loop thinking, there is a range of processes that can lead us into the depth of reflection required to complete the double loop. **Facilitative Questioning** (Butler & Edwards, 2004) is the most effective process we have developed to support a feedback culture. It is based on the work of Carl Rogers (1956; Rogers & Roethlisberger, 1991) and embodies his four core concepts: empathy, genuineness, unconditional respect for the other, and deep faith in people's natural capacity for self-healing and growth.

Facilitative Questioning is a way of questioning to help a person take a deeper look at their mental models (beliefs, values, and assumptions). It is a powerful process for double loop learning.

It is almost impossible to look deeply at these aspects on our own, as we cannot get sufficiently outside ourselves. Our mental models are embedded in our thinking. They are what we think with, so we usually need the help of another to reveal them. Having colleagues, friends, or partners who are willing and able to use this skill provides powerful opportunities for us to grow. Facilitative Questioning is one of the most deeply respectful things we can do for another person. It helps them switch on their reflection-on-action.

Facilitative Questioning: Key Elements

- Focus all of your attention on the person being questioned.
- Try to be aware of your own agendas and keep them out of the questioning.

- Your role is to help the other person to explore their own issues in their own ways.
- It is not your role to lead them to the solution you can see.
- Genuinely try to understand the other person.
- Ask questions to clarify what is being said.
- Have total respect for the other person and their ability to find their own answers to their own questions.

The aim of this questioning is to help the person being questioned to reflect as deeply and powerfully as possible on:

- What they have done and not done
- What they have learned
- What they now plan to do as a result of this learning
- What are their underlying mental models

Here is a short two-minute segment from a sample script using Facilitative Questioning:

Questioner: What area for improvement do you want to target?

Teacher: My time management.

Questioner: What exactly do you mean by time management?

Teacher: I would like to have a tidy desk.

Questioner: Why is that?

Teacher: Well, a tidy desk means a tidy mind.

Questioner: Do you believe that?

Teacher: No . . . but most other people do, and my desk is really untidy.

Questioner: What do you believe?

Teacher: Well . . . I don't feel on top of things.

Questioner: Can you give me some examples of this?

Teacher: When the end of the day comes I seem to have more jobs still to do than I had at the start of the day.

Questioner: How does that make you feel?

Teacher: I feel like pulling my hair out; I just feel things piling up and piling up.

Questioner: What do you think you might do about that?

Teacher: Well, Michael is really good at being organized and calm, and I see him keeping a planner.

Questioner:	What sort of planner?
Teacher:	I think he got it from some course he went on, so maybe I could ask him to show it to me and tell me how he uses it.
Questioner:	And how do you think that might help you?
Teacher:	If I could slow down and give myself time to plan, I think that would be a great start. I actually tried that a few years ago.
Questioner:	And what happened?
Teacher:	I got better for a while but I am not very good at sticking with things.
Questioner:	Why is that?
Teacher:	Both my parents were like that, but I guess I should not blame them. Maybe it is because I am not really convinced that it is worth the effort. I sort of get by as it is.
Questioner:	What would convince you?
Teacher:	Not sure really. Maybe checking at the start and end of each day to see how my stress levels are?
Questioner:	How might you do that?
Teacher:	Not sure, what would you do?
Questioner:	Have you tried measuring your stress levels before?
Teacher:	Yes, I just rated my levels on a ten-point scale.
Questioner:	Did that work?
Teacher:	Actually, it was quite simple. I think I could do that again.
Questioner:	And how would you use the data?
Teacher:	Maybe keep notes and see what patterns come up.
Questioner:	Do you have any other possibilities in mind?
Teacher:	Yes, I have thought about maybe. . . .

And on it goes . . .

It is vital that responsibility for learning, planning, and action stays with the person being questioned. This empowers them in the learning process. It is not the questioner's responsibility to "fix them up," come up with the best way forward, or make judgments. The role of the Facilitative Questioner is to provide a skilled "sounding board." As you can see in the example above, from the two minutes of Facilitative Questioning the teacher has revealed at least twenty mental models. Try counting them in the script:

1. I believe that my time management is poor.

2. I assume that people see my untidy desk and think that means I have an untidy mind.

3. I believe that I am not on top of things.

4. I value time and space to think.

5. I assume I can learn from my past experience with monitoring stress levels.

6. I believe I am not good at sticking with things.

These are just six mental models. Can you find the rest?

Both the teacher and the questioner can record the mental models they are inferring, or the teacher can invite a colleague to keep good notes for her.

Any one of these mental models would be a good starting point for the teacher to work on their authenticity and self-awareness and to design for action. The secret is to work on them one at a time and not try to take on more. The teacher can choose the one that they believe is the most important here and now.

Creating Our Own Rich Feedback Environment

Central to any process for dealing with the self-delusion we all share is receiving feedback. We all need data to tell us how we are doing at delivering on our promises.

We have found that the dominant mental model around feedback is deeply flawed.

It is based on **givers** (usually leaders or bosses or anyone superior or more powerful by nature of position) and **receivers** (who sit back and wait to be told).

This creates a power imbalance where the person who needs to be changing behavior is not the person in control of the process.

We have created a new feedback model: **productive feedback relationships.**

This model conceptualizes feedback differently.

There are

DRIVERS of feedback, and there are the

SOURCES that we choose to give us feedback.

To set up a productive feedback environment,

- As the driver, we choose the people we believe will be the best sources of feedback for us.
- Then we meet with them, usually individually.
- We explain the type of feedback we need from them and also why we chose them as a source. The feedback relationship is negotiated. These are usually enjoyable conversations with mutual respect in strong supply.

In many of the workplace settings where we have helped people make this mental model shift, a strong culture of personal responsibility has emerged.

Leaders in this process have a very different experience of feedback.

The staff member comes to them with the feedback data they have gathered on themselves and from their chosen sources. They have negotiated a consensus view from this process and used this to plan their action. They own this action plan as it comes from their self-designed feedback.

At times, it can become clear to a driver that the sources have not been wisely chosen. The feedback from these sources does not deliver powerfully. This can be a basis for in-depth questioning. All of this is part of the ongoing action learning in finding your most productive feedback environment.

Using such a self-driven process can enable staff to see their leader modeling good self-design of a feedback environment. Having a cross section of staff as selected sources of feedback for the principal has powerful modeling impact. My sources ranged from members of my leadership team to some of my strongest critics, who I knew would balance the feedback of more supportive colleagues. My critics often helped me see the history the staff had experienced, with failed attempts in the past to do what I was seeing as a new innovation. I would have missed this. To this mix of sources, I commonly added at least two respected outside sources who could see my performance with fresh eyes, albeit less frequently. This once again draws on our habit of always using multiple data sources and triangulating.

Gather Our Own Data and Trust It

I lived for three years in Malaysia, working as a curriculum specialist at the South East Asian Ministers of Education Centre for Science and Maths Education. During those years, I had the honor to work with some of the world's leading educational researchers. The Centre was very well funded so they could afford to bring out "the cream" of world educational researchers, usually for one-month visits.

One of these researchers had a profound influence on me: Professor Kenneth Lovell from Leeds University in the United Kingdom. He was one of the world's top Piagetian researchers and had spent time working closely with Bärbel Inhelder and Jean Piaget. His major piece of advice to me as a researcher was "always stay close to your data." As a beginning researcher, this was no problem. As I received larger and larger grants, this advice served me well. Many of my well-funded colleagues used research assistants to gather the data, while they sat in their offices, freed up from what they saw as "donkey work." I continued to gather much, if not most, of my own. So, if anyone interrogated my work I could actually remember the classroom or the teacher or the child: what was really said and the context, the tone of voice, and other nuances. I particularly remember a study I was doing to design a new set of tests to replace the Torrance Tests of Creative Thinking.

The Torrance Test was the most widely used test of creativity at the time and was continually cited in the literature. But I found when I used it, that most children did not cognitively engage with the test. It was boring! When trialing my new creativity tests that were co-designed with children, I had an interview with a bright young Indian girl, who had just scored very poorly on the test. When I started interviewing her about her responses to one of the items on the test, she told me, "Oh Dr. Edwards, I never write down anything that could possibly be wrong." So, now I understood why her fluency scores were so low. She was being constantly rated low on creativity. How valid was that measure of this girl? She had the ideas, and she then self-censored, so her thinking never got onto the paper. You can never know this if you do not stay close. What one learns from deep Facilitative Questioning is often pure gold. I can still picture this girl's face, her intonation as she quietly spoke with me. I easily recall the rich insights she provided as we explored this dysfunctional mental model she worked from, where she had learned it, and what she could do to address its influence on her output.

The message for us is to, where possible, gather our own data and be clear about what will really convince us. This is the data that matters.

We have learned to be wary of surveys. Teachers, and staff in many other organizations, tell us that they are "surveyed out." Too often they hear the call: "Let's do a survey" (and consume the time of many people).

Our experience is that much of what one gets from surveys is superficial. The inability to probe in response to a response is a major disadvantage. We have learned that three well-placed, in-depth interviews will reveal so much more than surveying twenty people.

The rural school is deep in the agriculture region of Western Australia. Because of its remote location, staff come and go; principals come and go. The current small staff of principal, two teachers, and an educational assistant decided to research how the school could become a better

(Continued)

(Continued)

community citizen. They decided to research this for a year. But their research was unique. They developed an interview protocol around how the school could become a better community citizen. This small and committed band interviewed fifty community members. There are only seventeen families on the school roll. They interviewed current parents. They interviewed parents of children who went to other schools. They interviewed past parents. They interviewed grandparents. They interviewed past students. The news of the interviews spread like wildfire across the wheat belt. **The close relationships that emerged made the school a good citizen.** On the day we witnessed the school presenting their findings, the audience included ten parents. They all participated in building the plan to ensure the school would be a good citizen well into the future based on the data generated—no matter how the teaching staff or school leader might change.

We have thought often about the joy that would be spread by banning surveys in schools. High-quality decisions can only be made from high-quality data. Have a close look at what you are getting from your surveys. Some colleagues have reported value in using survey data as the starting point for interviews.

We need to focus our collective attention on gathering and recording the high-quality data that matters and making it available for easy reuse by others.

Systems of Accountability

In most organizations, staff are concerned about an apparent lack of accountability. We have explored this with them over many years, and four levels of responsibility have emerged:

1. Personal

2. Team

3. School

4. Leader

The key to accountability always comes back to individual responsibility and individual accountability. The real power over performance and delivery lies inside each of us.

Argyris (1998) talks about empowerment as "the emperor's new clothes," an illusion that never reached us.

As Argyris explains,

The change programs and practices we employ are full of inner contradictions that cripple innovation, motivation, and drive. At the same time, CEOs subtly undermine empowerment. Managers love empowerment in theory, but the command-and-control model is what they trust and know best. For their part, employees are often ambivalent about empowerment—it is great as long as they are not held personally accountable. (p. 98)

From long leadership experience, de Geus (1988) argues that the level of thinking in most management teams is below the individual manager's capacities. His experience is that in institutional learning situations, the learning level of the team is often the lowest common denominator. This serves to focus our attention on how we build and maintain teams. The work of Patrick Lencioni (2002) and others provides ways to avoid the dysfunctions of teams. Lencioni alerts us to absence of trust, fear of conflict, lack of commitment, avoidance of accountability, and inattention to results.

There is no doubt that well-constructed aligned teacher teams are powerful levers for school improvement. In the research and implementation phases of our process, as outlined in Chapter 1, teacher teams foster shared responsibility as a basis for supporting individual responsibility. Each team is working on behalf of the whole school community:

- Delivering on the Shared Vision and Core Values provides an aligned focus for commitment and accountability.
- Results are reported and celebrated regularly.
- Emergent issues are raised and dealt with openly and collaboratively.
- Shared delivery drives the building of trust and shared momentum.

To look honestly at the effectiveness of your teacher teams is an important use of time and energy. The good news is that team skills are learnable.

WHAT DOES WHOLE SCHOOL ACCOUNTABILITY LOOK LIKE?

Schools that deliver walk their talk. Everyone on staff holds themselves accountable to do so. You can almost smell this in a school. Accountability for walking the talk envelops you as you walk the hallways and grounds.

Freshwater Bay in Perth, Western Australia, is an impressive school. Five years ago, it became a consolidated school. Two schools were merged into one. Each school staff was less than happy. Steve Ivey was named principal of the new merged school. He was charged with bringing angry staff members together into one new Freshwater Bay. Today, when you walk into the school reception, the school's Shared Vision looks down at you. A student is pictured announcing the school's Core Values with pride. As you walk deeper into the school, children's portraits adorn the walls. Each picture is accompanied by a statement from the Shared Vision defining the Freshwater Bay child. On classroom doors are the "Personal Philosophy and Pedagogy" statements of the teachers. They articulate with pride "the walk" you will see in these classrooms. As you meet children and staff, you are showered with the language of happiness, joy, and love of learning.

At Freshwater Bay, whole school accountability is delivered.

In his book, *Visible Learning* (2009), John Hattie's meta-analysis reveals that teacher-to-teacher feedback is one of the greatest factors ensuring student achievement.

There is a veritable arsenal of skills and tools available to the school leader in developing a feedback culture ensuring personal accountability.

Our belief is that the fuel for a powerful feedback culture is to be found in eyeball-to-eyeball conversation. As a principal, I invited each of my staff to be my partner in creating the best learning environments possible. Choosing to be partners both empowers and holds each of us accountable for the results we desire.

Empowerment means that the answers lie inside each of us. We are personally responsible for creating safe and successful learning journeys for ourselves and our students. There is no one else to take the joy or the blame. The outcomes and quality of cooperation and collaboration within a school are everyone's responsibility. Each partner is responsible for maintaining faith, hope, and spirit. The price of freedom that partnership offers is to take personal accountability for success and failure at our school.

The Stewardship Conference: Creating Learning Partnerships

I have eyeball-to-eyeball conversations annually with every staff member as a starting point. The conversations are focused on four central questions:

What parts of our Shared Vision are you most passionate about?

What are you going to do to help us achieve our Shared Vision?

What skills and resources will you bring to help us be successful?

What obstacles do you think could get in your way?

Dialogue around these questions covers the first half of the stewardship conversation.

The second half of the conversation often surprises staff initially. I ask this question:

"What do you need from us to enable you to do what you say you will do?"

I facilitatively question deeply to find out and clarify my role and that of my leaders team, with each individual staff member.

The partnership agreement is framed by asking the staff member,

"This is what you are going to do . . . Do I have this right?" And then,

"This is what we will do to support you . . . Do I have this right?"

A Stewardship Conference ends with a handshake.

Partnerships are formed and shared accountability is established.

Each Stewardship Conference takes around half an hour. In a large secondary school, they would take me one month to complete. I chose to do every staff member's conference myself. It was the bedrock for my ongoing professional relationship with each of them, and it kept me very well informed. It reminds me of Professor Lovell's advice to John, as shared earlier in this chapter. I stayed close to my data as well as to my people. They hold the fundamental responsibilities and provide the central data needed by leaders.

In some schools where we work, these Stewardship Conferences are shared among the leadership team.

In a school culture where each staff member is held accountable, continuous conversations need to be framed by the partnership agreements that emerge. If you observe a staff member delivering well on what was agreed, another conversation needs to take place.

Here is what we see happening . . . And here is what was agreed . . .

Know how much your contribution is valued, and here is why . . .

And then,

Am I delivering on what I said I would do?

If you observe a staff member not delivering what was agreed, a different conversation needs to take place.

Here is what we see happening . . . And here is what was agreed . . .

What is the problem? We need to get this clear so we can deliver as agreed.

This may also involve asking

Am I delivering on what I said I would do?

A similar conversation could be initiated by the staff member around me delivering, or failing to deliver, my leadership part of that Stewardship Conference agreement. Stewardship Conferences are based on open trusting relationships. They also develop trusting relationships.

Time spent practicing Facilitative Questioning, building partnerships in Stewardship Conferences, and finding areas of alignment with resisters (see Leadership Challenge 3 in Chapter 3) are central to successful school-wide accountability structures.

Stories born of walking the talk reverberate throughout a school community. Non-delivery stories travel even faster. What are you hearing?

Does your school deliver? Are you delivering on your promises?

SUMMARY

Have you ever been part of a team, a school, a department, a group, or a family that delivered something that really mattered to you? If so, you will recognize yourself in this book. If you want that experience again and again, you will find pathways in this book. If you have never or seldom experienced this deep satisfaction, then the book will be a revelation.

Think about a time when you really delivered something authentic. Remember, go back inside yourself and feel it. What set you off, what kept your momentum, and what ended it well for you? What were the feelings of action that embodied your delivery?

In Chapter 4, our aim is to raise to conscious awareness the gap that always exists between what we say and what we do. This is unavoidable. The key is to have systems around us to ensure our awareness. If each of us is not delivering on our promises, then the school bogs down in wishful thinking, good intentions, and empty words. When we do deliver, totally complete something together, that is a delicious feeling of professional satisfaction and achievement that we all deserve.

5

Core Values and Culture

I t is the collective values of each member of our school community that form our "culture as lived." Paying attention to culture ensures that it remains fresh and relevant. Paying attention to our shared values opens us to the quality of relationships that drive a school that delivers.

As one New Zealand principal put it to us earlier this year,

> I love the 'caretaker', or *kaitiaki* as we would call it, notion of nurturing culture.

Working on identifying, clarifying, defining, and living our Core Values brings us up against a critical tension. Tension exists between the culture and values we have been living and the new values and culture we want—our future. This is an essential, healthy tension. It is representative of the broader tension: between the ways we have been doing things around here and the ways we now need to be doing things. This is our focus in Chapter 2.

I learned the power of living by Core Values in the aftermath of the shooting at Langham Creek High School in 1985 (see the "Voices" section at the start of this book). As the shooting happened on a Friday, the community lived in fear of what would happen when we all returned to school on

(Continued)

(Continued)

Monday. The Leadership Team planned across the weekend on how to deal with the fear and prepare to support everyone's return to school. What was observed the following week was incredible. This tough high school transformed itself over the weekend into probably one of the safest schools in the country. I wondered why? Over time, I figured it out. When we all came back to school on Monday, each of us—staff, students, parents, community members—carried a new value seared inside our heads and hearts: "This will never happen to us again on our watch." Unknowingly, this formed our agreement of how we would live together. Each of us demonstrated and shared with one another, in open and honest ways, the behaviors that ensured "this would never happen on our watch again."

Sadly, after two years, the behavior of the school began to deteriorate to its old toughness once more. And I wondered, "Why?" What I figured out was that because we did not teach this Core Value, it was only in our heads. It gradually faded and we lost it. As students who were part of the shooting left the school, the new students who replaced them did not know this value. The same happened as staff moved on and new staff replaced them, and as families moved away and new families came in.

Because the Core Value was never taught, learned, and embedded in the culture, it was lost!

> Culture is an abstraction, yet the forces that are created in social and organizational situations that derive from culture are powerful. If we don't understand the operation of these forces, we become victim to them. (Schein, 2004, p. 3)

If something is working really well in the school, map it back to your Core Values; what light does it shine on them? If something is causing problems, do the same. Your Core Values are the touchstones of your culture. When staff come up against worrying issues, we suggest that they form into groups of three and facilitatively question each other (as outlined in Chapter 4). Through this process, the mental models of each staff member can be clarified, collected, and shared openly. This enables everyone to see "the culture as lived" up in front of them. Powerful dialogue around these mental models provides a sound base for decision making and action at the cultural level. As Edgar Schein's research shows, understanding these forces is crucial.

Schein's experience matches ours, in that it is generally easier to draw on the existing strengths of a culture than to overcome the constraints by changing the culture.

DOES YOUR SCHOOL LIVE
BY YOUR CORE VALUES?

You see them everywhere: in the reception area, on classroom walls, in the school prospectus. These are the posters proclaiming the school's Core Values. Many of them are commercially made and laminated on paper that sparkles at you. They have often been created by the education hierarchy or the latest commercial values program. One school we worked with had forty Core Values. Others are proud of their ten or fifteen. Often, dust has dimmed their brightness. Then you ask a staff member, "How do you teach your values?" Some will say that Self Esteem needs to be done at the start of the year: "How about we get them to draw portraits of themselves?" Respect is in March, and on through their values list. Others will give you a blank stare and say, "I am not really sure." And when you ask, "Can you name your values?" sometimes the same "I am not really sure" forms on the lips of the principal.

How important are your school's Core Values to you? As James Kouzes and Barry Posner (2012) explain,

> Because values are so deep-seated, we never actually "see" values themselves. What we "see" are the ways in which people's values manifest themselves: in opinions, attitudes, preferences, desires, fears, actions, strategies and so on. (p. 198)

Does your community see you modeling, articulating, and teaching your Core Values every day?

We know from experience across many schools that if your school community lives its Core Values, success will follow. Greg Morgan (personal communication, 2015), a principal in Tasmania, Australia, talks about

> where Core Values come from and the vital role Core Values play. My observation is that no matter what is espoused by whom, staff must feel respect and trust in the process. This stems from the quality of the professional culture and relationships in the organisation, especially those modelled by school leaders.

Schools that deliver clarify a common set of Core Values. They are contextual Core Values that come from the rich lived lives of their people. They come from their hearts and souls. They are few in number, no more than four to six. In our experience, it is almost the fewer the better. One Core Value fully lived actually brings other values as a trailing legacy. For example, living respect will often bring with it the values of loyalty, trust, and excellence.

How can anyone consciously live twenty values? Our school's Core Values must be modeled, articulated, and taught to everyone: staff to staff, staff to students, students to staff, students to students, school to community, and community to school. Our Core Values define who we are.

> One exciting thing is that our new PTA chairperson who came along to Thursday and part of Friday is so inspired by the Core Values. She wants to write these into the PTA constitution and is extremely inspired about the parents using them as well. She has them up on her fridge at home! She and I had a great meeting following the PD days. I feel really happy that she is so enthused. It will make that relationship with the PTA so much easier than it has been. The Core Values are up in every teacher office in the school. We start to unpack them at the staff meeting in 2 weeks' time.
>
> —Principal, New Zealand

Core Values Process

In Chapter 1, we have spelled out in detail one effective process for identifying a school's Core Values and how to use them as alignment tools.

We are often asked why the statements are written in the present tense, such as "We accept one another's differences."

We believe that when written using the future tense, "*We will accept one another's differences*," it is too easy to say we will live this value tomorrow, or sometime in the future. We can keep putting it off. Writing in the present tense influences us to **take action now**.

As mentioned in Chapter 1, once your Core Values are generated, staff teams develop operational definitions of them. These are drawn from observing what people really do, rather than developing theoretical definitions.

> The Core Value work which we had all around the staffroom for several weeks really did get things stirred up. It was fascinating to see the impact it had on the various personalities.
>
> —Primary School Principal, Western Australia

Descriptions developed by each group should describe clearly what members of the school community would see as someone lived this Core Value in all aspects of school life. Each group can develop and trial their descriptors through a number of iterations. This generates more descriptors, practical descriptors, our descriptors.

Modeling and articulating Core Values throughout the school community is one powerful focus for the first year of a Shared Vision journey.

The school staff introduce these Core Values to the children who then explore and agree on how they will live these values at their level in the school. Families and other community members are introduced to the Core Values and collect examples from their life in the school community. Examples of Core Values being lived out are publicized creatively around the school.

Each teacher can begin the new school year by discussing with their class or classes how the Core Values will be lived out in that class this year. Students should be very clear about what is acceptable and what is not acceptable in each classroom and across the school. I well remember hearing one of our physics teachers exploring with his class how they would live out "we respect each other's differences." Often, we could observe classes where students were role-playing a Core Value. Children would act out how the Core Value should be lived. And they would act out what the Core Value would look like when it was not being lived.

> Atmosfären på skolan har blivit mer positiv. Bara det faktum att vi satte upp skolans kärnvärderingar på dörrar och väggar bidrog till att det blev ett dagligt samtalsämne. Jag såg en förändring en dag när elever plötsligt började hålla upp dörren för mig. Detta hade aldrig hänt förut.
>
> —Rektor, Varberg, Sverige

> (It has become a more positive atmosphere at the school. Just the fact that we set up the school's Core Values on doors and walls helped that it became a daily topic of conversation. I noticed a change on a day when students suddenly began to hold the door open for me. It has never happened before.)
>
> —Headmaster, Varberg, Sweden

Many schools have told us that discipline referrals are reduced as teachers forge these Core Value agreements. Each teacher brings his or her own individuality to this process. The unity through diversity that this introduces only enriches the learning. This also brings the consistency of behavior that is so elusive in some school communities.

> Our Core Values have been collaboratively developed through input from parents, students, and teachers. We are delighted with our work. The Core Values are in all classrooms. The children have developed examples of how these are demonstrated in the playground and classroom. The Core Values are now part of our school logo and faction flags. Parents suggested that we have a section of the weekly newsletter. In it, we congratulate teachers,
>
> *(Continued)*

(Continued)

parents, and students for demonstrating the Core Values. With this work permeating all aspects of our teaching and how we conduct ourselves, I have been able to have some hard discussions with particular staff members. I always embed our Shared Vision and Core Values in these talks. Some have been uncomfortable and decided to jump ship. It is certainly uncomfortable but has to happen.

—Primary School Principal, Western Australia

This Core Values process, born of our Shared Vision, provides the solid bedrock on which to build effective patterns of behavior, and systems and structures. Our process, as outlined in Chapter 1, is only one way to articulate the link between Core Values and Shared Vision. Some schools develop their vision from their values and not the other way around. Their dream, their vision, emerges from their value platform; while in our process we articulate our values after first forming the vision. In reality, vision and values are in constant interaction. Values create a vision, and a vision makes values visible.

The vision is formed from the values people bring with them to the Shared Vision process. That is why people vote for some ideas over others in the Inquiry Probes process.

Core Values and Culture

Our lived Core Values are reflected in the culture of our school. Building culture and paying regular attention to it are key roles for leaders and staff of schools that deliver.

Our values are in place and aligned to the school's spirit. The students have embraced them well and know exactly what we are talking about. The most interesting result for me has been the reaction from the community. Everyone comments to me on how well the school is perceived by the local community. My boss keeps telling me we are doing a fantastic job. We have not suspended or excluded anyone. The perception is that we are a 'strict' school. We are not. We stick to our values and our vision and make it crystal clear to everyone. Our values are our basis for all decisions. It works. We have jumped from 383 students to 650 and from 15 classroom teachers to 28.

—Principal, Queensland, Australia

For Schein (2004),

Culture as a set of basic assumptions defines for us what to pay attention to, what things mean, how to react emotionally to what is going on, and what actions to take in various kinds of situations. (p. 32)

We understand school culture through our senses.

> It is very exciting here at the moment—lots of enthusiasm and positive feelings about each other. People are talking to each other, helping each other, laughing!!!! I no longer have a black cloud over my car as I drive up Spine Road! People are commenting on how much I am grinning. As a Year 1 child commented, 'You don't need to be grumpy in school anymore'. As you can tell I am a very happy head teacher at the moment. Yippee, indeed.
>
> —Primary School Head Teacher, United Kingdom

The Impact of a Leader

As a school principal, the first responsibility next to my name in the staff handbook was "Culture Builder and Caretaker." We have been surprised by how "foggy" the conversations can become when we engage educators in discussions about school culture. It is like "We know it's there and we know it's important but we can't quite grasp it or get our hands on it." It seems slippery and mystical. Culture seems to just happen, one way or another.

As a school leader, the mental models your life has taught you impact your performance, your colleagues, and the school. My long life experiences of "failure" have made me less judgmental than most people.

My mental model list includes

I am the most flawed person in this school.

I crave your feedback to ensure I get better.

I trust you.

The past is yesterday; let's build hope for tomorrow.

If it is good for a child, go for it!

I have learned over time, from personal reflection and from broad feedback, that these mental models formed one important kernel in becoming an innovative school.

This is one man's journey to leadership. Like all journeys, it is unique. In my case, I think that is probably fortunate for the planet. I worked from what I had, from my Personal Practical Knowledge (PPK). The self-awareness behind these mental models is hard earned. Needless to say, no staff member shared my idiosyncratic life. Each brings his or her own richness and his or her own set of hard-earned mental models. It is the unique combination of PPK and mental models we all bring that creates our unique culture.

As Schein (2004) sees it,

> A paradox of learning leadership is that the leader must be able not only to lead but also to listen, to involve the group in achieving its own insights into its own cultural dilemmas, and to be genuinely participative in his or her approach to learning and change. (p. 417)

What values and beliefs do you live every day that have seeped into the school culture?

Are you happy with what you see?

How do you together draw on the richness of your whole school community?

If your culture is not what you want it to be, what is your role in that?

A principal's mental models are central, foundational cultural building blocks, whether we like this or not. They often have a disproportionate impact. Some schools reflect their principals. And some principals are happy for this, particularly when things are working well.

Schools have the responsibility to use a rich tapestry of cultural elements to grow and sustain their culture. School culture becomes the landscape for healthy teaching and learning and for student achievement. Time spent drawing out, jointly crafting, and maintaining the culture is time well spent.

Two core cultural elements have been a foundation at every school I have led:

- **A culture of alignment and disciplined action**
- **A culture of delivery**

Alignment fuels delivery. Delivery produces achievement. These elements were the focus of Chapter 1 and Chapter 4.

Stephen Covey (2004) taught us the difference between productivity and productive capacity.

Productivity is about what you do, what you deliver.

Productive capacity is what you must build internally, to develop the constantly evolving capacity to keep delivering. You cannot have the first without the second. Cultures must be designed that do both: deliver and ensure the ongoing capacity to deliver.

There is a rhythm to culture building, a flow. School leadership requires an understanding of how one cultural element impacts the next. **Leading involves designing continuous and specific actions that make a cultural element a central part of school culture.**

Ask yourself,

Do we have an action plan for growing our culture?

Is a community member able to describe the elements of our culture?

Choosing the elements of culture is serious leadership work.

We have identified many elements of school culture as we work with schools around the world. Along with our in-school colleagues, we have distilled this to eleven Core Cultural Elements and the flow they create.

A CULTURE OF OWNERSHIP

To create a school that delivers involves tapping the skills and potential of everyone in our school community as well as we can. To do this, people need to be skillfully involved. The basis for this is shared ownership. Ownership is a central theme of this book. Through a culture of ownership, people get to sense their personal power. They experience how it feels when they impact their own work and the way it is done. They experience the way they can impact as a pair with one colleague, as a team of colleagues, as a whole staff together, and as a united school community.

Ownership is the simple process of people being free. Organizations hire people to do jobs for them. They come to us with their rich contextual abilities, skills, and personalities. The secret to ownership is to have a culture where we each go out and do something with what we bring. **The doing creates ownership.** Ownership can be personal or collective.

> How lucky for me to be able to work at a school on the "cutting edge" — exploring new frontiers. I've never been on the forefront, never been a pioneer, and never been the "first on my block . . ." I value this opportunity!
>
> —US Speech Teacher

For ownership, we need shared clarity. Clarity means we know where we are headed. Clarity means we understand our parameters of freedom. It means we have agreed what the end product should look like. Clarity enables collective responsibility and accountability to be the lived reality of culture.

Once clarity is achieved, staff know how, when, and where to align. They will take ownership confidently. We need specific structures in place that honor ownership for people across the school. As long as the systems and structures are aligned to where the school is going, people will take responsibility. The Shared Vision is the glue that binds clarity and responsibility together.

In one US school, some structures of ownership in successful action include

- A Delegation Protocol (described in Leadership Challenge 6 in Chapter 3) that gives leadership team members ownership of their responsibilities.
- A Student Government that mirrors the US national government, created by Student Council Sponsors. This allows students control over the adults in the school at appropriate times. Simply, an action is created in the Student Senate. If the Student House of Representatives pass the action as well, the students take the action to the adult decision-making body, the School-Site Council. They either veto or pass the student action. If vetoed, the Student Government can override the veto by a two-thirds majority vote of both the Senate and House of Representatives.

The high school timetable (order of classes through the day) had been set by adults for adults. The student government's first legislation was to change the timetable on late start days (due to snow or fog) to a timetable that fit their interests. After the adults vetoed this plan, the student government overrode the veto by using their two-thirds majority option. **The students' timetable was put in place.**

- A School-Site Council is made up of every segment of the school community. It is the decision-making body of the school. Their challenge is to ensure that all decisions are aligned to the Shared Vision.
- Stewardship Conferences build clear partnerships with every staff member each year. As outlined in Chapter 4, these are annual authentic one-on-one conversations about our work. These establish both the parameters of ownership as well as responsibilities. They determine how accountability will be managed. How to support one another is established.

Through participatory decision making the school is fueled by the people who do the work. What are the systems and structures in place in your school to influence and sustain ownership?

He was observed always simply teaching new thinking. An example of this is how he explains to staff how he is expecting them to hold each other accountable. This is a transformation from traditional thinking. He has given staff examples. In the past few months, people have expected him to put out their fires because he is the authority. He explains how this makes it nearly impossible for him to do his job well. He emphasizes that it is impossible to be the father to over one hundred staff and two thousand students. This leaves staff floundering at moments. It is difficult to change years of thinking and grasp the amount of courage it takes to confront other teachers and staff.

—US Art Teacher

I have grown so much. Part of that growth has been for you to notice and give your approval (the old me). I'm finding now that I am doing it for me, which is so exciting. Believe me, no matter who the principal is, I'm not turning back. I know too much to do that. I'm going to continue to change and improve.

—US Middle School Science Teacher

A CULTURE OF INCLUSION

To create a culture of ownership in a school requires inclusion. When we think of the great schools we have experienced over the last fifty years, one thing they share is their culture of inclusion. These schools are warm and caring places to be. They are welcoming places to be. They are open to fresh people and fresh thinking. Great schools know the richness that comes from including people in the decision-making processes. Such committed staff drive delivery of what they know is needed.

Andy Hargreaves and Michael Fullan (2013) refer to collaborative cultures, which build social capital and professional capital. They share knowledge and ideas as well as assistance and support. This helps teachers become more effective, increases their confidence, and encourages them to be more open to, and actively engaged in, improvement and change. Their simple key is *talk together, plan together, work together*.

From our experience, **to be an effective professional learning community, every voice must be heard.** What do we mean? You see this core mental model threaded throughout our story of schools that deliver. Everyone in a school community has a voice and a lived life to share. Far too often, schools only see and hear the strongest, loudest, and popular voices. The soft, quiet voices and personalities seldom have a forum. Their unique thinking is neglected as we travel toward the future. A culture of inclusion ensures systems and structures are present to bring these voices to the surface. That is the only way to ensure our school is generating and using the best of all of us.

Every school principal has supporters: staff, parents, and children who shower them with praise and good tidings. Our human nature drives us to spend time with these people. They make us feel good. They can also be the source of an organizational infection, "groupthink." How often do we seek advice from our resisters? How much time do we spend on building relationships with silent and quiet staff members? We will often get an unvarnished truth from these staff before we will get it from our advocates. Everyone must be included!

Time spent lifting marginal staff and building relationships with resisters can have significant value on a Shared Vision journey. Making time to have personal conversations with every staff member is the lifeblood of inclusion. These conversations, both structured and unstructured, are serious leadership work. A school's champions and enthusiasts will find the leader. Involving all staff in daily relationships through coaching, mentoring, or listening embodies a culture of inclusion.

A CULTURE OF CARING

For people to feel ownership and inclusion requires skillful ways of relating to each other. Some schools already have this as part of their culture. We have seen other schools pay attention to their culture of caring and grow it where it was not a strength initially.

Cultures of caring can manifest in many different ways. We have lived inside cultures that claimed to be caring, and they sure were not experienced in that way. It is the lived experience of caring that matters, not the espoused theory of caring or the intention of caring. If it is not received as caring, then it is not caring. This is complex. What can be experienced as caring by one person can be experienced as gross interference by another, or as neglect by another.

> "We value one another." One United Kingdom school had been working on this Core Value for a year while doing their research for the Shared Vision. They told us they were making great progress living the Core Value. At a staff meeting, we asked the staff, "Stand up if you feel valued at school." A handful of staff stood from the over forty staff. A loud buzz rose to the ceiling. A year later, when asked the same question, the entire staff rose in unison!

Caring can be as simple as just giving the other person the space to figure things out for themselves. Resist the temptation to rush in and solve problems for people or to rush to judgment. **People do not need our judgment; they need our feedback.**

As Carl Rogers (Rogers & Roethlisberger, 1991) puts it,

Through my experiences in counseling and psychotherapy, I've found that there is one main obstacle to communication: people's tendency to evaluate. Fortunately I've also discovered that if people can listen with understanding, they can mitigate their evaluative impulses and greatly improve their communication with others. (p. 206)

Caring begins by knowing the people we work with. Know each other's stories and express personal interest in each other. Make time for sustained conversations. Meet others in their space. Discover how we are the same and how we are different. We have observed schools where staff support one another, in any situation or condition, within the framework of who they are. Their antennae of caring are "on alert." They are comfortable to "put themselves in the shoes of the other person." They are clear about what support will be received well. Such attending and listening with empathy and understanding drive caring.

Caring can flow from sharing high expectations and helping hold ourselves accountable; believing in our collective abilities; stretching and challenging. Caring means the willingness to engage skillfully in sensitive conversations that may be uncomfortable. Caring happens when we take and share independent responsibilities and choices. Everyone gets a fair shake: a special hand to support learning from mistakes. This creates what Brené Brown (2012) refers to as "connection." She believes that connection is why we are here and it is what gives purpose and meaning to our lives.

An important time to practice caring is when a person is in "the pit." The more the pit becomes shared language, the more people will see pits and give help. Layers of understanding of the pit experience grow. Its validity is honored at a deeper level.

Schools reflect the people in them, and if one of us is hurting, the school is hurting.

> You rejoiced with me when I thought I was pregnant, and you held my hand when I thought I was having a miscarriage. You were very sensitive to my depression and you cared enough to come and talk with me.
>
> —US Special Education Teacher

It is important to pay attention to the "Rituals of Caring." A school is like a town. We have seen everything from tiny towns to very large ones.

The town is made up of people who experience all the joys and sorrows of life. In my years as principal, I experienced

- A school shooting
- Student suicides
- Untimely staff and family deaths
- Students killed in car accidents
- The need to expel children from school
- Students succeeding against unbelievable odds
- A school community supporting each other through crises
- Times when we were all confused and frustrated together
- Moments of collaborative learning and staff achievement that would take your breath away
- Leveraging together from small successes to major transformations

What caring protocols do you have in place to deal with life's harsh realities and to leverage your successes? Be clear, at "peak" moments the school community is watching you very carefully! How do you care for each other in hard times and in high times?

When caring is planned for, there is ongoing awareness of the personal impact of the school on its community members through the lived values. The plan ensures the delivery of caring, not just the thought.

Together, the elements of ownership, inclusion, and caring set a school culture in place to realize the power of the collective potential of every person. This is the culture that fuels a school from being simply good to one that is outstanding—a school that delivers.

A CULTURE OF TRUST

By attending to these first three elements, you are already building trust. We have learned that people will forgive you many things, but what are hardest to forgive are breaches of trust. It is so hard to mend these breaks. We have heard staff say to leaders, "We can forgive almost anything, just don't lie to us!"

A longitudinal study of more than 400 Chicago elementary schools by Anthony Bryk and Barbara Schneider (2003) showed the central role of relational trust in building effective education communities. The schools with greater achievement levels had higher levels of trust between teachers, students, parents, administrators, and colleagues. It is important to understand the factors that influence the development of trust, such as personal disposition, shared values and attitudes, organizational stage, institutional support, and assumptions (Tschannen-Moran, 2004).

For Wayne Hoy, Charles Gage, and C. John Tarter (2006),

A culture of trust should provide a setting in which people are not afraid of breaking new ground, taking risks and making errors. (p. 237)

They found that trust in a school fosters mindful actions.

Mindful administrators know that "believing is seeing," and they are on guard—wary of the obvious and searching for "the danger not yet arisen." They are suspicious of facile explanation as well as their own success. (p. 239)

Francis Fukuyama (1995) introduced us to the concept of a trust radius. Fukuyama's research shows that the success of a country, a culture, a family, a business, or a person can be indicated by the radius of trust that surrounds them. So, if your school culture involves no one being able to trust anyone else, then the chances of success are low indeed.

Think about yourself and your school, and the trust radius you have.

If a staff member can trust one best friend, the radius grows.

If they can trust a small group, the radius grows.

If all staff can trust each other, but not their leaders, the radius grows further.

If all staff trust their leaders as well, the radius grows again.

If the children, the community, and the staff trust each other, you are flying!

If you have strong trust with other schools as well, you are even better placed for success.

A whole district trusting each other—now you are talking!

As you can imagine, we could go on. Fukuyama's work is powerful to consider when looking at the culture we want to create and how to go about that. The two key elements of trust are character and competence. We have talked about competence in Chapter 4. Without competence, there will be no delivery, and this breaks down trust.

Competence is about delivering on your talk. Living in a sea of competence is a reassuring feeling for everyone in a school. It forms a bedrock, a basis for confidence throughout the school.

Let us focus here on the other key aspect of trust: character. A widely quoted maxim in organizational theory tells us to "hire for values and train for skills." Hop onto the Internet and you will find many examples of how this maxim is used. Many schools we observe send the Shared Vision, Core Values, and Long-Term School Development Plan out to prospective applicants. They hire for aligned character. Who most convinces them that they will bring new richness to the journey toward the Shared Vision?

For Kouzes and Posner (2012),

Leaders who build trusting relationships within their team feel comfortable with the group. They are willing to consider alternative viewpoints and utilize other people's expertise and abilities. They are also willing to let others exercise influence over their decisions. (p. 148)

Two other attributes that we have observed to build trust are being present, and openness with information.

Being present is commonly embodied in "leadership by wandering around." When people are out and about, leaders are out of their offices and with their people. They are talking, supporting, challenging, cheering, or commiserating with them.

Information is a source of power. If I possess information you don't have, I have more power than you. This is why, as much as humanly possible, we should openly share as much information as we can with everyone. If we all have the same information, we are sharing power.

Many staff naturally exhibit character, competence, presence, and openness. Leadership modeling encourages their expression more fully in the school culture. All four trust attributes work just as powerfully in classrooms as they do in the wider school environment.

- How happy are you with the trust radius of your school?
- What are your school's criteria for bringing new people into the culture?
- What are the key elements in your culture of trust?
- How trustworthy is your school in the eyes of your community?

A CULTURE OF QUESTIONING

Your culture creates a safe container made up of these first four elements. This is a good time to focus on opening up your practices to skillful feedback from others.

Schools that deliver never accept the status quo. One of my greatest sources of stimulation to innovate was questioning from our staff, our students, and our community. These open, honest questions are what Schein (2013) is asking for more of in current US culture. For Schein, "humble inquiry" is the skill and art of drawing someone out, of asking questions to which you do not already know the answer, of building relationships based on curiosity and interest in the other person.

Some schools refer to this as their culture of inquiry. Along with many other schools, we have observed, Baverstock Oaks School in New Zealand (Wilson, personal communication, 2015) has woven a culture of inquiry through all of their teaching. Over time, the school "becomes" the answers to its own questions and inquiries, and these answers help grow their common language.

Dominant questions that can challenge you daily include

- In what ways is this idea working for a child or a staff member?
- How are we living our Core Values today?
- How will we address this mismatch between external research and our experience and internal research?
- In what ways are we changing and how do we know?
- If we believe that every child can learn with quality, how is that evident in our practices?
- Are we on the best pathways to realize our vision?
- What are we doing to sustain hope for all members of our school community?

Peter Block (2008), in *Community: The Structure of Belonging*, recommends that a strong culture address several categories of questions: questions of possibility, questions of ownership, questions of dissent, questions of gifts, and questions of commitment.

"Is this about learning readiness, or is it about the way I have grouped them, or the environment as a whole, or is it about something completely different?" is a question of possibility. Such questions free people to innovate, challenge the status quo, and explore options and new futures.

"How have I contributed to this current reality?" is a question of ownership. For Block (2008), confusion, blame, and waiting for someone else to change, are a defense against ownership and personal power.

"How is this going to give me more information or better information on my students?" is a question of dissent. For Block, if we cannot say "no," then our "yes" has no meaning. Such questions give people the chance to express their doubts and reservations, to seek clarification of roles, needs, and yearnings within the vision being expressed.

"What has someone done today that has touched you?" is a question of gifts. As Block suggests, we must be willing to stop telling people about what they need to improve, what didn't go well, and how they should do it differently next time. Our diversity becomes our strength as we authentically acknowledge the gifts each person brings from PPK.

"What do you need from us in order to honor your commitments?" is a question of commitment. Such questions center on the promise we are willing to make to the shared enterprise and on the price we are willing to pay for the success of the whole effort. These are promises for the sake of a larger purpose, not for personal return.

We have found that

- school-based research addresses questions of possibility;
- stewardship conferences address questions of ownership, gifts, and commitment; and
- dealing with resistance addresses questions of dissent.

Questions are a crucial element of culture.

Questioning is a tool for stimulating thinking and enabling us to imagine other possibilities. Along with such skills as listening, paraphrasing, using silence, and building trust, these form the basis for coaching. We will elaborate on coaching in the next core element.

Marlys Witte (2013), from the University of Arizona School of Medicine, has taught us the value of attending to our ignorance. Witte, Ann Kerwin, and Charles Witte (1998) developed the Curriculum on Medical Ignorance. This introduces medical *ignoramics* (Witte, Crown, Bernas, & Garcia, 2008):

> the art and science of recognizing and dealing with medical ignorance, that is "managing" unanswered questions, unquestioned answers, and unmanageable questioners, and analyzing the indecision implicit in everyday medical practice and laboratory research. (p. 898)

We have found Witte's work to be a rich source for learning how to design powerful questions and to help people develop confidence in their own ability to pose good questions, contribute, and seek solutions. For us, there are four main fields of ignorance in the Ignorance Map she developed with Ann Kerwin (Witte, Kerwin, & Witte, 1998):

The things we know we do not know (such as a cure for AIDS)

The things we do not know that we do not know (things yet to be discovered)

The things we think we know but we do not (where we have misconceptions)

The things we do not know that we know (where we have tacit knowledge)

Each of these fields is ripe for genuine questioning to explore our ignorance.

In *The Fifth Discipline Fieldbook* (Senge, Kleiner, Roberts, Ross, & Smith, 1994), Rick Ross outlines the Five Whys Perspective (p. 108). This is a process of asking why five times, in a team setting with discussion, to help dig deep down for underlying root causes. I could introduce Ross to any of my nine grandchildren who could teach him "The 55 Whys" with which most mothers are very familiar. Asking questions is built into us.

Having a rich repertoire of questioning strategies, such as the five whys, the ignoramics questions, and others outlined throughout this book, ensures that time can be spent on root causes rather than superficialities.

All elements of culture provide a catalyst for questions that can drive a school forward. For example, what does a culture of ownership mean in the context of the daily life of our school? What are our most significant areas of ignorance in creating a culture of inclusion?

How central is questioning to the ongoing evolution of our school culture? As one high school student who attended the Summer Institute on Medical Ignorance (Witte et al., 2008) commented,

> This summer showed me I need to ask questions. I've learned that just sitting in the back of the room, taking in all of the information, is not going to help me; I need to be in the middle of it all, amid all the action, interacting with the person speaking. We need to investigate things and find out what's real, what's true. (p. 900)

A CULTURE OF COACHING

Openness and questioning are powerful elements in a culture. They also demand a range of nuanced skills. The learning of these skills requires a culture of coaching, where everyone is opened up to the challenge of ongoing growth and learning. This element of culture is directly linked to the trust radius; trust is at the base of a coaching relationship.

There are many forms of coaching and approaches to coaching. The forms of coaching that we have observed working best involve being a trusted, respected source of feedback and helping someone grow to be the best they can be. Our introduction to the true potential of coaching came through the powerful work of Arthur Costa and Robert Garmston (2002) on Cognitive Coaching. The mission of Cognitive Coaching is

> to produce self-directed persons with the cognitive capacity for high performance both independently and as members of a community. (p. 16)

Cognitive Coaching provides the skills and dispositions on which to base any effective coaching program. We have experienced it in action and seen its powerful positive impact. Its core mental models are personal responsibility and deep respect for any individual's ability to grow himself or herself. **The role for the coach is this: mediator of self-directed, self-managed, and self-monitored learning.**

John Hattie's (2009) research on meta-analysis alerts us that teacher-to-teacher coaching is a significant factor in ensuring high student achievement. We do not often see long-standing embedded cultures of coaching. When we do, the sense of collaboration is tangible. To achieve an effective coaching culture, these schools have commonly had to overcome limiting mental models such as these:

- As teachers, we already know how to coach adult colleagues.
- A coaching culture can be in place tomorrow.
- There are too many other things to worry about to make time for coaching.

- Academic freedom means that I have the right to be left alone.
- Teaching is a private, personal experience.
- Feedback and coaching is typically a negative experience.

Unskilled feedback can be the rule rather than the exception in many lives. Building a culture of skilled "fine-grained" feedback in a school is serious and vital work. Because much of the feedback we receive is unskilled, we become defensive and often fear receiving feedback. Paul Jackson and Mark McKergow (2007) show that most people leave a performance review diminished by the experience!

How often does someone pay close attention to you and to what you are doing and give you skillful fine-grained feedback?

> We facilitatively questioned a principal in front of his staff, with total focus on him for six minutes. Staff were listening carefully and recording and inferring his mental models. After the feedback, he said publicly that this was the first time in his leadership life that someone had paid him this "respect." (Remember we are talking about six minutes!) There were tears in his eyes and in the eyes of his staff who learned things they had never seen in the man over their ten years together.

As teachers, we draw the best from our students. As leaders, we draw the best from our staff. As colleagues, we draw the best from each other. Some of us are natural coaches; others learn to be effective coaches. Each of us has areas where we have the experience and insight to coach others. And we have our blind spots where we in turn need coaching. I hunger for coaching. Having a personal coach is a treat not to be missed. Establishing a culture of peer coaching is a strong step toward developing a staff who will deliver. Coaching is complex. Our experience teaches us that the most effective cultures of coaching evolve over time.

The essence of coaching is to help the staff to understand themselves. Costa and Garmston (2002) use the effective metaphor of a "stagecoach." Coaching conveys the person being coached to a destination: an understanding they seek, but which they cannot get to by themselves.

How do these processes compare to your school's evolution of a culture of coaching?

A STRONG ADULT PROFESSIONAL CULTURE

Through these first six cultural elements, you create a strong adult professional culture.

Jon Saphier, Mary Ann Haley-Speca, and Robert Gower (2008) highlight the role of strengthening adult professional culture as the surest way to ensure readiness for all of our students. To build and sustain such a culture demands school leadership for action. These actions represent an enduring commitment to improving classroom teaching and learning, deliberately, systematically, and continuously.

Saphier (2015) has identified twelve key components of a strong adult professional culture:

- Safety to take risks and be vulnerable in front of colleagues
- Non-defensive self-examination of teaching practice in relation to student results
- Constant use of evidence to refocus teaching
- Frequent teaching in the presence of other adults (Public Teaching)
- Constant learning about High Expertise Teaching (HET)
- Deep Collaboration and deliberate design for interdependent work and joint responsibility for student results
- Commitment to implement the belief that through effort, "Smart is something you can get" in classroom practice, class structures, and school policies and procedures
- Transparent and legitimate decision making
- Urgency and Press
- Honest, open communication and ability to have difficult conversations
- Human environment of caring, appreciation and recognition, celebration, traditions we look forward to . . . a starting point of getting to know one another
- Demanding and high standards for teaching expertise for all teachers

These are facilitated within a culture of trust in the leaders' competence, transparency, fairness, and motives. This is generated through leaders showing vulnerability and strength at the same time.

Saphier et al. (2008) provides a valuable resource for creating a culture of successful teaching and learning in their book *The Skillful Teacher*. They focus on areas of teaching performance and the teaching tasks they contain. This includes a repertoire or strategies for accomplishing both performance and tasks. Teachers mindfully match chosen strategies to the particular context (student, situation, or curriculum). As Saphier explains it, "Pick your spots and choose your shots." He has used the work of Michael Polanyi (1958) as a theoretical base. Polanyi writes about the distinction between tacit, implicit knowledge (what we call PPK) and codified knowledge such as the explicit research base Saphier provides. Both are important in professional growth and learning. For Polanyi and Saphier, professional knowledge is about repertoire and matching. It is not a list of things one should do. This parallels the work of Donald Schön as outlined in Chapters 2 and 4.

There is strong alignment between Saphier's work, our practical experience in schools, and our ongoing action research in schools. You will see examples of his twelve components for an adult professional culture throughout this book.

Mike Gillatt (2014) describes his experience as a principal with this cultural challenge:

> Our teachers are smart people who have neglected a focus on their own, deep learning in favour of the learning of their students. My role is to focus on my class, the most challenging in the school, the 33 teachers with whom I work. (p. 37)

He outlines six key mental models that they now use with great success in his school to impact teacher learning:

- Professional learning must be based on reflection on our own practice.
- Our professional learning must be undertaken with our fellow teachers, as we are the only ones who deeply understand our own context.
- We must generate a Shared Vision around which we align our professional learning.
- We must action learn together around issues in our own adult learning.
- We must shift our professional learning from information acquisition to theory building.
- We must create safe and effective professional learning environments where staff can explore and test their own learning together.

Collaborative learning experiences are part of forming a culture of adult professional learning. The most important challenge is to then transform the collective learning into personal learning for each staff member.

One teacher we worked with in Varberg, Sweden, responded to such an experience:

> Vi har tänkt en hel del tillsammans vilket är väldigt stärkande (jag hoppas att ni förstår vad jag menar). Vi brukar inte ha tid att göra det.
>
> (We have done a lot of thinking which is very "growing" [I hope you understand what I mean]. We don't usually have the time to do that.)

Elizabeth City, Richard Elmore, Sarah Fiarman, and Lee Teitel (2009) parallel the work of Gillatt (2014), through their use of instructional rounds to promote collaboration for improving instruction. They share a core mental model with our process:

We learn to do the work by doing the work, not by telling other people to do the work, not by having done the work at some time in the past, and not by hiring experts who can act as proxies for our knowledge about how to do the work. (p. 33)

They offer powerful ways to help a staff member be personally accountable to begin to demonstrate mastery of new skills and mental models.

Greg Morgan (personal communication, 2015), a principal in Tasmania, Australia, shares his experience:

I have come to an understanding that a conduit for this is shared values and key mental models. The culture of coaching and dialogue around a Shared Vision stimulates clarity, energy, hope, trust, and confidence in self and colleagues. It generates a greater sense of personal agency in people, and with that, a greater sense of personal and shared responsibility.

What processes do you have in place to ensure the ongoing evolution of a strong adult professional culture?

A CULTURE OF INNOVATION

With a strong adult professional learning culture in place, staff have the collective confidence and skill sets to explore new ways of working. Innovation means that your school is doing something new and fresh that has not existed before in your context. How have you dared to change, be different, from the way you have always been?

Oliver Wendell Holmes (1895) expressed it well:

A mind that is stretched by a new experience can never go back to its old dimensions.

Innovation demands that we create "safe spaces" for innovation to flourish. Edgar Schein (2004) calls these "practice fields." It can be disastrous to put a schoolwide innovation in place before trying it out on a smaller scale first. This allows us to see the obstacles and positive drivers of the innovation. It can be refined and refined prior to widescale implementation. In our work in high-performance sport, everyone understands practice fields. In the corporate world, most people understand to "never mess with your core business." They first try things out in pilot studies or on "practice fields." These are spaces for experimentation, for being safe to fail and learn. They are spaces without the normal time pressures, spaces free from the necessity of immediate public delivery. In the same way, every classroom can become a "safe space" for innovation.

At one Auckland Intermediate School, a staff research team was studying cooperative learning. They studied various cooperative learning models and chose three that piqued their interest. They broke the team down into three subgroups. Each subgroup tried one of the models out in their own classrooms for a period of time. They came back together and shared what they had learned in the trials. They designed their own contextual cooperative learning model. They took the model back to their own classrooms and trialed it. They came back together again, after time, and shared what they learned and refined their model. Back they went to trial it again. They came back together and settled on the final innovative cooperative learning model that was presented to staff. The next year, their own innovative cooperative learning model started to be embedded into the culture across the school.

An innovative culture rewards thoughtful, designed risk taking. It is characterized by support rather than punishment. Ideas come from anyone and they are valued and nurtured, particularly early in their life when they are most vulnerable.

> It is a privilege to work in an environment where thoughts and feelings flow freely. Our quest for excellence has created a culture that is like a deer searching for water. There is a thirst and determination to succeed.
>
> —US History Teacher

Innovation is the term commonly used for the lived expression of creativity. We value creativity, and we value this being lived out. Much creativity lies trapped in the minds of creative people without the cultural surround that supports the translation into innovation. Why does this happen?

We sometimes go into schools that are filled with people who are afraid: afraid to rock the boat, afraid of being bullied by other staff, afraid of upsetting others. Many expect to have their mistakes counted, collected, and used against them. A core leadership action is to eradicate these creativity crushers.

Being inside a school that lives with aligned energy, direction, passion, and enthusiasm is like another world. Leadership actions in such oases support the culture of freedom of expression, of skilled collaboration, and of robust safe challenge. This is the fertile ground where innovation flourishes.

> I am sonorous of emotions as I reflect on our school year. It has been awesome in so many special ways. The pace has been expeditious; the knowledge has been abundant; the accomplishments have been many; my growth, personal and professional, has been strong. I have grown even when it meant getting out of the safety zone and taking unfamiliar risks. I have probably taken more risk this year with faculty and parents than ever before!
>
> —US Literacy Teacher

Making purposeful time for "thinking outside the box" to bring to the surface our most audacious ideas is a vital structure for innovation in our schools. In our Texas middle school, we focused on helping every child and every staff member think at the highest levels. How powerful was this focus? Over four years, every teacher engaged in 290 hours of professional development in teaching thinking at a cost of $63,000. We committed to mastery of this one thing! This drew innovation from all of us. We thought we were innovative before we started. What we learned was that new thinking skills and dispositions can be learned. These delivered processes for innovation, and products of innovation, that enriched us all.

> The teaching of critical thinking skills is the major focus of Bleyl Middle School. A parent gave an example of her twins—one gifted and one average. Mom stated that the critical thinking skills program helped her average student tremendously while her gifted student pretty much used those skills. Also, special education staff and another parent stated the benefits of critical thinking skills. The school is willing to take risks to move toward its goals and truly teach critical thinking skills. It is on the "cutting edge" and can serve as a model school.
>
> —United States Department of Education
> Blue Ribbon School Site Reviewer

Nailing one thing really well as we did created that **wonderful sense of completion for all of us together**. It is so satisfying: a sense of real achievement and shared mastery. You find this then flows on through everything you do. Innovation becomes a living, breathing part of your culture.

A CULTURE OF SYMBOLS

I was to meet with the board of a large scientific organization. On arrival, I was ushered into the waiting room in their new building. It was freshly painted with a mural panel on each of the six walls. As I waited, I looked closely at each of the panels and asked myself: What messages are these symbols sending me about the organization? When I was finally invited into the boardroom, I asked if the board members could join me briefly in their waiting room. I asked them to look at the walls that I had been experiencing and to tell me what messages they were picking up from them. They were shocked; some were horrified. One mural told a story of "old fashioned scientists (lab coats, spectacles, Bunsen burners, and test tubes)" in an organization that wanted to pride itself on being cutting edge in science. All other murals had no people in them, just hills, pastures, animals. The organization wanted to pride itself on the quality of its people, top researchers. I could go on. The chairman demanded to know who had commissioned the mural, who had briefed the artist, who was the artist, how could this have happened? A massive cultural mismatch was on full show between the organization and its symbols.

Tomorrow, walk into your school. Observe and write down the symbols you see and what they shout to you. What do people experience and feel as they enter your school? What symbols do they see and what messages do they send? Look at the symbols in your teachers' classrooms. What are the messages they send? If you are like us, you have visited many schools and you will know the wide range of messages one receives as one enters different schools.

Once an innovative, safe, professional learning culture is in place, this manifests itself in many ways that can be seen and felt around the school.

A smile greets any visitor to Our Lady Star of the Sea Primary School in Esperance, Western Australia. The smiling clown outside the front door tells you the week's events. If you are a visitor that day, you receive a personal welcome note. And their Professional Learning Wall in the staff room proclaims their common language to anyone who enters. One of their Core Values is "We strive for excellence." Above the copy machine is a small sign, a symbol that reads, "Excellence is leaving the copy machine ready for the next person." Walking through Our Lady Star of the Sea becomes a feast for the eyes as you experience their Shared Vision journey through their symbols program!

A culture of symbols grows from creating, storing, and managing artifacts that promote the Shared Vision journey, the Core Values, and products of success. A symbols program depicts a Shared Vision journey in many different forms. The only limit to this is the collective imagination of the staff, and this is seldom in short supply. Leadership can play a key role in freeing time, orchestrating, and caretaking the stories the community want their symbols to tell.

A CULTURE OF STORY

Healthy growing cultures are rich in stories as well as symbols. Our stories carry our culture, and storytelling is central to any culture.

On a Shared Vision journey, "stuff" happens. There are interesting adventures and discoveries, fun moments, challenging times, and monumental mistakes. We need to collect these experiences and we need to tell the stories of them. Stories carry our culture and influence us to keep going, keep traveling forward. Once you have changed it is hard to remember being different, hard to remember the steps you walked and the varied landscape you traversed on the journey. You forget and often do not give yourself the credit or "bank" the learning.

> The last few weeks have been somewhat of a blur for me as I have grappled with the changes that are about to overtake me. CHANGE . . . that is something my four years here have taught me to understand and accept. A hard task at times for an old hand to deal with. But, it never ends, nor should it! That, alone, is an attitude adjustment of major proportion. It is so important for me, at forty-three, to see how much there is yet for me to do. With my own children bordering on adulthood, it would be so easy to let down my guard and think my job is done. It is reassuring to know, beyond a shadow of a doubt, that I have much yet to contribute in this changing world of education. Without our vision, I'm not sure I would have felt this way.
>
> —US History Teacher

Art Kleiner and George Roth (1996) from MIT suggest that all organizations need a learning historian, someone who will keep the artifacts and stories of the emerging culture. A natural part of going on a journey is telling the stories of the journey. As George Santayana (1908/2005) suggested, in one of his famous sayings,

Those who cannot remember the past are condemned to repeat it.

Who is writing your learning history? Such a history has value at many levels. By recording your journey as you live it, while it is fresh and clear, you have it for future reference. This enables you to store invaluable PPK. **You can make fresh new mistakes rather than the same old mistakes.** It also allows you to draw from, and build on, the powerful lessons you have lived through together.

Whether you like it or not, your culture has stories. You need to know what stories are being expressed through your culture. It is much better to be the author of your own stories, than to have stories happen to you.

In any school, it is important to be able to tell your story succinctly. Teachers often have a reputation for being "long-winded" with members of the public. How would you tell them the story of your school in around half a minute? Let's look at one example:

> We are creating a school that fully taps the potential of all our staff, our children, and our community. Already we are seeing positive shifts in student achievement, in staff passion for our work together, and in community joy at what is happening for our children. We have done this by creating a Shared Vision where the voices of all of the school community were heard. It took us a whole day to achieve. We then took a year to research the changes we needed to make. Now, we are into the second year of implementing those changes. It is exciting. These innovations are bringing world's best practice into our school. One of them has completely changed student behavior in our school. This is the most professional satisfaction I have ever had in my career.

Try speaking the words; it takes 35 seconds at a comfortable pace.
How would you respond to such a story?
What would be the story for you and for your school?
Give it a go. Explore how you would tell your story succinctly.

Many schools use drama to tell their stories at meetings or school functions. Teachers and students often have a great gift for drama. Here is a space to express that. Drama adds flesh to what can be bare-bone concepts before we start. It can communicate juicy gestalts rather than dry analytical chunks of what we are about.

The new media available to us create a range of new ways to tell our stories with impact that was not available before. What impacts today's students is worthy of exploration. Through their responses, students will soon show which media work for them. Which new media are you exploring?

The development of a shared language is a manifestation of growing alignment to mental models. Discipline in choosing the right language, the best language, brings a level of nuance to the way people interact. There is a shared joy in choosing just the right word or phrase. Knowing nods between people often recognize this precision and beauty of language well chosen, and the camaraderie this engenders.

A CULTURE OF CELEBRATING

How celebration works is markedly different across nations and across subcultures in nations. We are wary of generalizing in this book. For celebrations to work, they must be done in a valid way for those involved.

If you are in teaching and learning you have chosen one of the most complex professions. We love you for choosing it. Teaching is a demanding and unrelenting job. The pace is furious and often we work in isolation. Often, we cannot see how well or how poorly we are doing. Often, we feel uncomfortable, even jealous, when we see others being complimented. And some feel the world keeping score of their perceived deficiencies. The continuous stress sometimes drives people from the profession.

Our lifetime in schools has taught us that in every school, anywhere in the world, desired outcomes are being delivered. The key is to notice, to be aware, and bring achievements into the light. Positive deviants, or the "bright spots," are particularly instructive. They are happening within our own context and with all the constraints of resources and personnel and demographics. Some schools do not take time to celebrate these. These are opportunities not to be missed.

As Kouzes and Posner (2012) express this,

> Leaders give heart by visibly recognizing people's contributions to the common vision. (p. 239)

We need to take time to learn from, honor, celebrate, and talk about the positive things happening every day. Does your community know your culture of celebration? How are you making everyone aware of the good things going on inside your school?

We had an APPLAUSE, APPLAUSE board in our reception area. Community members, staff, and students could identify people who did an outstanding job living our Core Values and they would be recognized there. Contributions took many forms: photos with associated text, stories, and clippings. This was a meeting place for recognition. You can have applause walls in classrooms, in staff rooms, anywhere that people see as valid spaces for celebration.

Balancing this public form of celebrating are the more subtle, private forms of celebrating: noticing when colleagues or children or families are struggling and showing recognition quietly and privately for their struggles and successes. Moments of shared delight, noticing, quiet nods, "go next door and show Mrs. Matthews what you have just achieved"—the many small indicators of recognition for a job well done.

Together, everything builds a culture of celebration. Celebrating should be experienced at every step in a culture-building process. Teachers tend to be good at celebrating the achievements of children but not so good at celebrating their own achievements, both individual and collective.

In some cultures, celebration can also include gentle humor and the revelation of vulnerability. I was always happy to use examples of my own vulnerability as a leader to celebrate the vulnerability that is often essential to growth over time. The regular disasters in my own early learning journeys prepared me very well for such openness. The journey and the pits on the way are to be celebrated as well as the achievements.

LEARNING JOURNEYS

The core cultural elements we have shared in this chapter have been selected from a much longer list that we initially generated. So please do not see our list as exhaustive.

By paying attention to the cultural elements we currently live with, and the cultural elements we believe we need to add, we create a framework for the learning journey of each staff member.

Personal and Shared Visions establish the learning journey pinnacle. There is a beauty that develops from the synergy created by the alignment of a group's pursuit of both their Personal Visions and Shared Vision. Many staff and school leaders have reported major impacts from clarifying vision.

> Thank you for challenging me to find my place in the school. I've been run over by bureaucracy and lived a life of management (which I dislike immensely!). I'm ready to wear my heart on my sleeve and have it 'stroked' by those that join me in this wonderful opportunity. I am finding my real self in making a difference to the children who are trusted in our care. Our school motto is 'We are the future'. And my preferred future for them is the future they will find through a Shared Vision journey.
>
> —Principal, Western Australian

The skills and new mental models necessary to become what we want to be, personally and collectively, define our learning journey. Helping one another to "get there" is the essence of what it means to shout to the world, "I AM A TEACHER!"

Culture Is Built Around Long-Term Relationships

Culture is about people. Building relationships is essential.

Our relationships mentor and coach us. They give us quality feedback. They tell us truths. They support us through pits. Trust develops as we sustain relationships over the long term. The complexity of leadership creates a thirst for trust born of long-term relationships. Who can we count on for the truth? Who can we count on to have our backs?

W. Edwards Deming (cited in Walton, 1986), the "father" of quality management, suggests this: Seek out quality providers and build long-term relationships with them. Most of us have experienced the high-quality results that flow from working over time with the best people. They know us, we know them, and we work together with synergy and richer insights. You are not always going back repairing messes and trying to find yet another relationship you hope will deliver.

Gillatt (2013) describes the powerful impact on his leadership from forming such a long-term relationship with a personal coach:

> Having a coach seems to be in vogue for leaders in the business world. But it appears to be very rare in the world of educational leadership. Personally, I know of very few school leaders who are coached on an ongoing basis . . . as leaders we are all blinkered about our performance and we cannot readily see the mental models that drive performance. We need someone "outside" to help us to step over the boundaries that blinkered performance imposes upon us, and then see our current reality with fresh eyes. An ongoing personal professional coaching relationship is a powerful way of doing this. . . . I can ensure that my mental models are aligned with our Shared Vision and my Personal Vision. This ongoing, intensely rewarding, and at times uncomfortable, process provides me with continuous growth. (pp. 38–39)

Openness to Learning About Our Culture

Most people with experience in schools can sense the culture of the school from the moment they enter. Some call it the "tone" of the school. Classrooms are the same. What "tone" do people feel as they enter our school or our classrooms? How often do we ask for such feedback, set up opportunities to receive such feedback?

There are many forms this can take.

Because we work across education, the corporate world, and elite sport, we have been able to support creating a very wide range of quality feedback environments. We regularly bring in "naïve outsiders" from totally different cultural settings to work with an organization. We bring high-performance sports people and business people into education settings. We bring educators and business people into sporting contexts. And we bring educators and sports people into business settings. The feedback we have received from this very rare process has been universally positive. People enjoy having fresh minds present, fresh insights, fresh questions to reflect anew on their culture as lived. In our experience, they highly value both the commonalities of experience and the provocation of a new lens on their work.

Similarly, having people outside of the teaching staff on a Shared Vision Creation Day has been a significant benefit and appreciated. Parents sing the value of being invited, being respected, being listened to, having an equal voice. This is not hard, but it is rare in many educational settings.

Schools that deliver are open to challenge and to fresh ways of seeing and knowing.

Cultural Evolution

As culture builders and caretakers, school leadership teams ensure an ongoing focus on designing and maintaining the culture. A school's culture is directly related to adult professional learning and student achievement. Designing and steadily embedding core culture elements together has a major impact on aligned school performance.

A Cultural Activities Program, a structure for culture building and caretaking, is a valuable systemic structure to work on.

SUMMARY

A Shared Vision creates a journey. As we go on journeys, we must come to agreement on how we will live together. This is the focus of Chapter 5. We must agree on what set of Core Values we will live by. Our school's culture begins with our Core Values as the foundation. A leadership responsibility is to build, and be caretaker of, the school's culture. This requires a deliberate action plan to embed what becomes the fabric of daily life—the culture. Cultural elements evolve and blend with one another to create our school's capacity to deliver.

Sitting around, taking time defining Core Values, is not what this is about. Living the values, modeling them, articulating them, and teaching them delivers aligned action and results in the emergence of operational definitions of what we all stand for. This is what really matters: what do your values look like and feel like "on the hoof," as lived in your school community?

When you are living your Core Values, your culture comes alive.

6

Schools Are Part of the Community

The main hope of a nation lies in the proper education of its youth.

—Erasmus

There are rich examples from across the world of schools that challenge deeply the idea of the "classroom within four walls" model. Radical writers such as Paulo Freire, Ivan Illich, John Holt, Paul Goodman, A. S. Neill, D. H. Lawrence, and others have opened our minds to completely different approaches to education and its role.

Freire (1970, 1985) argued that education either promotes conformity and integrates young people into the present system, or it becomes "the practice of freedom" whereby people learn to deal critically and creatively with reality and discover how to participate in the transformation of their world.

Freire's call for freedom had a strong political element in dealing with oppression. This was later echoed from a different angle by Steve

Jobs in the iconic advertisement to initiate Apple's Think Different campaign in 1997:

> Here's to the crazy ones. The misfits. The rebels. The trouble-makers. The round pegs in the square holes.
>
> The ones who see things differently. They're not fond of rules. And they have no respect for the status quo.
>
> You can quote them, disagree with them, glorify or vilify them. About the only thing you can't do is ignore them.
>
> Because they change things. They push the human race forward. While some may see them as the crazy ones, we see genius. Because the people who are crazy enough to think they can change the world, are the ones who do.

BALANCING LIFE'S COMPLEXITIES

We share the mental models of freedom, respect, and equity, as you will have read so far. In this book, we are focusing on a more contained target than Freire and his colleagues. We are aiming to help teachers and school communities exercise their freedom to achieve together what they want for their children and their community. In this respect, our work is more closely linked to recent work on cultural proficiency (see Lindsey, Nuri-Robins, & Terrell, 2009). Our concern is for the collective well-being of the whole school community. Our respected colleague, Jon Saphier (personal communication, 2015), on reviewing this chapter for us, shared this:

> For educators who have studied what we are calling "cultural proficiency" and "culturally relevant teaching" these days in the States, this chapter will resonate like a beautiful Chinese gong.

We believe the family is the "first educator" of a child. All other institutions are designed to support the family in the pursuit of Erasmus's (1523) hope for a nation. Schools are essential "community citizens" in this effort. A school's responsibilities are breathtaking, as is the nobility of the task and its privilege.

Almost everyone thinks schools and teachers should be doing more or doing things differently. Everyone, that is, except for those who actually have to do the work every day of setting free the potential of each child. For them, this involves educating, disciplining, and caring for a school filled with our community's children.

As our colleague Brendan Spillane (personal communication, 2015) reminds us,

> Where do we stand up for these people, young and old, for the complexity of their professional task, for the nobility of the daily footsteps that these people take every day? Schools that deliver create conditions for human flourishing—not just for students but for staff also. Isn't one dependent on the other, equally aligned in flourishing or in languishing? Aren't they places of hope with leaders who believe that tomorrow can be better than today? My hope is that in this book you manage to honour schools, prod them for sure and provide them with real ways forward that are both **wise and achievable** in the maelstrom of contemporary school life.

Many times we have shared with families a job analysis of the life of a teacher. As we do, their eyes grow wider. Most parents have little idea of the realities of the life of a teacher both inside the classroom and out. When I have responsibility for thirty students, I sit in front of 435 separate relationships between individuals, let alone all those between groups. I manage that and the perceptions of sixty parents, my leaders, and the pedagogical demands of government and systems. Secondary school teachers commonly have 160 children in their classes, each to be helped on their learning journey. Try calculating how much time that gives them for each child each week outside the classroom.

Building more productive relationships between our school and our community helps us get to know each other better. It helps families better understand teacher life realities and helps teachers better understand family life realities. Walking for a time in each other's shoes helps us design systems together that are realistic for us both. Schools are partners with the family in helping each precious child maximize his or her potential. We want to address this crucial partnership in this final chapter. To do so, we all need to keep the realities in the forefront of our minds.

Every school and teacher action speaks loudly to your community. Sandra Russell (personal communication, 2015) draws attention to this responsibility:

> Every system you put in place
>
> Every decision you make
>
> Every decision you communicate and the emphasis you give it
>
> Every newsletter, notice, or pamphlet you send home
>
> Every connection every member of your whole school staff has with your wider community

Is a clear communication of who you are as a school and what you hold as valuable.

Try not to be misunderstood.

WORKING TOGETHER

As we work with schools across the world, we see families willing to do almost anything to help their children and their school. Often, they share with us that they are unsure what to do, how to best help. How can we best tap this goodwill and willingness to be involved? Mavis Sanders (2003) provides valuable background for anyone wanting to explore the link between the concept and the practice of community involvement in schools.

Everyone associated with a community has an opinion of how well the local school is meeting this responsibility of educating "our children." Schools are never separate from the community. They are forever embedded deep within community.

The UK school is located in a tough part of the central region of the country. It is a highly industrialized area with high rates of unemployment. It has a tough-minded mentality. The primary school has mostly female staff. Dads rarely show up or participate in school activities. The staff were concerned that the children had no adult male role models at school. They decided to go out into the community and interview the dads. The interviews established positive relationships that influenced the dads to assume a much more visible role in all school activities.

In Chapter 2, we briefly shared the story of Murupara Primary School, in a small Māori community about 40 km south of Rotorua on the North Island of New Zealand. The Murupara School principal believed the school needed to play a leadership role in the community. The area economics had been devastated by the dwindling timber industry that once flourished. The school developed their Murupara Thinking Program using the thinking skills that are embedded deeply in the stories and legends of their local culture. The community live these stories through their culture, so the community responded. The synergy between the school and the community grew around this sharing of what matters in their culture. Family life and school life were drawing on the same cultural sources. Traditionally from within *Te Ao Maori* (The Māori world view), there is a responsibility and commitment to upholding the *mana* (personal integrity) of people, to developing *whānau, hapū,* and *iwi* (family, extended family, and tribe) and to look after *Papa-tū-ā-nuku* (Mother Earth). The school was reminding the community of its deep roots, and the children were focusing on living their culture more deeply. This impacted families and the community, as well as the school. Interdependence and

> a sense of belonging was the community prize (Mandy Bird, personal communication, 2015). We listened as the chair of their school board reported on the positive impact the school, its staff, and children were having on this community.

Two schools at different ends of the world making efforts to connect with their community in ways that are valid for them.

A school richly linked to its community taps into a vein of relevant, diverse experience that is hard to imagine unless you have traveled this path. There are questions to resolve. Forging the answers is leadership work for all of us.

- How are you generating community involvement?
- What are the benefits flowing from this involvement?
- How wide is your definition of *community*?
- Are you clear about every community member's role within your framework of community?
- In what ways does your community play an authentic part in each child's learning journey?
- How does your community see their school?
- What data do you gather to inform your understanding of their views?
- Would you rather keep the school separate so it can focus on its work?
- If families have a choice of school, are you that choice?

Communities develop and live cultural norms. Each community provides a unique context. We see schools across many countries tapping into this uniqueness in an astonishing array of ways. They dig deeply into their community: they know the history, know the environment, know the work, know the norms, and know the politics. They are sensitive to community nuances, and give time to understanding the power structures, both formal and informal. They seek to understand their community and to be understood by their community.

> I was in town for the board of trustees' meeting where I was appointed principal. I was staying at the home of a good friend, and asked him the best way to start to know this community. He suggested visiting some of the neighborhood hotels. I am known to like a good bar and a pint! I told my friend that this might be the only time I could go into a bar unrecognized. So off we went. We visited six bars in all. In each one, rich conversations about the school emerged naturally with the men and women I met. The insights were priceless, for them and for me. My understanding of our community had begun. As had their understanding of me!

Abundance and Scarcity Mind-Sets

In his book *The Seven Habits of Highly Effective People*, Stephen Covey (2004) describes the differences between scarcity and abundance mind-sets:

> Most people are deeply scripted in what I call the Scarcity Mentality. They see life as having only so much, as though there were only one pie out there. And if someone were to get a big piece of the pie, it would mean less for everybody else.
>
> The Scarcity Mentality is the zero-sum paradigm of life. People with a Scarcity Mentality have a very difficult time sharing recognition and credit, power or profit—even with those who help in the production. They also have a very hard time being genuinely happy for the success of other people. (p. 219)
>
> The Abundance Mentality, on the other hand, flows out of a deep inner sense of personal worth and security. It is the paradigm that there is plenty out there and enough to spare for everybody. It results in sharing of prestige, of recognition, of profits, of decision-making. It opens possibilities, options, alternatives, and creativity. (p. 220)

Community creates a sense of belonging. This flows from small groups of community members having powerful conversations around the possibilities of community: "How can we each bring our rich life experiences to bear on the education we can offer together?" Tapping into such an abundance mentality adds curriculum elements that bring new learning, and pride, to children and their families. At Junction Park State School in Brisbane, parents run "J-Clubs." They share their range of talents with children through voluntary programs. These are highly sought after by the children and well attended. With an abundance mentality, we believe we have enough to meet everyone's needs. Each of us reaches out to support one another, individually and collectively.

Such approaches are not easy to accomplish in cultures fueled by a scarcity mentality where there is not enough time in the school day, or in busy lives, or there is competition and we must fight for our fair share.

When our school opened, we had a vision of it being 'the well in the centre of the village'. We endeavoured to be warm and welcoming. However, we struggled to get some parents to attend any of our planned events to encourage and grow learning partnerships. After trialling many strategies with little or varying success, we decided to ask our community why this was the case. What we discovered was one of the cultural communities within our wider community had real difficulty attending anything in the evening during dinner time. It clashed with the beliefs and values they had around this time. Another discovery (that we should have worked out) was due to the high immigration in our area, there was little opportunity to find babysitters. This was an easy one to solve—staff offered rostered childcare to cover this role for such events. This was truly living our Core Value of 'a sense of family and learning partnerships'. As a consequence, we have been able to get a much higher degree of parental engagement in our learning programmes. Parent evenings have a strong student presence and input.

A scarcity mind-set breeds a culture of isolation, blaming, and self-interest. Scarcity surfaces in conversations driven by our fear. Scarcity abounds in fragmented communities where everyone lives in a silo separated from one another. Busy lives can support the lifestyle of scarcity. Scarcity occurs when there is only time to solve problems instead of acting to build the future.

Where on the abundance–scarcity continuum are your community relationships? And how does this balance with where you are on the continuum with your own family life?

Our Shared Vision provides a vehicle for new conversations around an abundance mentality. "We are all in this together and together we are strong." A Shared Vision gives our community a language of possibilities. This allows us to design innovative and fresh ways of being together. The school becomes a community citizen. Peter Block (2008) in his book, *Community: The Structure of Belonging*, says a citizen

- Holds themselves accountable for the well-being of the larger collective of which they are a part
- Chooses to own and exercise power rather than defer or delegate it to others
- Enters into a shared sense of "collective possibility"—for us, the creation together of a Shared Vision
- Acknowledges that community grows out of "the possibility" of citizens
- Attends to the gifts and capacities of all others, and acts to bring the gifts of those on the margins to the center

Schools are inherently about the well-being of the larger collective and about exercising citizenship. Block's five challenges can help dig more deeply into this role.

An abundance mind-set within a community is one catalyst for moving forward. Many conversations over time, and the actions that flow from them, slowly build momentum through the community and the school.

Mary Catherine Bateson (2000) expresses well what we have learned in our work with schools and their communities:

> The encounter with persons, one on one, rather than categories and generalities, is still the best way to cross lines of strangeness. (p. 81)

Understanding where your school is placed on the continuum between an abundance and scarcity mind-set requires ongoing attention. Think through these questions:

- How often do we invite our community to come and talk about the future of our school?
- How often does the community invite the school into its context?
- How do we structure quality time and space for these conversations?
- How often do we take our large group of community members and break them down into small groups to have powerful conversations about the school's possibilities?

I attended one of those sessions on the proposed block scheduling plan. We were asked for our concerns and they were written up on chart paper. The staff research was summarized. The teachers' needs for this kind of scheduling were outlined. We returned to the list of concerns to make sure each was resolved. After the discussion, our at first angry and confused audience was asked to vote on the proposal. An overwhelming majority voted in favor. It is a school in which the whole of the learning community is involved.

—US Mother

Abundance conversations

- Generate the actions each community member will take to move the Shared Vision forward
- Surface the agreements and disagreements that define our current reality
- Enable actions that use our collective gifts
- Enable a small group to have a conversation around a profound question
- Sustain a culture of interdependence and shared ownership; this grows a sense of belonging

Through sharing our gifts, our actions embody personal commitment, personal responsibility, and personal investment in our community.

Schools require a clear action plan to be a community citizen. School leaders build credibility as they demonstrate skills and dispositions to interact successfully with diverse constituencies. This taps the richness of the community and anticipates and prevents crises. Leaders sustain quality communications between the school and home. They respond to special interest groups. The action plan is driven by abundance conversations defining a future of possibilities. Your Shared Vision provides energy for the deep conversations.

James Kouzes and Barry Posner (2012) explain the importance of such openness with the community:

> Commitment is more likely if choices are made visible. Taking public action is tangible, undeniable evidence of people's belief in the purposefulness of their behavior. In addition, by making our choices and actions public, we become subject to other people's review and observation. (p. 228)

Simon Sinek (2009) argues that more information is always better than less. When people know the reason things are happening, even if it's bad news, they can adjust their expectations and react accordingly. For Sinek, keeping people in the dark only serves negative emotions.

Knowing our community leaders and sharing the learning journey with them is a win for everyone:

- Who are the visible leaders in your community?
- Who are the invisible leaders in your community?
- Who are the emerging leaders in your community?

Community will outlast any school principal. **Principals who take** *their vision* **to the school community are already in deep trouble.** When we are working with principals to develop a school's Shared Vision they sometimes ask, "What if the community's vision for the school is different than mine?"

We always, with humor, say that the principal should sharpen up his or her résumé. If the principal's vision and the community's vision are so different from one another, there will only be one departure. And it will not be the community! **Communities set the mission, the purpose for the school to exist.** The school is responsible for weaving its way to being part of the history and fabric of the community. To do this, it is imperative for the school to be proactive. To sit and wait for the community to come to you can lead to a long wait. At the same time, the community and its leaders have a similar responsibility. They better know their members and how to mobilize them in collaboration with the school. In this respect, committed community members and leaders are as important as those in the school. It can be sad to see efforts by schools not picked up by families and communities. When the flow between the two is right, as shared in quotes in this chapter, everyone benefits—particularly the children.

Here are some current community voices:

> A pity as children, we didn't come out of school saying 'wasn't that exciting what we learned today, I'm going to think about that. I'm going to tell my friend/mum/dad about that'.
>
> It's good to know change will happen. For years, I've felt so frustrated with the methods of teaching with the apparent 'why change if it's not broken?' It's so stimulating to know the teachers are committed to change and that we have a headmistress open to changing the status quo.
>
> —Parent, Sydney, Australia

This parent was part of the Shared Vision creation process and wants a school that dares to break the mold.

> I went away remembering and wanting to remind everyone that Less = More, Slower = Faster, Quality is better than Quantity, Simple is sometimes best, Balance, and We can be whatever we want to be.
>
> —Parent, Western Australia

This parent was part of the Shared Vision creation process and wants the school to work with quality and balance: to take its time and to do well whatever it decides to do.

> At a primary school in Sydney, parents and staff in this diverse community surfaced balance in the lives of families and children as a topic for research to achieve their Shared Vision. They formed a team to research homework. A parent, and high-profile Australian businessman, was made team leader. As he traveled the world on business, he would learn about homework in different countries and send information back to the team. The school did away with traditional homework and implemented their new "Home Work" policy. This was a rich, diverse menu of activities the child and family could choose to do "at home" each night. One such "Home Work" activity was to participate in cooking dinner with a parent.

This school is using the gifts of the community. These gifts can flow both ways. One principal shared this experience with us:

We had formed around our Shared Vision with great excitement. Our Core Values were identified and we displayed them and talked about them. However, a year passed and our Core Values had not become part of everyday life. We decided to start again and truly unpack them one at a time. We gained shared meaning with staff, students, and families, looking for examples being lived each day and celebrate these. We started to share these examples in our newsletters, at assemblies, with each other, and in the community. A mother stopped me one day on crossing duty and told me the impact of our Core Values on their family. The children were coming home wanting to share the experiences of their school life and the unpacking of our Core Values. The children had called the family back to dinner around the table together rather than on laps in front of television. They were teaching the family the lessons of the Core Values and looking for connections in their life as a family. The mother became quite emotional as she described the difference this was making to their lives. Who says schools can't make a difference to the wider community?

—Primary School Principal, New Zealand

A school's life plays out in a glass house. Through your children and staff, the community sees into the school every waking moment. Understanding the perception the community has about the school is critical. I found it valuable to work with the mind-set that every community member was observing me. Your community's perception is built every time a child goes home at the end of a day and with every interaction a staff member has with the community.

In a similar way, some families are concerned about the insights they believe the school may be gathering about their family life. Openness, discretion, and genuine partnership can help to allay the fears in both directions.

FAMILY: THE PARENT/CAREGIVER AS LEARNER

There are many and varied "families" in which children live. In this text, we use the generic terms *family* and *parent* to embody this wide range of support structures that children bring with them.

Our experiences and observations across many schools have taught us clear lessons about the relationships between families and schools.

- Parents are most likely to participate in school if the experience is related to their child.

(Continued)

(Continued)

- Parents move into the school when they see the experience is of value.
- Parents move away from the school when they believe their time spent is meaningless.
- Parents will always be at the school if they feel children are unsafe.
- Parents who come to the school and leave satisfied will spread their satisfaction like wildfire.
- Parents who come to school and leave unhappy will spread their unhappiness like wildfire.
- Parents can always tell when the school is trying to hide or cover up issues.

The school–parent–child relationship can be seen as a "quality of engagement" triangle. The triangle forms a stable base.

Our community is a melting pot of many cultures, all clustered together in a newly subdivided valley. Forty-five nationalities are represented in our family makeup. We had been investigating across the school what makes us who we are as people and how our family cultures and traditions have moulded us. Students, staff, and parents were encouraged to share their stories throughout this time. At the end of term, we had an 'open school evening' and invited in the community to share in our learning. There were static displays as well as student live presentations. As I walked through the school, a father stopped me. He told me that I would never fully realise the impact of his eight-year-old daughter's learning during this time. He described that she was the only member of their family born in New Zealand and she would not engage in their family cultural traditions. She appeared embarrassed to acknowledge her heritage because their country of origin was often in the media due to unrest and the atrocities of war. This inquiry had unearthed her understanding of her family heritage and started a journey of discovery for her that was growing pride in her newfound biculturalism. By this stage, both the father and I were shedding tears. Who needed an assessment task to know this was powerful learning for this child?

—Primary School Principal, New Zealand

How do you create this level of openness at a schoolwide level?

Do you ask your parents and caregivers what they need from the school to engage in partnership with you?

Parents are not a homogeneous entity with a definable set of wants. Each family is unique just as is each child. They each hunger to know how to support their child's learning journey. They are often also interested to know how their child fits into the bigger picture of their age cohort. This creates many questions of possibility. Here are some regularly encountered:

- How can home learning and school learning best enrich each other?
- What can we do together to support the child's next learning steps?
- How can we best help the child to think about, monitor, and assess their own learning progress?
- What are our separate and shared roles in homework?
- How is my child performing when compared with classmates?
- What do we see as our parent–teacher relationship?
- What are our separate and shared roles in keeping each child safe?

Parents commonly want more clarity about

- How to master the school's systems and structures
- How the school works
- How to help their child move within the school culture comfortably
- How to help their child behave within the school norms and how to help their child have friends
- How the school will respect the individuality of their child at the same time as respecting the whole body of children

Joyce Epstein's ongoing work (e.g., Epstein, 2011) provides a broad exploration of ways to establish positive productive partnerships between the school, the family, and the community to "care for the children we share." She highlights that the way schools care about children is reflected in the way they care about their families. If children are seen as "students," then the family is likely to be seen as separate from the school. Debbie Zacarian and Michael Silverstone (2015) use practical examples from across the United States and Canada in K–12 settings to describe

> how working together to connect students' personal, social, cultural, language and world experiences to the curriculum is a powerful tool for closing the achievement gap. (p. 7)

They support Epstein's emphasis on the importance of building relationships between students, teachers, families, the school community, and the community at large. They share ways to explore the interconnecting spheres of influence and to allow expertise and contributions to flow in multiple directions from multiple sources, to support the learning of all students. Similar to our work, this forms new networks of possibilities.

Edgar Schein's (2013) humble inquiry, which we referred to at the end of Chapter 1, is a powerful frame for conversations with parents:

> We all live in a culture of tell and find it difficult to ask, especially to ask in a humble way. What is so wrong with telling? The short answer is a sociological one. Telling puts the other person down. It implies that the other person does not already know what I am telling and that the other person ought to know it. Often when I am told something that I did not ask about, I find that I already know that and wonder why the person assumes that I don't. When I am told things I already know or have thought of, at the minimum I get impatient and at the maximum I get offended. The fact that the other person says, "But I was only trying to help—you might not have thought of it," does not end up being helpful or reassuring. (p. 8)

Schein has found that humble inquiry, in both directions, produces a climate in which people will speak up. It has always bothered Schein that even "ordinary" conversations tend to be defined by what we tell rather than what we ask.

Never assume that you know the needs of a family or a community. Building relationships enables such understanding to emerge. We learn from and with each other and with the school. There is a strong positive response when parents can safely be learners:

> I wish both my kids were beginning school instead of just one of them. I'm sure they will both be better thinkers and hopefully never get stuck in 'the pit' (as I did). I'm going home tonight to show my son 'the pit' graph. I'm excited for the teachers.
>
> —Parent, Brisbane, Australia

> It has given me as a parent a real self-awareness as a mother and wife. I have also learned to be more appreciative of my children's teachers and staff. I would appreciate more information on how I as a parent can work with teachers and other parents on being passionate in making a difference.
>
> —Parent, Western Australia

At times in our interactions with a school staff, we hear about the problems they have with children coming to school from dysfunctional families. These "dysfunctions" are articulated in a variety of ways: low socioeconomic status, privileged parents from high socioeconomic areas who are too busy with careers, non-English-speaking parents, inner-city disadvantaged families, parents who let their children run feral.

We have never heard a staff member articulate the problems families have with children coming home from dysfunctional schools.

Neither of these judgments is helpful. There is a balance here that needs deeper thought, if we are genuinely in this learning journey together. Picture functional parents connected to functional schools. This is what children need.

> At parent information evenings, we try to have interpreters who speak the various languages within our community. These interpreters are generally parents who have been with us for a while and know our school values well. Through one of these interpreters, I met a new mother who had twin children in our school camp group. She was visibly upset about the prospect of her children attending. On inquiring through an interpreter, she asked me, 'Can you promise me the helicopters will not land and steal my children?' I was shaken to say the least. In all the years I had organised and led camps, I had never been asked that question. I ensured she was reassured strongly that this did not happen here. I made a strong mental note about what we needed to add to our camp preparation and communication that was currently missing. Building trusting relationships is paramount for us. We have learned to listen, be flexible, and to refocus our own lens to be open to learning.

Life for families can be much more complex than many of us imagine.

PARENTS AS PARTNERS IN THEIR CHILD'S LEARNING

The role for many parents in their child's learning journey has been to oversee that the homework gets done or in some cases to do it themselves. Often parents are unhappy with the grades they get for that long and conscientious work! Parents often feel responsible for influencing further "school" learning for their child from the data given to them at the traditional parent–teacher conference. Sometimes, the resulting parent–teacher relationship is uncomfortable. The parent is uncomfortable because they don't feel competent in the new ways of school that have evolved since they were students. The teacher is uncomfortable because they don't feel competent in giving critical feedback to parents regarding their child's learning. For this scenario to change requires a mental model shift in teachers and school leaders. The child, teacher, and parent need to all be active and aligned partners in the child's learning journey.

> Congratulations on the commitment to the 3 Way Meetings with parents which have been almost 100% successful in engaging parents and students in conversations led by students about their learning and progress.
>
> —Principal, Brisbane, Australia

Parents Sharing Their Gifts

Parents can contribute their commitment, talents, and life experience as gifts to our school in a multitude of ways. Andy Hargreaves and Michael Fullan (2013) have found

> We know that both human and social capital have links to student achievement. (p. 37)

Anyone serious about mining social capital cannot fail to notice the mother lode to be found in the broader school community.

Norma González, Luis Moll, and Cathy Amanti (2005) share the rich tradition of longitudinal field-based research, which they have used to reveal the "funds of knowledge" that are present in the community. Their approach of helping teachers go into the community, to learn about the rich culture embedded in the lives of children and their families, has clear benefits. As expressed by Moll, Amanti, González, and Deborah Neff (1992),

> These are neither casual visits nor school-business visits, but visits in which the teachers assume the role of the learner, and in doing so, help establish a fundamentally new, more symmetrical relationship with the parents of the students. (p. 139)

Parents are vital in helping our school live our Core Values. Being aware of this is important for each of us. Our values emerge from our mouth every time we speak, and others see them in our actions. Seeing them emerge in the language and actions of our parents and our wider community, as well as our staff and children, is a reassuring indicator of success. What systemic structures do you have in place to enable your parents to be deeply involved in living the school's Core Values?

As mentioned earlier in this chapter, parents can contribute their gifts by volunteering to support school initiatives and activities. The pattern of behavior we observe is that parents seek opportunities to serve the school as their child begins school. Slowly, as the child moves through the system, parents can begin to disappear from the landscape. An exception to this pattern is a live performance by their child. Within this reality, parent volunteer programs are common to schools. The caliber of programs varies widely. The most meaningful programs ensure there are a variety of options for parents so they can define "meaningful" on a personal level. Any second a parent can gift a school is valued in schools that deliver. And that parent will become crystal clear of that value, feeding a growing valid involvement.

> I couldn't imagine a more inspirational and motivational two days, not only for this school but as a parent, for my life. When the principal mentioned that this opportunity was available I had little idea that it would change the way I see my own personal and professional life (as a doctor). I feel extremely privileged to help make this school what I believe it will become.
>
> —Primary School Parent, Sydney, Australia

Our experience is that it is often the parents with the most packed lives that help the school. Their lives can often be even busier than ours inside the school. Remembering this is an important aspect in helping them design their involvement. It should also feed into the acknowledgment that flows from the involvement, through avenues such as newsletters and assemblies.

Parents as Participants in Decision Making

Schools benefit from according parents meaningful roles in the decision-making process. Robert Fritz (1987) explains that the best way to experience the power of fundamental choices is to make them. Our colleague, Mary Wilson (personal communication, 2015), principal of Baverstock Oaks School in New Zealand, shares how their collaborative culture has grown:

> Our staff, students, and families form a partnership. The entire community is working together towards a Shared Vision. Our students understand what learning is, and learn how to learn. Learning experiences are authentic so learning has purpose. An open door policy exists which enables the community to celebrate and invest some of themselves into the success of the school. Best learning happens when parent, child, and teacher work together. Together they value what each child already knows, identifying their needs and talents within a rich learning environment. The 'family' is at the heart of what we do. The sense of family and the integrity of these values are of paramount importance at Baverstock Oaks. Family will be considered in all decisions made.

The trust radius grows as people are validly involved. In our Shared Vision process, we encourage school leaders to invite parents to be part of the process. Never have the parents who accepted done anything except praise the school.

> I am convinced that we are going to see some amazing changes at the school over the next few years. I believe we are going to see motivated, enthusiastic kids being taught brilliantly by teachers who have the time and the freedom to do what they do best. My son is in pre-school this year and I wasn't sure which primary school to send him to. Now I have no doubt that *** State Primary School is the best possible choice for these vitally important learning years.
>
> —Primary School Parent, Brisbane, Australia

When they are invited to be part of the school's decision-making process, parents become powerful school advocates throughout the community. When controversy arises, parents who have had meaningful roles are the school's allies. When new initiatives are implemented, parents who have been accorded meaningful roles are supporters.

Kent Peterson and Terrence Deal (1998) report

> School leaders from every level are key to shaping school culture. Principals communicate core values in their everyday work. Teachers reinforce values in their actions and words. Parents bolster spirit when they visit the school, participate in governance, and celebrate success. In the strongest schools leadership comes from many sources. (p. 30)

Ragnhild Isachsen is the retired, wise ex-principal of Hogsnes Kindergarten and Primary School in Tønsberg, Norway. Their Shared Vision was their North Star and created a strong bond between parents and staff. Hogsnes was a valued community member. For three years, the community politicians wanted to close the school down because of decreasing enrollments throughout the kommune. For three years, the collective strength of the unified voice of parents and staff caused the politicians to leave the school open.

Parent Complaints

Often a child will have a bad day with a teacher. The child comes home and shares their bad day with Mom or Dad. They commiserate. The parent feels the need to intervene and call the school. They lodge a complaint with a leadership team member. What happens next? Often a note is put in the teacher's inbox or staff mailbox, "I need you to come and meet with me about Bobby Bynum." The teacher knows that they are about to endure a parent complaint. Time and energy for all parties is about to be consumed. Often, trust is about to be eroded.

Why do some school leaders do this to our teachers? The complaint originated in the relationship between teacher and child in the classroom. The first place to seek resolution and understanding should be at the source. The teacher has all the data. The school leader has none except the second hand information from the parent through the unhappy child. Systems and structures should be in place that require a parent to meet with a teacher first. We have found that leaders who put energy into designing effective systems and structures can create wonderfully productive meetings with parents around issues of genuine concern.

I experienced this phenomenon when I became principal. It seemed I had parents lined up "around the block" to complain about something to me. They had learned to expect the principal to resolve every problem. This mental model is a "principal killer" in any school. We put a system and structure in place that influenced parents to begin at the source of their concern. This involved staff professional development and parent education. We designed layers of response. If satisfaction could not be found at one level, there was a process to negotiate a shift to the next level. As principal, I became the last resource at the school level. The first two months of such a new system are always a challenge. Everyone knowingly entered the learning pit together.

A culture of mutual trust evolves as teachers master the complex skills associated with being the "first responders." These skills are learnable across a staff. They require focus and serious practice with feedback. They also require sensitivity to the parent experience. Many parents report to us discomfort, and a lack of skill, in approaching a teacher with whom their child is having difficulty. This is especially the case if they have experienced a "serial offender" in their past, or if the teacher becomes defensive. Different cultures also bring differing expectations of hierarchy. So, mastering this area is a challenge for both parents and school to embrace together. This is best addressed by well-designed systems and associated skill development for both parents and staff.

THUNDERBOLTS WILL CHALLENGE US ALL

An absolute parent priority is that their child will be safe when they go to school. What is the community perception of "feeling safe" in your school?

In his book *The Winner Within*, Pat Riley (1994) defines a thunderbolt as "something beyond your control, a phenomenon that one day strikes you, your team, your business, your city, even your nation. It rocks you; it blows you into a crater. You have no choice but to take the hit" (p. 80). Our communities experience thunderbolts. Schools are not immune.

How the school deals with crises and thunderbolts is another influence on how the school is perceived in the community. What happens when your school is struck by a thunderbolt?

There are many options:

Believe this is fate.

Wallow in self-pity and feel sorry for yourself.

Believe it is someone else's fault and place blame.

Or

Live your Shared Vision and Core Values stronger than ever.

Use the thunderbolt as a vital source of new learning.

Involve the entire community for support.

What is your school's crisis management plan? These plans influence the school to take action to

- Have deep knowledge of the community culture.
- Anticipate and prevent crises.
- Look for opportunities to learn.
- Help everyone assume responsibility the first thirty minutes after a thunderbolt strikes.
- Lean on your Core Values more than ever.

The best antidote in a crisis is to be an integral citizen of your community. Being "among and with the community" gives you sensitive antennae, allowing you to act proactively and anticipate and prevent many crises. Brené Brown (2012) argues that the willingness to show up changes us. It makes us a little braver each time. In this way, relations between school and community continue to grow as we each keep showing up.

Our best learning often happens in our darkest moments. It is important, during a crisis, to keep your senses aware of learning opportunities. This is not easy to do when there is so much emotion and chaos at play. Personal and collective reflection-in-action and reflection-on-action are critical during and after a thunderbolt.

Living through crises taught me that the most important time in a crisis is the first thirty minutes after it happens. If everyone knows what to do, and assumes responsibility as soon as a thunderbolt strikes, you are better able to move through the event more quickly and often soften its severity.

Most schools have plans in place for the significant crises to be expected within their community's context. Each crisis reveals the gaps in your present plan! We learn one iteration, one crisis, after another.

Skilled Response to Emergencies

A tree falls, crushing a wing of the building. A parent kidnaps a child from the school site. Someone collapses with a sudden medical illness. How a leader handles such emergencies has a profound effect on teacher and community trust in one's competence. Gossip spreads like wildfire. Leadership requires that the community gets vital "needs to know" information effectively and quickly. The communication out from the school to various constituencies needs to bear in mind "who needs to know what, and when." This is different for students, parents, staff, media, and community members.

Naturally, an emergency makes us feel we must move fast. There is some truth to this. Staff and student training in CPR, fire drills, bomb threats, and 911 calls enable automatic and immediate responses. Regular practice of these strategies is an absolute in the school business. But, living the mental model of "slower is faster" is required as well. Leadership means acting fast during an emergency. At the same time, we can slow down the ongoing drama, enabling us all to see the "big picture" and observe the emerging nuances. Leaders do this by orchestrating a gathering of emergency responders. Together we identify all the needs that must be met, and the best pace for these, as the emergency is worked through. The decisions flowing from this "collaboration on the run" ensure that no one is overlooked. Our care taking and communication chain ensure a reasonable and sensible culmination of an emergency journey.

RELATIONSHIPS WITH THE MEDIA

A school's reputation is in large part based on the perception of the community. In some communities, this reputation can flow from negative observations of the school in stories by local media. Think about it. When do we see schools in the headlines? Schools report to us that the first school news is commonly the negative news. If you are in the negative spotlight, the media will do all they can to keep the issue alive. These negative stories sell newspapers and headline the afternoon newscasts. The school that waits for positive media coverage may wait forever. Why is this so?

Our schools are so "busy" engaging in teaching and learning that our time and energy is focused inward. We seldom take time to look outside ourselves. This creates the pattern of behavior of always reacting to single negative events or issues. Then, if the media thinks you are hiding something, they swarm like sharks looking for blood. Perception rules over reality. This is a choice we make. There is another choice.

Schools can have the mental model that they will create an honest picture of their school in the minds of their community. For those concerned about the reputation of educators, better alignment between the school and the community is even more urgent. This requires school leaders to reach out. Making public the achievements and stories of your school as an ongoing priority usually pays back the energy many times over. We know school leaders who see this as marketing and shy away from it. Honestly and skillfully managing perceptions of your school is important to all who care about your school community.

How is your school's relationship with the media? Are you passive and reactive and simply wait for the hits? Or are you future focused and the maker of your own news?

Public relations is a leadership responsibility. Great new stories happen in every school every day. Few people know about them. Schools can identify the community media sources: newspapers, radio stations, television networks, and other sources. A system and structure can be designed to collect positive school news. These stories can then be sent out regularly as press releases to the media outlets.

The tendency of many school leaders is to be cautious around communicating with local media. Building relationships with the people who cover the school in the local media is essential. Talk with the media sources personally. What is their process for printing press releases? Who handles education news? What kinds of stories are they interested in printing or talking about?

Tell them the truth about the school in a positive, open way. Quality media relationships will serve a school well in tough times.

How are you sharing the stories of your school?

MUTUALLY PRODUCTIVE ACTIVITIES WITH THE WIDER COMMUNITY

What messages do we send to our wider communities? Each country and subculture has its own traditions that have been built over years.

We often find schools flourishing in their traditional community activities. At the same time, we have found schools trapped in traditional activities that no longer work. They drain a school staff of their time and energy. We seldom see schools delete activities; they commonly keep adding more.

Schools that deliver find innovative and satisfying ways to build authentic relationships with their community. They examine closely how this precious "relationship time" is spent. Some schools use the Pareto Principle. If 80 percent of our impact is generated by 20 percent of our effort, do we know what this 20 percent is? Do we know why it works so well and how to replicate it? If 80 percent of our effort gives us little delivery on vision—how do we prune this non-delivering clutter?

We saw a mental model shift of this type in a middle school in New Zealand. They were experiencing "drowning in traditional activities." They listed all of the community activities they had traditionally engaged in over a school year. They analyzed each activity through the lens of their Shared Vision. Does this activity help move us toward our vision or not? They started "decluttering" activities that they could see had limited value within their vision. This caused many hot internal debates among staff with special interests. "What? How can we not have our annual school production?" There was a belief that parents loved this performance by their children. On questioning, it was found that most parents were as jaded about the production as were the staff. It took a massive amount of energy from everyone each year. A one-year trial break was agreed. The freeing up of energy, from trying out this shift in priorities for staff time, brought a freshness and vitality to the staff. Synergy the school had been missing for many years returned.

Exploring and experimenting with fresh approaches to how staff time is used in interaction with the community can bring an air of innovation and blow away staleness.

Community as Expanded Classroom

Beyond the school gate is another vibrant learning environment. Many radical authors, such as those mentioned at the start of this chapter, suggest that this is where schooling should take place. As Ivan Illich (1971) expresses it,

> Most learning is not the result of instruction. It is rather the result of unhampered participation in a meaningful setting. Most people learn best by being "with it," yet school makes them identify their personal, cognitive growth with elaborate planning and manipulation.

In traditional schooling, the field trip offers a way for teachers to expand the classroom into the community. The worth of these trips is commonly decided by how the staff design the teaching and learning strategies for the experience. They can provide rich learning not possible inside classroom walls.

The community offers a different type of classroom. A learning opportunity can be found around every community corner. How innovative is your school in seeking them out? Some parent groups have created a directory of community parent skills and the experiences they can provide for children. Co-designing such experiences with staff usually provides shared learning of a high order.

The Shared Vision is the school lens for becoming a community citizen. The vision defines the mental models that we all need to live to make the school interdependent with the community.

One school's Long-Term School Development Plan identified eight tasks designed to ensure that the school was a vital part of the community:

- We will model, articulate and teach our Core Values to everyone in our community.
- We accord meaningful roles in the decision-making process to parents and other community members.
- The school will engage students' families as partners in the students' education.
- The school will establish political and financial relationships with individuals and organizations in the community.
- The academic program will take advantage of learning opportunities outside the four walls of the building.
- The school will foster productive business partnerships.
- The school will require each student to participate in a service program in the community.
- The school will report annually to the community.

Communities change constantly. We must ensure that we are always an active participant within the community culture. One significant benefit from this is the formation of long-term relationships with quality people.

At Lilydale District School, in Tasmania, Australia, a strong source of the school's engagement in the community and of community support of the school is a unique partnership. Lilydale has developed a special relationship with the small, local branch of the RSL (Returned & Services League). It began with the school inviting members to speak at ANZAC (Memorial) Day assemblies. The group responded to requests for such help as public address equipment and chairs for the club's official commemorations on ANZAC Day. This has now evolved into a strong bond which sees Lilydale students playing central roles each year in the Club's official commemorations. The children vie for the privilege of doing so. Members of the RSL attend every official school function as honoured guests. At the school's own ANZAC ceremony each year, the RSL Club—in lieu of a wreath—make a donation of a large, hard-cover book to the school's library. The RSL have ongoing value to students' learning. There is no greater champion of the school than this group of war veterans. (Morgan, personal communication, 2015)

Schools that deliver become, and stay, part of their community through thoughtful, skilled co-design and collaboration. They become integral citizens of the community. They belong.

SUMMARY

The community is the cloak in which your school is wrapped. This creates a culture of belonging. Schools are essential community citizens as partners with the family to ensure the education of the community's children. Each school creates its own community identity as embodied in the examples in this chapter.

Ignoring the values of the broader community ignores the heritage of each child and separates home and school, in an arbitrary way that does not exist in the lived learning of a child. We have no right to do this.

The school is an important partner with the family in the education of each child. These partnerships require the building of productive relationships and sharing of the deep insights we each bring to the learning of each child and group of children.

When the whole community aligns around the school they want for their children, you have a school that delivers.

Appendix 1

Consensus Building

Inquiry Probe Tools

During the Inquiry Probes experience it is essential that "every voice is heard" equally and with respect. Participants must come to consensus about the best ideas that come to the surface during the inquiry. Below are the best two consensus-building tools we know. We continue to search for better tools and trial them. To date, these still work best. They have passed the test of regular use over time.

As outlined in Step 4 in Chapter 1, these processes are used with groups of six to eight people with a facilitator familiar with these processes.

CLASSIC BRAINSTORMING: TAPPING THE EXPERIENCE (PPK) AND MENTAL MODELS OF THE GROUP

- Collect ideas from members of your group, by asking each person in turn for one idea, going in a clockwise direction. It helps if you can be succinct.
- Each idea is written down exactly as spoken. No editing. This can require patience to listen carefully and respect exactly what has been said.
- If a person does not have an idea to contribute, they can say "pass."
- Continue collecting ideas from group members until everyone passes.

- Record the ideas on a sheet of chart paper.
- Number each idea contributed. This allows people to easily refer to any idea.
- There must be no discussion at all.
- The facilitator also votes when it is his or her turn.

Once you have all of the ideas for an Inquiry Probe, check whether anyone needs clarification of an idea put forward. The only person who can respond to this query is the person who put forward the idea. If the person wants to change the wording to make it clearer, they can do so. **There must be no discussion.**

Then check that no one believes any other idea on the list is the same as their idea.

The group is about to vote on which ideas they most value. **You do not want to split the vote** on any idea by having two different versions of essentially the same idea on the list. This would mean that an idea that is highly valued would not be voted to the top.

So, any person who believes that there is another idea that is so similar to theirs that it would split the vote should bring this up. The person who put up the second idea is then asked if they agree. If they agree, then their idea is removed from the list, and its number is written next to "same" idea. (From here on those two ideas stay together—if they are chosen as priority ideas by the group then when they are typed up—the second idea is included under the first with an asterisk.) If the second person does not agree that they are the same, then both ideas are left on the list. **Only the two people who put up the ideas can speak.** They either agree or disagree that the ideas are the same and you move on quickly. **There must be no discussion.**

Once you have your final list of ideas, you need to achieve consensus using 10/4 voting.

10/4 VOTING: GENERATING CONSENSUS IN THE GROUP

- Each person has 10 votes, including the facilitator.
- There are three rounds of voting.
- Each person can use a maximum of 4 votes in any one round of voting. That means they can use 4 votes in the first round, 4 in the second and 2 in the third round; or 4, 3, and 3; or 2, 4, and 4; or 3, 4, and 3; whatever they like. They cannot use 2, 3, and 5.
- The votes can be distributed any way the person likes among the items on the list, for example, 4 votes all for one item; or 1 vote for each of four different items; or 2 votes, 1 vote, 1 vote for three different items; whatever they like.

- The person can, over the three rounds, give all of their votes to the same item; or they can spread them as widely as they like. Keep a record of how many votes you use in each round so you know how many you have left.

IDENTIFYING PRIORITY DATA

After the voting is complete, add the scores for each idea or item on the list.

We need you to separate out the top 3 or 4 ideas on your list. With small organizations, take the top 4 ideas from each group, but once you get above five groups identify only your top 3 ideas from each group. If you have ideas that are voted equal third or equal fourth, you need to submit these "tied ideas" as well.

Appendix 2

Sample Shared Visions and Research (Preparation for Action) Themes

Shared Visions are rich descriptions of the future. They are normally one page in length and written in the present tense. They enable everyone to "see" what people will be doing as they live the Shared Vision. After each Shared Vision, we have listed the research themes each school identified from their Shared Vision. These are the themes they believe must be researched to shift the school from where it is now toward the Shared Vision. This "preparation for action" becomes the central work for the school for twelve months.

MONROE HIGH SCHOOL (US): SHARED VISION

Our school is a learning community committing itself to maximizing individual growth for our student population. We expect demonstrated academic achievement for every student in accord with the highest standards that stand up to national scrutiny. A professional, enthusiastic, and energetic team challenges students to become the best they can be intellectually, socially, and behaviorally. A strong work ethic permeates the learning environment. Working hard in a warm, caring atmosphere motivates each community member to become a life-long learner by continually thinking productively at the highest levels.

We function as a transitional experience, getting each student ready for the next stage of life, whatever it may be for that individual. We are a gateway of multiple options for our learners. The entire school community practices decency which encompasses fairness, care taking, and tolerance towards each other. Positive individual responsibility is learned through immediate, sensitive, and consistent interactions about conduct.

We lay the foundation for each learner to participate comfortably in an increasingly technological society. Our pursuit of the goal of excellence is fueled by cooperation, communication, and teamwork. Success in attaining our goals will be measured by the degree of self-esteem possessed by each community member, the quality of engagement that occurs on a daily basis, and the demonstrated mastery of essential transformational skills by our learners.

We equip our learners for life in a country and a world in which interdependency links their destiny to that of others, however different those others may be from them.

Preparation for Action Themes

- 21st Century Teaching and Learning Best Practice
- Behaving off of our Core Values
- Advocating for Students and Staff
- Making a Large School Feel Small
- Expanding Our Classrooms into the Community
- Communication and Feedback
- Student Voice

TORÅSSKOLAN, GRUNDSKOLA 1–9 (SVERIGE): GEMENSAM VISION

På Toråsskolan arbetar vi aktivt med att skapa trygghet för eleverna. Vi skapar en miljö där alla vågar vara delaktiga och vågar säga eller göra fel. Vi tar alla ett gemensamt ansvar för en god lärandemiljö. Eleverna känner sig trygga i sina grupper och respekterade för den de är. Olikheter ses som en tillgång och tron på allas förmåga är alltid närvarande.

På Toråsskolan är vi en motiverad personalgrupp. Här finns en positiv anda med arbetsglädje som väcker nyfikenhet, inspirerar och motiverar våra elever. Vi ser möjligheter och alla känner sig sedda och trygga i personalgruppen. Vi har en god gemenskap kollegor emellan. Med ett öppet klimat, tillit samt förankrade och synliga spelregler ser vi möjligheter tillsammans.

På Toråsskolan för vi en tydlig kommunikation där alla berörda medarbetare får nödvändig information för att skapa en gemensam utgångspunkt. Genom ett tydligt ledarskap från ledningen skapas en trygghet och tillit på skolan. Skolledarna lyssnar på pedagogernas önskemål och formar verksamheten därefter.

På Toråsskolan har vi en stimulerande skolgård, ett uppehållsrum och en caféverksamhet som erbjuder eleverna olika aktiviteter. Vi har ett aktivt elevråd, med ett verkligt inflytande, som arbetar under demokratiska former där alla respekterar de beslut som fattas. Genom detta arbete får eleverna träna demokratiska arbetssätt, lära sig hur man påverkar och vara delaktiga i en aktiv elevorganisation som går från klassrum till ledning.

På Toråsskolan strävar vi efter ett gemensamt förhållningssätt. Här finns tid för planering tillsammans i arbetslag och ämnesgrupper där pedagoger tar del av varandras idéer vilket leder till att vi blir *en* skola. Genom gemensam planeringstid tar vi till vara allas kompetens i arbetslagen. Alla ges möjlighet att vara med på utbildning, planering, husmöte, APT mm.

På Toråsskolan är vi måna om att ge eleverna goda basfärdigheter i läsning, skrivning och matematik. Vi gör eleverna medvetna om vilka målen är på ett tydligt sätt så att alla förstår vad som förväntas av dem. Vi arbetar med exempel på vad som krävs för att nå målen, både före, under och efter arbetet samt ger återkoppling kontinuerligt i verksamheten.

På Toråsskolan har vi elevgrupper som storleksmässigt medför att varje barn får den tid de behöver. Detta ger möjlighet till snabb återkoppling som gynnar elevernas lärande. Eleverna är med och väljer arbetssätt och redovisningsform utifrån tydliga mål med stöd av pedagogen. De utvärderar även sitt arbete, kamratbedömning och självbedömning är en naturlig del i detta arbete. På Toråsskolan har vi höga förväntningar på eleverna. Genom samarbete mellan pedagoger och mellan pedagoger och elever skapar vi en likvärdig kunskapsbedömning.

Med elevernas bästa för ögonen tränar vi dem i att uttrycka sina åsikter och att även respektera andras. Vi visar att vi har höga förväntningar på eleverna och gör dem delaktiga i vårt arbete med nolltolerans kring våld och kränkningar. På Toråsskolan är alla barn och elever *allas* barn och elever.

Förberedelse för handlingsteman

- Gemensamt förhållningssätt
- Positiv lärmiljö
- Ledarskap och kommunikation
- Trygg miljö
- Formativ undervisning/bedömning
- Elevdemokrati och elevers medverkan

TORÅSSKOLAN COMPULSORY SCHOOL (SWEDEN): SHARED VISION

At Toråsskolan, we work actively to create security for the pupils. We create an environment where everyone dares to be involved and dares to push his ability. We all take shared responsibility for a good learning environment. Pupils feel safe in their groups and respected for who they are. Differences are seen as an asset.

At Toråsskolan, we are a motivated staff group. There is a positive spirit with the joy that arouses curiosity, inspires and motivates our pupils. Everyone feels cared for and safe in the staff group. We have a good relationship between colleagues. With an open climate, trust, and anchored and visible game rules, we see opportunities together.

At Toråsskolan, we have a clear communication with all employees. They receive the necessary information to create the prerequisites for good activities and a common approach. Clear leadership, security, and trust ensure participation at school. Teachers listen to thoughts and wishes and take them into account in the development of the school.

At Toråsskolan, we have a stimulating school playground, a lounge and a café business that offers pupils a variety of activities. We have an active Pupil Council, with a real influence, which works democratically with all respect for the decisions taken. Through this work, the pupils practice the democratic approach, and learn how to influence and be involved in an active pupil organization that goes from classroom to leadership.

At Toråsskolan, we strive for a common approach. There is time for planning individually and together in teams and groups of substance. Educators are sharing each other's ideas and expertise so that we become *a* school. Everyone is given the opportunity to participate in training, planning, House meeting, APT, etc.

At Toråsskolan, we are keen to provide pupils with good basic skills in reading, writing, and mathematics. We make pupils aware of the targets in a clear manner so that everyone understands what is expected of them. We work with examples of what is required to achieve these goals, both before, during and after work, as well as provide feedback continuously in operation.

At Toråsskolan, we have pupil class groups that mean that each child gets the time they need. This allows for quick feedback that promotes pupil learning. Pupils are using and choose work procedures and accounting forms based on clear objectives, with the support of the teacher. They also evaluate their work. Peer assessment and self-assessment are an integral part of this work. At Toråsskolan, we have high expectations of the pupils. Through cooperation between teachers and between teachers and pupils, we seek comparable knowledge assessment.

With the pupils' best interests at heart we train them to express their opinions and to respect others. We make pupils involved in our work with zero tolerance on violence and violations. At Toråsskolan, all children and pupils are *everyone's* children and pupils.

Preparation for Action Themes

- Common Approach
- Good Learning Environment
- Leadership and Communication
- Safe Environment
- Formative Teaching/Assessment
- Pupil Democracy and Pupil Participation

JUNCTION PARK STATE SCHOOL (AUSTRALIA): SHARED VISION

Junction Park State School is a creative and vibrant learning environment. Learning is stimulating, innovative and exciting. We support each other and care for each other. Our strength is our welcoming and inclusive community. We value individuals from all social and cultural backgrounds; everyone has ownership. We share the courage to change; to challenge the way we have always done things and to innovate in our teaching. We are a school where great ideas are embraced. We find and support the spark in every student.

All members of our community share our vision to develop a love of learning and a lifelong learner. We believe that learning outcomes are maximised by working collaboratively. We value strong partnerships between staff, students, parents, and community who are involved in and committed to our school. Communication in our school is open; all voices are heard and respected.

We have the best staff with specialised skills. They are role models who inspire students to be the best they can be. Our teaching builds on students' interests, strengths and learning styles. Strategic early intervention sets the foundation for learning. Engaging learning occurs both inside and outside the classroom.

We have well-resourced classrooms with up-to-date technology. Our students are eager to progress and reach new heights. Our school is recognised as a place where there are high expectations for students and staff. Our students have a rich repertoire of thinking skills and can generate ideas for themselves. Everyone is willing to give new ideas a go.

We value the history of Junction Park State School. Our heritage buildings, school song and school motto, Fortitude and Fidelity, richly represent the history of our school. We are all part of the Junction Park extended family; together we care for our school resources, our outdoor environment and we are not wasteful. Our school environment is lush and green, supporting sustainable practices. Our whole school community takes responsibility for our environment.

We relate to each other with professional respect, courtesy and good humour. We work as a team and value different ideas. All staff are encouraged and mentored. Our Professional Development is targeted to specific goals that reinforce our whole school vision. It is continuous, consistent and has ongoing support. Through this, our staff keep up with international best practice. We play to our strengths and always strive to improve.

We ensure that there are daily opportunities for every student to shine.

Preparation for Action Themes

- Designing and implementing innovative classroom teaching.
- Quality professional development.
- Creative, vibrant, dynamic learning environments.
- Using the richness of our community: working together through collaboration, communication and consultation.

LINCOLN HEIGHTS PRIMARY SCHOOL (NEW ZEALAND): SHARED VISION

We are a school community where enjoyment and fun are valued. We ensure that learning is dynamic and that students, staff and parents enjoy a sense of belonging. The quality of relationships among us creates powerful connections.

We advertise openly what we are doing, and publicly celebrate the life of the school. The physical environment of the school is clean and safe. This ensures the physical, emotional, spiritual and social health of our school community.

Our staff is a most precious resource. He aha te mea nui i roto i tenei oa? He tangata! He tangata! He tangata! (It may be asked, what is the biggest thing in the world? 'Tis people! 'Tis people! 'Tis people!) They are valued and appreciated. Creating balance in the lives of all members of our school community is central to our way of living and learning together. Lincoln Heights is a school with strong, supportive, caring and positive leaders. Lead teachers provide in-class support for other teachers. Teachers are supported with effective behaviour management resources so that every learner is successful. Achievements are celebrated for all members in our community.

At Lincoln Heights, diversity is our strength. We set high expectations for achievement for every child. Our curriculum is matched to our students; it is relevant to their lives and their futures. We gather quality data to inform our planning, to keep an accurate track of what has been achieved, and to continuously improve the learning environment for each child in our care. Children willingly take risks as they learn and understand that mistakes are opportunities towards success. Literacy and numeracy assessment data as well as national and international data prove our students are successful.

Quality teaching and learning is our way of life. Our staff is the energy source for teaching and infusing thinking skills throughout our curriculum. Our learners have the courage to explore and source their own knowledge. They question skilfully and make up their own minds using global and analytical thinking. Parents and community leaders are invited to participate and help make decisions to sustain our culture of thinking.

Celebration events, extra-curricular activities (e.g., Sporting programmes, Mathematics Challenges, Music School, and Care Program), open days, and social gatherings are designed as opportunities for our community to think and learn together—kotahitanga. Our classrooms are real-life thinking environments where students are continually challenged to make decisions and constantly solve problems. A continuous professional learning programme assures that our teachers are expert in the thinking processes that our children take into the world. At Lincoln Heights we are 'Developers of Inquiring Minds'.

Preparation for Action Themes

- Authentic Assessment
- Lead Management: Creating a Lincoln Heights Culture of Leadership
- Lincoln Heights Thinking Skills Curriculum: Teaching and Learning Thinking Skills
- Communication, Collaboration and Participation in Supportive/ Thoughtful Communities
- Enhancing Positive Behaviour and Cultural Diversity

Appendix 3

The Long-Term School Development Plan

> The Long-Term School Development Plan is where vision and action can come together to transform the school.

There are three steps in this process:

1. Preparing and presenting Task Descriptors
2. Critiquing and analyzing Task Descriptors
3. Designing and implementing the plan

PREPARING AND PRESENTING TASK DESCRIPTORS

Over the last year, each team has been researching their theme on behalf of the whole school community. They now recommend what must be implemented to enable achievement of their part of the Shared Vision. Each team presents a maximum of two Task Descriptors—recommendations of the tasks to be undertaken in their theme area to lead the school forward. They provide clear evidence to support their Task Descriptors and show how they link to the Shared Vision.

A Task Descriptor answers this focus question in the present tense, as if it is happening now:

What will our school look like when this Task Descriptor is implemented?

So, for example, our Task Descriptor could be

> We have three-way conferences among parents, students, and teachers as a basis for designing individual learning programs.

Or

> Each of our students learns a core set of Thinking Skills and Thinking Dispositions that have been designed by us to fit our culture.

Or

> We have a feedback culture where every staff member and every student receives rich, skilled daily feedback.

The quality of the Task Descriptors is crucial. The school community has committed to implement what the team creates. The Task Descriptors represent the best of the team's creativity and intellect, and what they are convinced will work best in their school context.

CRITIQUING AND ANALYZING TASK DESCRIPTORS

Each team presents their Task Descriptors to the school community. Each person rates the Task Descriptor as ready for implementation or in need of more work. They also provide more detailed feedback on the strength of the Task Descriptors and any suggestions for improvement. The school leadership team uses these ratings and feedback as input to their plan design process.

The leadership team also rates each Task Descriptor against a set of their own criteria. Commonly used criteria include the following:

> The Level of Perspective (Vision Level, Mental Model Level, Systemic Structure Level, Pattern of Behavior Level, or Event Level, as outlined in the "Explanatory Power" section of Chapter 1)
>
> Perceived impact on student learning
>
> How long it would take to implement
>
> Cost to implement
>
> Amount of staff development required

DESIGNING AND IMPLEMENTING THE PLAN

The Task Descriptors that are ready to implement are sequenced into the plan.

This sequence is dependent on the interaction of many factors, such as the criteria listed above. This demands "big picture" synthetic thinking from the leadership team. Here are some design lessons we have learned:

- Look for initial tasks that have both a high rating on Levels of Perspective and high impact on student learning. These are absolute winners if implemented early.
- Look for tasks that can be accomplished with little cost, time, energy, and/or training. These offer "easy wins."
- Always remember you are on a journey. Be careful about doing too much too fast, especially if it involves staff development.
- Complex tasks may need to be implemented over two or three years.
- Every task, before implementation, must be "fit for your context." This may involve a period of trialing, gathering data, and action learning, to get it "just right" for you.
- Implement ONE TASK at a time, and see it right through to the finish.
- Be VERY careful. You must not overload staff or disperse their energies and passion.
- The draft implementation plan is taken back to staff for feedback before the final version is agreed.
- Implementation teams are formed, with a "sponsor" from the leadership team to keep them connected to leadership.
- Implementation teams commonly elect their own leader and design their own operational structure.
- Each year, you need to revisit your plan to match it against what you have learned from the year, any changes to your context, and what may now make better sense.

Appendix 4

Sample Personal Visions

(Shared with permission from three teachers.)

TEACHER 1: PERSONAL VISION 2012

After thinking 2011 would be a year of consolidation, the things I achieved surpassed my personal vision: bought a house, completed my degree, hit sub 90s in golf, lost 13kg in weight, dating, and professionally developing in confidence to tackle those difficult conversations.

This year will not involve any external study but will allow me time to read more professionally for the maths and leadership development we are involved in. One of my main challenges at work is to ensure the team collaborate and share responsibilities. I will ensure the leaders in our team take their responsibility seriously in tracking data and student achievement across the team. I also ensure teachers understand the personal and collective responsibility we all have to make a difference. I enjoy my role in developing home/school partnerships and am excited by the positive way the staff support this initiative already.

Being in your 50s and thinner is a great place to be. I am more confident with who I am as a person and ensure I have time for the things I want to do and with the people I want to do this with. 2012 is a year for me. One of my main aims is to reduce my golf handicap and enjoy representing my club in the pennants team and at the same time meet new people and improve my golf.

I still need to develop a stronger backbone when dealing with my dysfunctional kids. There is no rescuing of them this year, as they need to learn how to manage themselves and save to meet the demands life throws at them. Rescuing them only creates issues.

Spending time with friends is important to me and in doing so ensures balance in my life—a skill I am improving at all the time.

As I did enjoy study last year I will take this up again in 2013 and do some post grad leadership papers.

I love overseas travel but finances don't allow it at present. I am putting money away so this can become a reality in 2013 and beyond.

TEACHER 2: MY PERSONAL VISION FOR 2014

This year is DIFFERENT. Different at home, different at work and different for me. I no longer want to feel that I just exist and life is happening to me.

A light bulb went off in my head at retreat this year when discussing the need to learn, unlearn and relearn to be learners and educators in the 21st century, as this is exactly what I am going to do with my own life to move forward.

So how am I going to make this year different? I have taken the first step by changing age levels this year. I cannot run my programme the way I have run it for the past five years so I have to change my way of thinking and teaching and that is a good thing.

Like many books I have read, I had read 'The Fish Philosophy' a few years ago and been inspired by it but had forgotten that in order to live it, I needed to practice it daily. This is my tool for this year.

At Home

Choose My Attitude. I take the time to stop, get changed and adjust into my family role when I come home.

Make Someone's Day. I notice what we do well, how we have helped each other and celebrate our little successes.

Be Present. I actually listen instead of just nodding when asking someone about his or her day and make an effort to enquire further.

Play. I go swimming, go out for coffee and ice cream, walk the dog, and watch my son play tennis and rugby and my daughter swim. I also help my husband with the home DIY when I can.

At Work

Choose My Attitude. I use the drive to and from home to stop and adjust my attitude.

Make Someone's Day. I ensure I notice and thank colleagues, friends, students and parents, for all they do.

Be Present. I stop to listen and talk with others, rather than continuing to walk on.

Play. I enjoy playing, dancing, making, drawing, colouring and learning alongside my class of younger learners.

Me

Choose My Attitude. I make a conscious effort to quieten the negative voice in my head by actually saying STOP when I hear it. I have been told in the past to thank it for trying to protect me but it is not true and at the very least, it is just opinion—not fact.

Make My Day. I enjoy the hugs and hand holding ☺. Young children do not do these things unless they want to, there is no ulterior motive, just a need to be connected and secure.

Be Present. Instead of worrying about what is ahead, I remember that by focusing on the now and the lesson at hand, things will fall into place—and if they don't I will handle that too.

Play. I walk, read, go to the movies, go window-shopping, swim and take the occasional nana nap when needed.

So to 2014 . . . BRING IT ON ☺.

TEACHER 3: PERSONAL VISION 2015

The year 2015 promises to be quite different from any other at our school to date due to the focus on stronger collaboration, both in planning and teaching, the wide spread use of Google Drive as a tool for sharing, collaborative curriculum planning and assessment and the introduction of electronic devices in everyday classroom learning situations.

My philosophy for learning is: I believe learning flourishes when learners feel safe, valued and encouraged to 'give things a go'. This has guided my actions from week one. I am taking the time to observe the children in our room and truly get to know them. I am able to have discussions with them about their lives and their learning so that I can relate to them in a way that can best meet their individual needs.

Also, this year I am more open with parents from early in the term—sharing any concerns as well as successes. Our team meetings work well. We are able to speak freely and make decisions after dialogue. We focus on listening to each other and talking through any issues that develop each week.

Six words that come to mind when I consider this year are: openness, candidness, support, questioning, perseverance and balance. Openness to the different personalities, thinking and practices of the teachers and students in the team; candidness during team meetings and allowing others to be candid in return; support—encouraging others when the going gets tough; questioning—how can I best tackle ideas and activities that are challenging; perseverance to keep the balance in my life so that I remain positive.

This year I am further building my skills in teaching writing and so I am having some discussions with colleagues regarding successes they have experienced. I am observing their teaching practices so that I am an effective teacher of writing across the team.

With the arrival of our third daughter home permanently, family life has been given a rather large boost, which is great. This year, at the end of March my husband and I will celebrate our 40th anniversary. He will also reach retirement age at the end of the year—so a few milestones are ahead of us in 2015.

I will continue to pursue gardening and sport this year and build on friendships at every opportunity. The gift of a Kindle has opened up a world of reading material that is affordable. I devoured fiction books over the holidays and now have a copy of the Bible installed so that spiritually I can be fed at the touch of a screen.

As I reflect on the year ahead I feel it will be a defining one in many ways. There is no doubt in my mind that there are a number of challenges facing me. Through prayer, commitment and support from my family and colleagues I look forward to meeting these as and when they arrive and am able to look back and smile at the opportunities that have come my way to help me grow.

References

Argyris, C. (1991). Teaching smart people how to learn. *Harvard Business Review, 69*(3), 99–109. Retrieved from https://hbr.org/1991/05/teaching-smart-people-how-to-learn/ar/1

Argyris, C. (1992). *On organizational learning.* Oxford, UK: Blackwell.

Argyris, C. (1993). *Knowledge for action: A guide to overcoming barriers to organizational change.* San Francisco, CA: Jossey-Bass.

Argyris, C. (1994). Good communication that blocks learning. *Harvard Business Review, 72*(4), 77–85. Retrieved from https://hbr.org/1994/07/good-communication-that-blocks-learning/ar/1

Argyris, C. (1998, May/June). Empowerment: The emperor's new clothes. *Harvard Business Review* [Reprint Number 98302]. Retrieved from http://orion2020.org/archivo/TO/liderazgo/empowerment.pdf

Balatti, J., Edwards, J., & Andrew, P. (1997, November). Mentoring structures within a professional development program. *Training and Development in Australia, 24*(2), 8–14.

Barker, J. (1990). *The power of vision* [DVD]. Minneapolis, MN: Starthrower.

Bateson, M. C. (2000). *Full circles, overlapping lives: Culture and generation in transition.* New York, NY: Random House.

Blackwell, L., Trzesniewski, K., & Dweck, C. S. (2007). Implicit theories of intelligence predict achievement across an adolescent transition: A longitudinal study and intervention. *Child Development, 78,* 246–263.

Block, P. (1993). *Stewardship: Choosing service over self-interest.* San Francisco, CA: Berrett-Koehler.

Block, P. (2008). *Community: The structure of belonging.* San Francisco, CA: Berrett-Koehler.

Brown, B. (2010). *The gifts of imperfection: Let go of who you think you're supposed to be and embrace who you are.* Center City, MN: Hazelden.

Brown, B. (2012). *Daring greatly: How the courage to be vulnerable transforms the way we live, love, parent, and lead.* New York, NY: Gotham.

Bruner, J. (1986). *Actual minds, possible worlds.* Cambridge, MA: Harvard University Press.

Bryk, A. S., & Schneider, B. (2003). Trust in schools: A core resource for school reform. *Educational Leadership, 60*(6), 40–45. Retrieved from http://www.ascd.org/publications/educational-leadership/mar03/vol60/num06/Trust-in-Schools@-A-Core-Resource-for-School-Reform.aspx

Butler, J. (1994). From action to thought: The fulfilment of human potential. In J. Edwards (Ed.), *Thinking: International interdisciplinary perspectives* (pp. 16–22). Melbourne, Australia: Hawker Brownlow.

Butler, J., & Edwards, J. (2004). *Facilitative questioning.* Brisbane, Australia: Edwards Explorations.

Cain, S. (2012). *Quiet: The power of introverts in a world that can't stop talking.* New York, NY: Crown.

Carr, N. (2011). *The shallows: What the Internet is doing to our brains.* New York, NY: W. W. Norton.

Carr, N. (2015). *The glass cage: How our computers are changing us.* New York, NY: W. W. Norton.

City, E. A., Elmore, R. F., Fiarman, S. E., & Teitel, L. (2009). *Instructional rounds in education: A network approach to improving teaching and learning.* Cambridge, MA: Harvard Education Press.

Collins, J. (2001). *Good to great: Why some companies make the leap. . . and others don't.* New York, NY: HarperBusiness.

Costa, A. L., & Garmston, R. J. (2002). *Cognitive coaching: A foundation for renaissance schools* (2nd ed.). Norwood: MA: Christopher-Gordon.

Costa, A. L., & Kallick, B. (Eds.). (2008). *Learning and leading with habits of mind: 16 essential characteristics for success.* Alexandria, VA: ASCD.

Covey, S. R. (2004). *The seven habits of highly effective people.* New York, NY: Free Press.

Csikszentmihalyi, M. (1990). *Flow: The psychology of optimal experience.* New York, NY: Harper & Row.

Daloz, L. (1986). *Effective teaching and mentoring: Realizing the transformational power of adult learning experiences.* San Francisco, CA: Jossey-Bass.

de Bono, E. (1992). *Serious creativity.* London, UK: HarperCollins.

de Bono, E. (2009). *CoRT thinking lessons* (vols. 1–6) [CoRT Thinking Lessons series]. Glendale, CA: McQuaig Group.

de Bono, E. (2010). *Teach yourself to think.* London, UK: Penguin.

de Geus, A. (1988, March/April). Planning as learning. *Harvard Business Review, 66,* 70–74.

de Mille, A. (1991). *Martha: The life and work of Martha Graham.* New York, NY: Random House.

Dweck, C. S. (2010, January). Mindsets and equitable education. *Principal Leadership, 10*(5), 26–29.

Earl, L. (2003). *Assessment as learning: Using classroom assessment to maximize student learning.* Thousand Oaks, CA: Corwin.

Edwards, J. (1991a). The direct teaching of thinking skills. In G. Evans (Ed.), *Learning and teaching cognitive skills* (pp. 87–106). Victoria, Australia: ACER.

Edwards, J. (1991b). Research work on the CoRT method. In S. Maclure & P. Davies (Eds.), *Learning to think: Thinking to learn* (pp. 19–30). Oxford, UK: Pergamon.

Edwards, J. (1994). Thinking and change. In S. Dingli (Ed.), *Creative thinking: A multi-faceted approach* (pp. 16–29). Msida: Malta University Press.

Edwards, J. (1996). The direct teaching of thinking in education and in business. In S. Dingli (Ed.), *Creative thinking: New perspectives* (pp. 82–95). Msida: Malta University Press.

Edwards, J. (2001). Learning and thinking in the workplace. In A. L. Costa (Ed.), *Developing minds* (pp. 23–28). Alexandra, VA: ASCD.

Edwards, J., Butler, J., Hill, B., & Russell, S. (1997). *People rules for rocket scientists.* Brisbane, Australia: Samford Research Associates.

Edwards, J., & Marland, P. (1982). Student thinking in a secondary biology classroom. *Research in Science Education, 12*, 32–41.

Edwards, J., Martin, B., & Russell, S. (2009). *Forming a personal vision.* Brisbane, Australia: Edwards Explorations.

Epstein, J. L. (2011). *School, family and community partnerships: Preparing educators and improving schools.* Boulder, CO: Westview Press.

Erasmus, D. (2008). *A handbook on good manners for children* [De civilitate morum puerilium libellus] (E. Merchant, Trans.). London, UK: Preface. (Original work published 1523)

Forsyth, P. B., & Adams, C. M. (2004). Social capital in education. In W. K. Hoy & C. G. Miskel (Eds.), *Educational administration, policy and reform: Research and measurement.* Charlotte, NC: Information Age.

Freire, P. (1970). *Pedagogy of the oppressed.* New York, NY: Continuum.

Freire, P. (1985). *The politics of education* (D. Macedo, Trans.). Westport, CT: Bergin & Garvey.

Fritz, R. (1987). *The path of least resistance.* Salem, MA: Stillpoint.

Fukuyama, F. (1995). *Trust: The social virtues and the creation of prosperity.* New York, NY: Free Press.

Fullan, M. (1993). *Change forces.* London, UK: Falmer Press.

Fullan, M., & Quinn, J. (2015). *Coherence: The right drivers in action for schools, districts, and systems.* Thousand Oaks, CA: Corwin.

Gillatt, M. W. (2013). The self-construction of a leader: Changing the waters in which we swim. *Australian Educational Leader, 35*(4), 36–39.

Gillatt, M. W. (2014). A new face on the old: Teaching smart people how to learn. *Australian Educational Leader, 36*(2), 34–37.

Godin, S. (2008). *Tribes.* New York, NY: Portfolio.

González, N., Moll, L. C., & Amanti, C. (Eds.). (2005). *Funds of knowledge: Theorizing practices in households, communities, and classrooms.* Mahwah, NJ: Lawrence Erlbaum.

Hampden-Turner, C. (1981). *Maps of the mind.* New York, NY: Scribner.

Hargreaves, A., & Fullan, M. (2012). *Professional capital: Transforming teaching in every school.* New York, NY: Teachers College Press.

Hargreaves. A., & Fullan, M. (2013). The power of professional capital. *Journal of Staff Development, 34*(3), 36–39. Retrieved from http://www.michaelfullan.ca/wp-content/uploads/2013/08/JSD-Power-of-Professional-Capital.pdf

Hattie, J. (2009). *Visible learning: A synthesis of over 800 meta-analyses relating to achievement.* Abingdon, Oxon, UK: Routledge.

Hill, B. (1994). Growing people, growing crystals. In S. Dingli (Ed.), *Creative thinking: A multifaceted approach* (pp. 215–223). Msida: Malta University Press.

Holmes, O. W. (1895). *Autocrat of the breakfast table.* Boston, MA: Donahue & Co.

Hoy, W. K., Gage, C. Q., & Tarter, C. J. (2006). School mindfulness and faculty trust: Necessary conditions for each other? *Educational Administration Quarterly, 42*, 236–255.

Illich, I. (1971). *Deschooling society.* New York, NY: Harper & Row.

Isaacs, W. (1999). *Dialogue: The art of thinking together.* New York, NY: Currency.

Jackson, P. Z., & McKergow, M. (2007). *The solutions focus: Making coaching and change simple.* Boston, MA: Nicholas Brealey.

Jobs, S. (1997). *Here's to the crazy ones* [poster]. Cupertino, CA: Apple.

Jung, C. (1969). *Man and his symbols.* New York, NY: Doubleday.

Kim, D. H. (2001). *Organizing for learning: Strategies for knowledge creation and enduring change.* Waltham, MA: Pegasus Communications.

Kirschner, P., & Lai, K.-W. (2007). Online communities of practice in education [Special issue]. *Technology, Pedagogy and Education, 16*(2), 127–131.

Kleiner, A., & Roth, G. (1996). *Field manual for learning historians.* Cambridge, MA: MIT-COL and Reflection Learning Associates.

Kotter, J. (1996). *Leading change.* Boston, MA: HarvardBusiness.

Kouzes, J. M., & Posner, B. (2012). *The leadership challenge: How to make extraordinary things happen in organizations* (5th ed.). San Francisco, CA: Jossey-Bass.

Lencioni, P. (2002). *The five dysfunctions of a team: A leadership fable.* San Francisco, CA: Jossey-Bass.

Lindsey, R. B., Nuri-Robins, K. N., & Terrell, R. D. (2009). *Cultural proficiency: A manual for school leaders* (3rd ed.). Thousand Oaks, CA: Corwin.

Machiavelli, N. (1961). *The prince* (R. M. Adams, Trans.). London, UK: Penguin. (Original work published 1532)

Moll, L. C. (2013). *L. S. Vygotsky and education.* Abingdon, Oxon, UK: Routledge.

Moll, L. C., Amanti, C., Neff, D., & González, N. (1992). Funds of knowledge for teaching: Using a qualitative approach to connect homes and classrooms. *Theory Into Practice, 31*(2), 132–141.

Morgan, G. (2013). Leading with leverage: Transforming organisations by engaging the passions and aspirations of stakeholders. *Theory into Practice, 12,* 103–113.

Nottingham, J. A. (2010). *Challenging learning.* Berwick-upon-Tweed, UK: JN Publishing.

Peterson, K., & Deal. T. (1998). How leaders influence the culture of schools. *Educational Leadership, 56*(1), 28–30.

Piaget, J. (1964). *The early growth of logic in the child.* London, UK: Routledge & Kegan Paul.

Pierson, R. (2013, May). *Rita Pierson: Every kid needs a champion* [TED Talk]. Retrieved from http://www.ted.com/talks/rita_pierson_every_kid_needs_a_champion

Pink, D. H. (2009). *Drive: The surprising truth about what motivates us.* New York, NY: Riverhead Books.

Polanyi, M. (1958). *Personal knowledge: Towards a post-critical philosophy.* Chicago, IL: University of Chicago Press.

Rath, T., & Conchie, B. (2008). *Strengths-based leadership: Great leaders, teams, and why people follow.* New York, NY: Gallup Press.

Revans, R. (2011). *ABC of action learning.* Burlington, VT: Gower.

Reynolds, M. (2014). *The discomfort zone: How leaders turn difficult conversations into breakthroughs.* San Francisco, CA: Berrett-Koehler.

Riley, P. (1994). *The winner within: A life plan for team players.* New York, NY: Berkeley.

Rogers, C. (1956). *Client-centered therapy* (3rd ed.). Boston, MA: Houghton-Mifflin.

Rogers, C., & Roethlisberger, F. (1991, November/December). Barriers and gateways to communication. *Harvard Business Review, 69,* 105–111.

Russell, S. (1996). *The things we steal from children* [original version]. Brisbane, Australia: Edwards Explorations.

Ryan, R. M., & Deci, E. L. (2000). Self-determination theory and the facilitation of intrinsic motivation, social development, and well-being. *American Psychologist, 55*(1), 68–78.

Ryan, R. M., & La Guardia, J. G. (2000). What is being optimized over development? A self-determination theory perspective on basic psychological needs across the life span. In S. H. Qualls & R. Abeles (Eds.), *Psychology and the aging revolution: How we adapt to longer life* (pp. 145–172). Washington, DC: American Psychological Association.

Sanders, M. G. (2003). Community involvement in schools: From concept to practice. *Education and Urban Society, 35*(2), 161–180.

Santayana, G. (2005). Reason in common sense. In G. Santayana, *The life of reason* (vol. 1) [e-Book, Project Gutenberg]. New York, NY: Dover. Retrieved from http://www.gutenberg.org/files/15000/15000-h/vol1.html (Original work published 1908)

Saphier, J. (2015). *12 observable features of a strong adult professional culture.* Retrieved from http://www.rbteach.com/blogs/12-observable-features-strong-adult-professional-culture

Saphier, J., Haley-Speca, M. A., & Gower, R. (2008). *The skillful teacher: Building your teaching skills* (6th ed.). Acton, MA: Research for Better Teaching.

Schein, E. H. (2004). *Organizational culture and leadership.* San Francisco, CA: Jossey-Bass.

Schein, E. H. (2013). *Humble inquiry: The gentle art of asking instead of telling.* San Francisco, CA: Berrett-Koehler.

Schön, D. A. (1987). *Educating the reflective practitioner.* San Francisco, CA: Jossey-Bass.

Schön, D. A. (1991). *The reflective practitioner: How professionals think in action.* Farnham, Surrey, UK: Ashgate.

Scott, S. (2011). *Fierce leadership: A bold alternative to the worst "best" practices of business today.* New York, NY: Crown Business.

Scriven, M. (1967). The methodology of evaluation. In R. Tyler, R. Gagné, & M. Scriven (Eds.), *Perspectives of curriculum evaluation* (AERA Monograph Series on Curriculum Evaluation). Chicago, IL: Rand McNally.

Senge, P. M. (1990). *The fifth discipline.* New York, NY: Currency.

Senge, P. M., Kleiner, A., Roberts, C., Ross, R. B., & Smith, B. J. (1994). *The fifth discipline fieldbook: Strategies and tools for building the learning organization.* London, UK: Nicholas Brealey.

Senge, P. M., Scharmer, C. O., Jaworski, J., & Flowers, B. S. (2005). *Presence: An exploration of profound change in people, organizations and society.* New York, NY: Currency.

Senge, P. M., Smith, B., Kruschwitz, N., Laur, J., & Schley, S. (2010). *The necessary revolution.* New York, NY: Crown.

Sinek, S. (2009). *Start with the why: How great leaders inspire action.* New York, NY: Penguin.

Toporek, S. (1999, November 26). Monroe high school is a blue ribbon school. *Monroe Guardian.*

Tschannen-Moran, M. (2004). *Trust matters.* San Francisco, CA: Jossey-Bass.

Tuckman, B. W. (1965). Developmental sequence of small groups. *Psychological Bulletin, 63*(6), 384–399.

Walton, M. (1986). *The Deming management method.* New York, NY: Penguin Putnam.

Wellman, B. (2014, November). *Handbook.* Amplifying the power of social capital conference. Guilford, VT: MiraVia.

Wellman, B., & Lipton, L. (2012). *Data-driven dialogue: A facilitator's guide to collaborative inquiry.* Guilford, VT: MiraVia.

Wenger, E., McDermott, R., & Snyder, W. (2002). *Cultivating communities of practice: A guide to managing knowledge.* Boston, MA: Harvard Business School Press.

Williams, M. (1922). *The velveteen rabbit.* New York, NY: Doubleday.

Witte, M. (2013). *A curriculum on medical ignorance* [Video]. TEDxBloomington. Retrieved from https://www.youtube.com/watch?v=u3SGNvMcNdI

Witte, M., Crown, P., Bernas, M., & Garcia, F. A. R. (2008). Ignoramics in medical and premedical education. *Journal of Investigative Medicine, 56*(7), 897–901.

Witte, M., Kerwin, A., & Witte, C. (1998). Curriculum on medical and other ignorance: Shifting paradigms on learning and discovery. In M. Intons-Peterson & D. Best, *Memory distortions and their prevention* (pp. 125–156). Mahwah, NJ: Lawrence Erlbaum.

Zacarian, D., & Silverstone, M. (2015). *In it together.* Thousand Oaks, CA: Corwin.

Index

A SAGE Publishing Company

Helping educators make the greatest impact

CORWIN HAS ONE MISSION: to enhance education through intentional professional learning.

We build long-term relationships with our authors, educators, clients, and associations who partner with us to develop and continuously improve the best evidence-based practices that establish and support lifelong learning.

Solutions you want. Experts you trust. Results you need.